Public ~~~~~~~~~~~~ **Contempt**

'David Hooper has combined a penetrating
examination of their defects (of the libel laws)
with a witty account of some recent cases that
will provide admirable bedside reading'
Sunday Telegraph

'He makes some invariably sensible suggestions
about the reforms needed ... Mostly it's a book
of stories. Some are very funny. Some are rather
alarming'
Sunday Times

'In a style occasionally witty, occasionally
instructive and always entertaining he recalls
some of the more famous libel trials of recent
years ... Mr Hooper provides the reader with the
opportunity from the safety of the sidelines to
savour some of the excitement'
Standard

'A superb parody of contemporary libellers and
libelled ranging from Alfie Hinds through
Randolph Churchill to Goldenballs'
Punch

About the Author

David Hooper was born in Lisbon in 1949 and
educated at Eton and Balliol College, Oxford.
He practised at the Bar for a few years before
becoming a solicitor. He is a partner with Biddle
and Co in the City of London. He has two sons
and lives in London.

Public Scandal, Odium and Contempt

An investigation of recent libel cases

David Hooper

CORONET BOOKS
Hodder and Stoughton

Copyright © David Hooper 1984

First published in England in 1984 by
Martin Secker & Warburg Limited

Coronet edition 1986

British Library C.I.P.

Hooper, David, *1949–*
    Public scandal, odium and contempt : an
    investigation of recent libel cases.
    1. Libel and slander—England—Cases
    I. Title
    344.2063'0264   KD1960.A7

ISBN 0-340-38506-5

Printed and bound in Great Britain for
Hodder and Stoughton Paperbacks, a
division of Hodder and Stoughton Ltd.,
Mill Road, Dunton Green, Sevenoaks,
Kent (Editorial Office: 47 Bedford
Square, London, WC1B 3DP) by
Cox & Wyman Ltd., Reading

For Philippa, Edward and James

Acknowledgements

I would like to thank the many people who have assisted me in the preparation of this book. The views expressed are entirely my own and in some cases very different from the views of those who have kindly responded to my requests for information.

I would like to thank the following for their help: Iain Adamson, Anthony Bambridge, the late Luigi Barzini, Nora Beloff, Captain Jack Broome, Peter Carter-Ruck, Alexander Chancellor, Patricia Cork, Hugh Corrie, Harry Cox, T G Crone, Patrick Crosse, Paul Davies, The Right Hon William Deedes, Charles Dix, Henry Douglas, The Hon Gwyneth Dunwoody MP, Lady Falkender, Desmond Flower, The Right Hon Michael Foot MP, Michael Gillard, The Right Hon Sir Ian Gilmour Bt MP, J Glover, Sir James Goldsmith, Mark Hill, Frank Goldsworthy, Sir Jack Hayward, Martin Hooper, Percy Hoskins, H Montgomery Hyde, Brian Inglis, David Irving, the late John King, Simon King, Alan Leighton Davis, Bernard Levin, Sir David Llewellyn, The Countess Lloyd George of Dwyfor, The Viscount Norwich, Kenneth Parker, Barrie Penrose, Anthony Powell, the late Captain S W Roskill, J R Spencer, Marion Stewart, Alaistair Stewart Richardson, Paul Stockton, Major H H Sykes, The Rev Gordon Taylor, Auberon Waugh, David Whitaker, Sally Whitaker, Richard White, Hilary Whyte, Norman Williams and The Right Hon Lord Wilson of Rievaulx.

I would also like to thank the French and United States Embassies for their assistance and the Daily Telegraph Ltd, Express Newspapers Ltd, Mirror Group Newspapers Ltd and The Spectator Ltd for access to their libraries and Times Newspapers Ltd for permission to use their law and general reports of the cases referred to in the book. I am very grateful to Churchill College, Cambridge for access to the papers deposited by the late Captain Stephen Roskill and to the Benchers of the Inner Temple for access to the Inner Temple library. I would also like to acknowledge the assistance of the British Library and the London Library and the information provided by W H Allen & Co Ltd, the British Broadcasting Corporation, Frederick Muller Ltd, the Royal and Ancient Golf Club and Russell Jones & Walker. I do appreciate the assistance of the other people who have helped me with this book and who would probably prefer to remain anonymous.

Particular thanks are due to Peter Grose of Martin Secker & Warburg Ltd, Aubrey Davis and Pendleton Campbell for their enormous assistance in the creation and moulding of this book and to Justin Walford for reading the proofs and his helpful suggestions and to Ian Chapman and Peter Straus of Coronet.

My thanks are also due to the manufacturers of Smirnoff for their permission to reproduce the Marc cartoon and likewise to Mark Boxer its creator and Sarah Smith of Young and Rubicam Ltd.

I am also very grateful to Angela Bowley, Sarah Bolton and Diana Roberts for converting my manuscript into typescript. I am indebted to Weidenfeld & Nicolson and editor Mark Amory for permission to quote pages 21–22 from *The Letters of Evelyn Waugh*. I would also like to thank Weidenfeld and Nicolson and Richard Hough for permission to quote on pages 136–137 from *Edwina, Countess Mountbatten of Burma*.

Contents

One

A Bird's Eye View of the Law of Libel

The traditional test for spotting a libel is whether the words bring a person into hatred, ridicule or contempt. This has been found to be somewhat perplexing, so a more modern test is whether the words lower a person in the estimation of right-thinking people.

You can libel a person not only by the written or spoken word, but also by image, theme or, even more curiously, by juxtaposition.

Libel by image or theme recently secured a travel firm damages from the BBC when complaints about its dictatorial bill of fare on the Costa del Sol were accentuated by the theme music of the 'Colditz' series. In another case a CID officer was awarded £20,000 damages when he had the ill, or good, fortune to be filmed by a television crew leaving West Central police station. The film clip lasted two and a half seconds. At that moment the programme's reporter was speaking in general terms of CID men taking bribes. The programme did not identify or make accusations against that particular officer.

Libel by juxtaposition won a Mr Monson the princely sum of one farthing's damages against Madame Tussauds in 1894. They had placed a waxwork of him in the anteroom of the Chamber of Horrors, notwithstanding his acquittal on a murder charge by that grudging Scottish verdict of not proven – a verdict which is a halfway house between a conviction and an acquittal. A further example occurred in 1935 when the Duchess of Marlborough received undisclosed damages for a horticultural libel which had her in a

bed with the Rev F Page Roberts (another strain of rose
bush). To complicate matters the libel referred to a
gentleman called the Rev H Robertson Page (*see* chapter 4).

A recent manifestation of the variety of the means of
libelling people was to be found in the case of the libellous
Kissagram. An injunction was granted against a businessman who hired Kissagram girls to recite a poem accusing a
finance company of being 'Shylocks' as they stripped off. His
complaint was that the company had not paid him
commission on a lucrative deal with the Church Commissioners. The injunction was granted first before the
deliberations of the Church Commissioners were enlivened
by the arrival of the Kissagram girls.

You do not have to be human to have a reputation which
can be protected by the law of libel, but clearly it helps.
Property companies and dogs' homes have feelings. Each
has successfully sued for allegations regarding their
unwanted tenants. In the one case, it was suggested that they
were winkling out rent-protected old ladies, in the other, that
they were despatching their dogs for medical research. A
food guide won a libel action when a reviewer wrote, 'I have
no doubt that they are paid for their stars.' A Central
London hotel received damages for its entry in a hotel guide.
The company's 'impressive modern hotel' was described as
really 'a dosshouse for down and outs'. The guide was the
appropriately named *London Dossier* by Len Deighton.

Even a restaurant has sued. This improbable action arose
out of a cartoon in *Men Only* where some ladies in a cocktail
bar, described in court as 'extravagantly made-up and
indecently attired in inadequate dresses', were greeting a
customer with the words 'Welcome to the Spider's Web'.
This offended the 'high-class and well-arranged licensed
restaurant and roadhouse' on the Watford bypass called The
Spider's Web. The only similarity was its name. References
were made to the children's nursery rhyme, 'The Spider and
the Fly' and to the books of Isaiah and Job to show that the
phrase 'Spider's Web' was part of the English language.
Nevertheless, the restaurant was awarded £500 damages.

Even an Attorney General, Sir Hartley Shawcross, has

run foul of the libel laws. In 1946 he was conducting a vigorous campaign against the press. He had made a speech concentrating on the 'campaign of calumny and mis-representation by the Tory Party and the stooge press'.

'No-one cares a straw what the opinions of the proprietors of gutter press, Beaverbrook, Kemsley and owners of the *News of The World* are ... they are distorting views, suppressing the evidence and the facts.'

When Lord Kemsley threatened to issue a writ, Shawcross backed down with some alacrity writing in these less than heartfelt terms:

'Dear Lord Kemsley,
I learn with regret that certain words of mine in speeches which I made on the 19th and 30th July have given you the impression that I intended to impugn your business and professional integrity in the conduct of your newspaper and in particular to allege that you were part of the gutter press and intentionally distorting and suppressing facts.

I can assure you that I did not intend to make any of these imputations upon you, and if any words of mine appeared to make them, I desire unreservedly to withdraw them and express my regret.

I have always been strongly opposed to the introduction of personalities into political controversies and I should be sorry to think I myself had introduced them.'

This letter was prominently published with some relish on the front page of every newspaper owned by Lord Kemsley.

One of the first acts of Harold Wilson on becoming Prime Minister in 1964 was to apologize in open court to Herbert Hill, the chairman of Hardy Spicer Ltd, for libelling him during the election campaign. In a moment of over-exuberance Wilson had accused Hill of fomenting a strike at their Birmingham factory for political purposes and had said that if elected, he would hold a searching enquiry. He was elected but did no more than pay Mr Hill's legal costs.

Libel can arise in all sorts of different places. Canon
Collins was sued for libel by the Empire Loyalists for unkind
things he had said about them in the pulpit at St Paul's
Cathedral, following the Notting Hill riots. A D Peters, the
literary agent, sued a guest at a dinner party for his
slanderous remarks about his financial integrity.

Those two cases were slander. The distinction between
libel and slander is archaic. The difference used to be
between the written word in permanent form and the spoken
in ephemeral form. However, that ran foul of technology for
it was discovered that you could libel people by the
permanent broadcast word and slander them by ephemeral
skywriting. The practical distinction nowadays is that with
slander, a plaintiff also has to prove what was actually said
as well as showing that it was defamatory. In a slander
action, the plaintiff usually has to prove that the words
caused damage. However, the exceptions are so wide-
ranging – from a slander of a person in his profession or
vocation to the more intriguing imputations of criminal
offences, contagious diseases or unchastity – that the
distinction is more apparent than real. A case was recently
before the courts where the slander contained, for good
measure, all four ingredients. Any one would have sufficed.

A writer or publisher can be liable for libelling a person
quite unwittingly even when he has no knowledge of that
person's existence (*see* chapter 9). A number of cases arise
purely accidentally. Sometimes they cause considerable
annoyance and embarrassment to the victim, sometimes
they produce a windfall award of damages. An example of a
minor error which did cause considerable annoyance was the
headline in a case where the head of a large car distribution
business had had to pay damages to a wronged husband in a
divorce case. The headline read 'Car thief to pay £1,000 to
husband'. Another cropped up in an article entitled 'Vice
Den in Snob Square'. An arrow helpfully drawn on the
accompanying photograph pointed to a highly respectable
lady's flat in Hans Place.

Another curious feature of the law of libel is that lightning
does tend to strike twice or thrice. An example of this is the

action brought by a British police officer in Palestine in 1951 for an untrue allegation that he had been responsible for shooting in cold blood Abraham Stern, the leader of the notorious Stern Gang. W H Allen, who settled out of court, was the first publisher to pay him damages for publishing this allegation in a book called *The Revolt* written by Menachem Begin, then the leader of the Irgun. In 1972 Secker & Warburg repeated the allegation when they published *The Terrorists* by Roland Gautier, translated from French. This time the officer recovered £4,000. The allegation surfaced yet again in 1978 when Weidenfeld & Nicolson published *Ben Gurion* by Michael Bar Zohar. It meant another trip to the Law Courts and further undisclosed damages for the much-maligned officer.

The fact that someone else has published a similar allegation does not necessarily mean that action will not be taken. Every person involved in the process of publication is liable for what is written. It is by no means unusual for editors, printers and distributors to be made parties to libel actions, even though they may have given no thought to what was being published. Every repetition of the libel can be the subject of separate proceedings, although you can rely on earlier awards to reduce damages for the later libel.

The record for multiple successful libel actions appears to be a close-run thing between Dr John Bodkin Adams and Princess Elizabeth Bagaya of Toro. The cases were wholly dissimilar except for the amount of damages awarded. Dr John Bodkin Adams sued thirteen newspapers for their suggestions that he was guilty of the poisoning of wealthy Eastbourne widows during the preceding twenty years. Without the legal restraints that now exist on the reporting of criminal proceedings, Fleet Street, with very few exceptions (such as Percy Hoskins of the *Daily Express*), had little hesitation in convicting Dr Adams of the murders of Mrs Morrell, Mrs Hullett and a few others beside. The headlines in the *Daily Mail* were particularly lurid. 'Yard probe mass poisoning. Twenty-five deaths in the great mystery of Eastbourne – inquiry into four hundred wills – rich women believed to have been the victims.' If there was any doubt as to who might be the subject of this interest there was an adjacent headline concerning the inquest into the death of Mrs Morrell which read 'Coroner talks of careless treatment. Doctor tells of £1,000 cheque.' In that story Dr Adams was named.

After the seventeen-day trial, during which Dr Adams, with commendable reticence, had confined himself to six words: 'I am not guilty, my Lord', the jury took only fortyfour minutes to acquit him of Mrs Morrell's murder. The Hullett case was not proceeded with. So the field was open for him to seek redress from Fleet Street. In 1961, he received in an out of court settlement £50,000 damages. It was a term of the settlement that he did not proceed with any of the other libel actions and presumably the other papers contributed to the settlement. When the doctor died in 1983 he left £402,970. In addition to his libel actions he had benefited from no less than one hundred and thirtytwo of his patients' wills.

Princess Elizabeth Bagaya of Toro was the victim of a number of scurrilous accusations suggesting misconduct at Orly airport. It seems that this was based on nothing more substantial than the word of that notoriously unreliable source, President Idi Amin. She brought six libel actions in this country against the *Daily Express*, the *Daily Mirror*, *The Sun*, the *Sunday Telegraph*, the *Daily Mail* and even *Der Spiegel*. She received £50,000 damages as well as DM 23,000 and undisclosed damages in France and Italy.

In a libel action the plaintiff must prove three things. The words must be defamatory of him, they must have been so understood by other people and they must have been published to a third party. Merely insulting a person face to face is insufficient. To invite a person to repeat the remark to a third party is in law dangerous, as you may thereby have consented to the publication. Proving that the words actually caused you damage is an optional extra.

Normally there is little difficulty in deciding whether the words were defamatory. If you write of an hotelier that in occupied France during the last war he was in the habit of turning his guests over to the Gestapo, there can be little doubt that you have libelled him. Where it is less clear-cut, the judge rules on whether the words are capable of being defamatory and the jury decides if they were in fact defamatory. Words can be libellous either in their natural and ordinary meaning or by way of special innuendo (*see* chapter 2). Libel by innuendo means that there are particular facts known to a number of readers of the libel that would render an apparently innocent remark libellous. An example of this was a rather curious photograph of a pregnant woman which appeared on a breakfast cereal packet with the caption: 'A pregnant mum does not have to be constipated'. It was, on the face of it, harmless, if tasteless, first thing in the morning. It was libellous, because the photograph was of an unmarried nurse and had been altered so as to make her appear pregnant. As she was single, not pregnant, not a mum nor, one imagines, constipated, she recovered libel damages.

It is fairly easy to libel a person. The question is: How can a libel action be resisted or defended? There are a number of defences, some of which are unduly technical.

The principal defence is that of justification. This means that, if you can prove that what you said was true, you can defeat the claim for libel, the problem for the writer of the libel is that he has the burden of proving that the words were true. In the law of libel, truth is essentially a practical rather than an abstract matter: it is what you can prove to be true. It is sometimes wrongly said that the greater the truth, the greater the libel. If you can prove the facts, you will have a complete defence to a claim for libel. However, if you try and fail, it can prove very expensive in terms of increased damages and legal costs (*see* chapter 12).

One of the clearest examples of the expense involved even in successfully defending a libel action is to be found in the recent Moonies case. There the *Daily Mail* defended its claim that the church was in the habit of brainwashing its converts. It was a fiercely fought case with the unusual spectacle of the defendants periodically being granted increasingly large sums as security for their legal costs, as the court was persuaded that the plaintiff, Dennis Orme, was really a nominal plaintiff on behalf of the Korean-based church. Disaffected Moonies had to be flown in from all over the world and, when it ended after a six-months' trial and an appeal, legal costs were reckoned to total £750,000.

As will be shown in chapter 13, the position regarding justification is different in criminal libel. Libel is essentially a civil matter where damages and possibly an injunction against the repetition of the libel can be ordered. Criminal libel involves a prosecution under the criminal law and under an 1843 Act of Parliament a maximum penalty of two years' imprisonment. Such prosecutions are very rare nowadays and normally require the leave of a High Court judge before they can be brought.

Criminal libel is an archaic survival from the days of the Court of Star Chamber. It dates from the time when it was felt that the state must protect itself against publications that might lead to a breach of the peace. As will be seen in chapter 13, the authorities gave themselves the benefit of the doubt and criminal libel was used as a political weapon. It now exists only for what are considered by the courts particularly serious libels or cases where an action for civil libel may be inappropriate, such as a person with no means of paying damages persistently libelling a member of the Royal Family. In criminal libel truth alone is not a defence. You also have to prove that it was in the public interest to publish what was written. By contrast in civil cases you can, if you can prove them, rake up any ancient indiscretions (with the exception of spent criminal convictions, where you can be guilty of libel, if they are published out of a sense of malice).

You have a defence to an action for libel if you can prove that what you wrote was fair comment on a subject of public interest. You must establish that what you said was comment as opposed to fact (*see* chapters 4 and 11) and that the comment represented your honestly held belief, however prejudiced your views may have been.

The other main defence is that of privilege, of which there are two varieties: absolute and qualified. Absolute privilege means there can be no libel action for what was said, however outrageous or malicious. It covers what is said in Parliament and in the courts. It explains why the challenge is often made, but rarely accepted, to repeat an allegation outside Parliament. Qualified privilege is a defence which enables people, who are felt to have a legitimate interest in communicating freely, to do so without the fear of being sued for libel – such as giving trade or credit references or testimonials about former employees. So you cannot be sued for libel even if your reference turns out to be wrong, provided that you were not motivated by malice and that you did not pass it to someone who had no business to receive it. This defence has been extended by Parliament to such matters as the fair and accurate reporting of the proceedings of Parliament and the courts and of company and council meetings. In some instances a person who is aggrieved at what is said about him may have the right of reply in explanation or contradiction.

There are a number of other defences. There is a highly technical defence under the Defamation Act to cover accidental libels. It is so unsatisfactory that it has only arisen in one reported case in thirty years (*see* chapter 9), when it failed.

If you are unwise enough to consent to a libel about yourself being published you cannot sue. For example, if you sell your story to a Sunday newspaper, you may have to take the consequences of the less than flattering picture they may draw, as with the headline, 'Bully boasts, I beat up tragic deb' (*see* chapter 13).

If you or the person you are suing die, that too is the end of the matter. An otherwise unmemorable case about caravans in Luton brought by Frederick Webb against George Holder came to an abrupt halt in 1958, when the plaintiff collapsed and died in the court corridor, after he had completed his evidence. However, it sometimes happens that those who are assumed to be dead, and therefore unable to sue, are alive and well and drafting a libel writ. It may have come as something of a surprise to Rolf Hochhuth to be sued in 1970 by Edward Prchal, the pilot of the Liberator aeroplane that crashed in July 1943 killing all the other fifteen persons on board. Hochhuth alleged this was part of a plot to assassinate the Polish Prime Minister, General Sikorski.

That was untrue and grotesquely libellous. The pilot turned out to have survived despite two broken legs and numerous other injuries, having been found clinging to his lifebelt by one arm. He came from California to sue for libel in this country, and was awarded £50,000 against Hochhuth. Subsequently he won four other awards of undisclosed sizes against assorted impresarios, theatre producers and publishers.

One way round the rule against bringing actions on behalf of dead persons was discovered in the case of Wright v Lord Gladstone. In 1925 Captain Peter Wright had written very disparagingly of the then dead W E Gladstone. He contrasted Gladstone's public moral stance regarding women with his visits to the prostitutes who knew him as 'Old Gladeye'. Gladstone's descendants could not sue for libel, as he was dead. They therefore wrote a series of letters aimed at compelling Wright to sue them for libel, culminating in one to the Secretary of the Bath Club accusing Wright of being a liar and a coward. He was expelled from the club. He sued for libel but lost. The trial was an unqualified triumph for the memory of the late W E Gladstone. The jury added a rider vindicating Gladstone's reputation, which was greeted with loud applause.

In a slander action, mere vulgar abuse is a defence. When a lady was called 'You tramp' in the foyer of the Cumberland Hotel this was thought to be mere vulgar abuse and not a reflection on her morals.

If the libel action surmounts these hurdles, the remedy will be an award of damages and possibly an injunction. Damages may be contemptuous (*see* chapter 5), nominal, compensatory (*see* Appendix), aggravated or punitive (*see* chapter 12). If a libel has been published it is prudent to take steps to mitigate the damage to the plaintiff's reputation by publishing an apology (*see* chapter 10).

It is not necessary in a libel action to prove that the words actually caused you financial loss. If they are libellous, it is assumed that the words must have caused you damage and the jury awards an appropriate sum. If you have lost money as a result of the libel by, for example, losing your job, you receive compensation for that by way of special damages on top of your general damages.

The amount of damages awarded is something of a lottery, as no one in court is able to suggest a figure to the jury. All the jury can do is to try to recollect the awards they have heard about. These tend to be the larger and possibly excessive ones which have been reported in the newspapers. In the action brought by Sir Oswald Mosley against the *Star* in 1934 each juror wrote down a figure and the total was divided by twelve, producing an award of £5,000. That is probably the way many juries approach the question of damages. Very often the case is settled out of court with damages not normally being disclosed and a statement in open court being read in front of the judge, vindicating the plaintiff's reputation. The advantage of such a statement is that it can be published in newspapers as a report of court proceedings.

Injunctions are granted rather less frequently in libel actions nowadays. An injunction against repeating the libel will not normally be given before the action has been tried, if the defendant says, with some prospect of success, that he will justify what he has written. In such cases freedom of expression triumphs over the desire to suppress upon the basis that either what was said was true or damages are likely to be increased appropriately for the unsuccessful plea of justification.

The principle is illustrated by two similar cases in 1975. In one, a man was so outraged by the quality of the cherry-red paint on the front door of his £28,000 home that he unscrewed the door and fixed it to the front of his Rolls Royce having daubed on it in yellow paint:

This door fitted by Crest Homes is typical of the poor quality materials used and as with all other paint work needed renovating within twelve months.

Another man had found fault with the quality of the tasteful Vandyke brown paint he had chosen for his home, which turned green after six months and presented, according to the judge, 'a multi-coloured appearance not unlike military camouflage'. His reaction had been to paint prominently on his flaking paintwork abutting the South Circular: 'This house is painted with Carson's paint'.

In both cases, these aspersions against their goods were disputed by the manufacturers; but, as the homeowners maintained that what they said was true, no injunction was granted and the cases had to proceed to trial.

Two

What is Libellous?

Libels come in two varieties. Either the words are clearly libellous in their 'natural and ordinary meaning', or they are libellous by innuendo – this arises where there are special facts known to a particular group of people which can render some innocuous statement libellous. For example, it might seem unobjectionable to refer to someone as 'Fatty Arbuckle's latest lady love', until it emerges that she is a happily married woman.

A libel can crop up in any area of a person's life. Passion may well be an ingredient of a libel whether it occurs in the council chamber, a dog show or elsewhere. However, the vast majority of libel actions concern people's livelihoods and usually there is no ambiguity about what was said. In recent times a professional boxer has successfully brought an action when he was described as a fat and horizontal layabout, flabby and overweight. So, too, has a Liberal parliamentary candidate who, in a particularly imaginative libel, was accused of having given his daughter the African name of Kwame to curry favour with his constituents. The truth of the matter was that he had a son who had the singularly un-African names of Marc Montague.

The permutations are infinite. A prison governor recovered damages for an untrue suggestion that he used to invite to his house outside the prison to play bridge the former diplomat George Blake (who was briefly enjoying Her Majesty's maximum security hospitality, prior to escaping). It is not clear from the report of the case whether the two prison guards who accompanied Blake were there purely to escort him or to make up a four. A press photographer recovered damages for the suggestion that he was fast asleep, when he should have been photographing the action at Silverstone. A competitor at the Badminton Horse Trials successfully sued when it was said that he had given his horse a sound thrashing each of three times it refused to take a jump. A racehorse trainer took justifiable exception to a false report that he had been warned off for doping. In fact, it had been pure misfortune the horse had been doped. The only reason his licence had been withdrawn was that he failed to ensure that a horse under his charge was not doped.

In 1963 Scobie Breasley, the champion jockey, sued when it was suggested that he had not been trying in the Byfleet Stakes. He said it was just another case of being beaten on an odds-on favourite. He recovered £250, but had unwisely turned down an out of court settlement of £500. Recently the trainer Michael Dickinson was awarded £7,500 when a similar allegation was made against him when he was a jockey – a startling 3,000 per cent increase.

Still in the racing world, but less obviously libellous, was the case where Clive Graham, the *Daily Express* tipster known as The Scout, obtained damages for being accused of being too modest in his tips. It was suggested he had tried to ensure his own horse raced at good odds by stressing its three-legged qualities.

Most professions have been the subject of libel actions. A doctor sued when he was accused of being 'the menace of a quickie quack'. A barrister, Sir Andrew Clark QC, sued when it was suggested that he begged for a truce in one action so that he could take on another. The case he was accused of wishing to escape was one where he faced a particularly persistent litigant in the form of Anthony Wedgwood Benn (earlier Viscount Stansgate and later Tony Benn) who was forcefully presenting his election petition following the renunciation of his title. A claims assessor successfully sued when he was called a claims chaser and a glib white-haired vulture. The Duke of Marlborough took the Communist paper, the *Daily Worker*, to court for suggesting that his pheasants were receiving preferential treatment during wartime, while he was trying to have poachers sent to prison.

Even a firm making dresses for the Queen sued when it was suggested that one of its special creations for a Royal Tour was to be found on sale in Bond Street for £5.

Libel by way of innuendo is a rather more difficult matter. Normally the words speak for themselves, but sometimes evidence is needed to prove a special meaning. In 1943 the Court of Appeal had to decide the slang meaning of the word 'pansy'.

The milliner, Mr Thaarup, had been awarded damages after bringing a case against the magazine *Lilliput* which published two photographs: one showed a member of the Home Guard shouting fiercely, 'Get out of my garden' towards the other picture which was clearly recognizable as Mr Thaarup, who was holding a model of a lady's head with a hat bedecked with artificial flowers. It was captioned: 'I only wanted a few pansies'. This led to a remarkable passage in the judgment of Lord Justice Scott:

> I personally was not alive to the slang meaning of the word, nor, I think, was my brother Mackinnon but my brother Goddard fortunately was quite alive to it, having had judicial experience as a result of which he had come to know about it.

There were in the 1920s and 1930s a number of libel actions with little apparent merit where newspapers were sued for purely accidental libel. In 1928 a man known as Michael Dennis Corrigan, a racehorse owner and reputedly a general in the Mexican army, accosted Stanley Richardson of the News Illustration Press Agency at Hurst Park races and informed Richardson that he was engaged to the lady on his arm. Corrigan invited him to photograph them and announce the engagement. Richardson duly did so and the happy news was reported in the *Daily Mirror* gossip column. Imagine the distress this caused to Mrs Mildred Anna Cassidy, for – unbeknownst to the newspaper – Corrigan was none other than her husband, Kettering Edward Cassidy. Not surprisingly their relationship was not the happiest and they no longer lived together, although apparently he did visit her at the shop at which she was employed.

With mixed emotions she and her three witnesses went to see her solicitor. Her witnesses told him that after reading the article they had come to the conclusion that their friend Mrs Cassidy had been deceiving them and masquerading as Cassidy's wife, while cohabiting with him as his mistress. It was a winning deduction. They did, however, have the grace to admit in cross-examination that they knew Cassidy to be a blackguard who had treated her badly and had been unfaithful to her. For this improbable libel Mrs Cassidy recovered £500. It was a marked improvement on the rather paltry sums of £37 10s she had received in each of her two earlier libel actions against other newspapers.

The Court of Appeal by a majority upheld the decision, although Lord Justice Greer in his dissenting judgment did not much care for the jury's decision, commenting acidly:

> They appear to have jumped to the conclusion that she was a dishonest woman who had been deceiving them and had been living in concubinage with the scoundrel who occasionally visited her at the shop where she was employed.

On the strength of this case, a number of gold-digging actions were subsequently settled out of court and the claimants paid off. The position has been slightly improved by the defence of unintentional defamation under Section 4, Defamation Act 1952, but that is not without its technicalities. Even under the Act, a gossip columnist might be required to be a little more careful when describing a reputed Mexican general's intentions towards his girlfriend.

Most of the cases brought on the basis of a libellous innuendo are, however, every bit as meritorious as those arising out of the natural and ordinary meaning of the words. One such case was brought by Cyril Tolley.

On 20th June 1928 Cyril James Hasting Tolley, one of the leading amateur golfers of the day, was horrified to discover that his name was being used to advertise a sixpenny chocolate bar called Fry's Carteret. The advertisement had a picture of his golf swing with a caddy behaving in a most uncaddylike way. It was accompanied by a limerick which Lord Justice Scrutton was to describe as an 'offensive piece of vulgarity, reflecting little credit on those who control the advertising of Messrs Fry'. It ran as follows:

> The caddy to Tolley said 'Oh Sir
> Good shot, sir, that ball, see it go sir
> My word how it flies
> Like a carteret of Fry's
> They're handy, they're good and priced low sir.'

This less than immortal piece of verse appeared in no less than sixtyfour publications including the *Daily Sketch* and the *Daily Mail*. Fry's were using famous names such as Asquith, Woodrow Wilson and Gerald du Maurier to promote the sales of these chocolate bars. Mr Tolley felt that people seeing the advertisement would conclude that he was being paid and thus was receiving payment for his sport in contravention of his amateur status.

Tolley was chosen to appear in this advertisement because he was a well-known figure. In 1920 he had won the British Amateur Golf Championship at Muirfield in an epic match that ended at the thirty seventh hole. He regularly played in international matches, had won the Military Cross in the first world war, but he had since the war become a stockbroker. He belonged, therefore, to that profession which is particularly sensitive on matters of libel and like Mr Blennerhassett and Captain Canning (*see* chapter 9), he was not amused.

He did, however, approach the matter in a restrained way. He said he would not take proceedings if Fry's published a statement in one morning and one evening newspaper that he had not received any payment for appearing in this advertisement. Fry's politely declined expressing their regret that Mr Tolley found the advertisement offensive. Their reply was castigated as entire humbug by Tolley's counsel, Rayner Goddard QC.

Cyril Tolley therefore sued. Shortly before the case was heard on 20 July 1929 by Mr Justice Acton, Tolley again won the British Amateur Championship. His amateur status was therefore scarcely in doubt; like many others Fry's were to find it was an expensive business to treat a leading sportsman so shabbily.

The case lasted no more than a day and produced an interesting contest between Rayner Goddard QC and Norman Birkett QC. In sporting terms it was the contest of a former Oxford athletics blue against an occasional golfer. In legal terms, however, the issue was whether the special facts applicable to Tolley, namely that he was a well-known amateur sportsman and people would assume he was being paid for lending his name, could render libellous this harmless advertisement rather than its actual words or pictures.

The case was opened with suitable gravity by Rayner Goddard QC. He said the advertisement suggested that Tolley had prostituted his reputation as an amateur golfer and that he was guilty of conduct unworthy of his status as a leading golfer. Cyril Tolley gave evidence of the annoyance and the embarrassment the advertisement had caused him. He explained he had not been asked to give his permission nor had he received any payment. Not only did the article call into question his amateur status, but he complained it looked as if the shot had gone to the right. No golfer of his standing would play a round with a bar of chocolate sticking out of his pocket. At the very least, he explained, he would get the caddy to carry his chocolate. As it was, it looked as if he went round the course chewing chocolate. It was also a very bad limerick, he commented.

Two witnesses were called on his behalf. The first, Edward Storry, was a Walker Cup golfer. If an amateur golfer appeared in an advertisement of a company's goods, people would think he was infringing his amateur status. He was very surprised to see the plaintiff's name in the advertisement. The second was Henry Hobson, a former secretary of Stoke Poges Golf Club and then of Le Touquet Golf Club. If a golfer involved himself in the advertising of people's goods, he would be called upon to resign from any reputable club, including Le Touquet.

The defendants were represented by Norman Birkett QC. He took the line that the action should never have been brought. Such caricatures were an occupational risk of being a public figure. He pointed out to Tolley that he was in distinguished company with such figures as the Lord Privy Seal and the Home Secretary and that they had not complained. 'But they were professionals', he countered.

The defence might have succeeded but for the ill-considered correspondence between Fry's and their advertising agents. This showed that they were well aware of the risk of libel and had made a cynical calculation as to the prospects of being sued for libel. Counsel's opinion had been taken on the question of libel. As a result of his advice, six of the caricatures were not used, although counsel did pass the Tolley advertisement. With commendable foresight, the advertising agents did suggest sending the proofs to the people caricatured for their consent. This was rejected by Fry's in a letter that was to cause them some embarrassment:

> We feel this is rather bad form and are not agreeable to this procedure.

There was also correspondence which stated that it was safer to use the name of Suzanne Lenglen, a former Wimbledon champion who had turned professional, rather than two amateurs, Miss Betty Nutthall and the reigning Wimbledon champion, Miss Helen Wills. The agents commented that as tennis players their amateur status had to be even more carefully guarded than that of golfers.

It was difficult, therefore, for the defendants to argue that such an advertisement could not affect a sportsman's amateur status. They called no evidence. The jury did not think much of the way they behaved and they awarded Tolley the then not inconsiderable sum of £1,000 damages.

The defendants successfully appealed to the Court of Appeal where all three judges felt the damages were excessive. Two of the three judges, Slesser and Greer (sporting activities: croquet and golf), held that on the evidence the advertisement was not defamatory. Lord Justice Scrutton (no sporting activities) held that the advertisement was defamatory.

Tolley was more successful in the House of Lords where four of the five judges decided that the advertisement was defamatory. The one dissenter, Lord Blanesburgh, was of the view that the advertisement was so vulgar no one would seriously think Tolley could have been paid for it.

The result of all this litigation was that Tolley had his verdict that he had been libelled, but there had to be a retrial on the question of damages. Tolley had not contested the Court of Appeal's decision that damages were excessive. He was back at square one and had, despite his success in the House of Lords, to pay his legal costs in the Court of Appeal.

It was only in 1952-4, while Cyril Tolley was a member of the Committee of the rules of Golf, that the rules relating to amateur status were altered so that anyone who benefits by allowing their likeness or name as a golfing personality to be used in any advertisement, whether relating to golf or not, forfeits their amateur status.

A more modern example of a libellous innuendo concerned Michael Foot MP. In 1978 the *Daily Mail* alleged that he received private medical treatment in a National Health hospital. On the face of it there was nothing wrong with that; the libel arose out of the fact that Michael Foot was a member of a Labour Cabinet firmly committed to the abolition of 'pay-beds'. The article was, therefore, accusing him of hypocrisy and using his political position to obtain an unfair personal advantage. In fact, nothing of the kind had happened and the allegations were shown to be ill-founded. Happily, the National Health Service restored his health and the *Daily Mail's* libel damages, his reputation.

The problem for the plaintiff in many cases of libellous innuendo is proving that he has 'been lowered in the estimation of right-thinking people' because usually a plaintiff can only produce people in court who know him well and will think none the worse of him as a result of what they have read. Consequently, a jury is often left guessing how everyone else would have understood the words.

Three

What Makes People Sue for Libel?

There are many examples in this book of serious allegations being made against highly respectable persons, which compelled them to take libel proceedings to clear their names. Captain Jack Broome and Jack Hayward are just two examples (*see* chapters 12 and 14).

Not all libel actions are born of such worthy motives. A writ can be issued for a very modest fee and it was, and to some extent still is, used to stifle further comment. The matter is said to become sub judice, and therefore cannot be discussed until the case is concluded – an excellent means of curtailing discussion. In 1974 Lord Denning reduced the scope of gagging writs in a case concerning a financier called Dr Wallersteiner.

When a stockbroker criticized the way in which he handled his companies, including the august-sounding Rothschild Trust which turned out to be 'an obscure concern of little worth, registered in Liechtenstein' and wholly unconnected with the well-known banking family, Dr Wallersteiner sued him for libel. Lord Denning dispelled any suggestion that discussion of the issues should then cease and poured scorn on what he called the abracadabra that the matter was sub judice.

One of the more elaborate means of using the law of libel to stifle criticism was that employed by Horatio Bottomley who wanted to suppress a pamphlet by Clarence Henry Norman entitled *Horatio Bottomley Exposed*. Bottomley could not sue Norman because what was written was true. He therefore hit upon the idea of suing a tame printer who would print a few copies of Norman's pamphlet and admit he had libelled Bottomley; anyone planning to distribute Norman's publication would then be aware of the fact it had been adjudged libellous. He therefore approached his friend Reuben Bigland to find a printer he could sue. Bigland obliged with an ex-convict called John Greaney who was paid £50 for producing six copies.

Bottomley then sued 'this reckless printer' who did not appear at the trial, although he was waiting outside the court to receive another £50, when Bottomley obtained his verdict for £500. It did Bottomley little good, as he was soon to fall out with Bigland who himself wrote a similar pamphlet. *The Downfall of Horatio Bottomley MP* – His Latest Greatest Swindle. Bigland denounced Bottomley's latest investment scheme as a swindle. He had gulled poor subscribers to invest £1 notes in his great Victory War Bond Club. Bottomley issued proceedings for criminal libel against Bigland, although he offered no evidence and he had to pay £1,600 costs. In the end he was himself successfully prosecuted for fraudently converting part of the proceeds of his Victory War Bond Club subscriptions.

It is highly unlikely anyone would ever emulate Bottomley's example. However, the issue of a writ for libel is still a simple matter and there are even nowadays well-known figures whose speed with a writ has ensured excessive caution in what is written about them. A writ for libel can also serve a useful purpose in that its issue may well be reported and it gives the impression that the allegations made will be fiercely resisted and that it would be extremely unwise to repeat the libel, even though no further action may be intended.

In some respects the law of libel is slanted in favour of the unmeritorious plaintiff. The issue of any writ for libel is a source of worry and expense to most defendants. It is the plaintiff who has control over the proceedings. Even if he ultimately loses the case, it will be some time before the defendant recovers his legal costs. However strong the defendant's case is, the court is very unlikely to allow him to recoup more than three-quarters of the fees he has had to pay his own lawyer. It is, therefore, a brave defendant who refuses to make any retraction.

No corresponding demand is made of such a plaintiff. One very sensible suggestion made by the Faulks Committee on the Law of Defamation was that, if a plaintiff demanded that a book be withdrawn, he should have to undertake to pay the costs of this being done, should his action fail. At present publishers normally feel compelled to withdraw or withhold the publication of a book when they receive a claim for libel, except in all but the most spurious cases.

Another unworthy motive for bringing a libel action is the attraction of tax-free money. Nowadays, with the high cost of litigation, this will depend upon the case being settled out of court. In practice nearly all libel actions are settled out of court, often with all the plaintiff's legal costs being reimbursed to him. However, if the case goes to, or very near to, court, the legal costs can be horrendous.

There are many reasons why people bring libel actions. Sometimes anger or a desire to teach the other side a lesson may play a part. However, it is very rare for such feelings to be admitted. One outstanding and somewhat tongue-in-cheek exception was the action that Evelyn Waugh brought against Beaverbrook Newspapers and their literary critic Nancy Spain, which he described with irreverent humour.

The facts were suitably bizarre. In June 1955, Nancy Spain, accompanied by Lord Noel-Buxton, was on what Miss Spain was pleased to refer to in the *Daily Express* as a 'pilgrimage'. She had been to see the Poet Laureate John Masefield and had then driven eighty miles to Evelyn Waugh's house near Dursley in Gloucestershire. She braved the sign on the gate saying 'No admittance on business'. Mrs Waugh had warned her on the telephone, before she embarked on her odyssey, of Evelyn Waugh's dislike of such calls. Mrs Waugh's forecast of Evelyn Waugh's reaction to this visit turned out to be correct, as he became extremely angry and said, 'Clear off, both of you', or as the law report coyly added, 'words to that effect'. Waugh's evidence was that the peer remonstrated: 'I am not here on business. I am a member of the House of Lords', although this was disputed.

The upshot of this incident was an unkind article in *The Spectator* by Evelyn Waugh, entitled 'Awake my soul! It is a Lord!'. While at the outset of the encounter, Evelyn Waugh

claimed not to have heard of Miss Spain, he made up for lost
time when he wrote: 'Has the Editor of the *Daily Express* no
horsewhip?' Miss Spain, as literary critic of the *Daily
Express*, was particularly upset by a suggestion in a review
Waugh subsequently wrote for *The Spectator* about P G
Wodehouse that literary criticism at Beaverbrook News-
papers had taken a nosedive since the days of Arnold
Bennett at the *Evening Standard* and D H Lawrence at the
Daily Express.

Miss Spain's reply was an article in the *Daily Express* on
17 March 1956 which started, 'THERE IS A WAR between
Evelyn Waugh and me' and which proceeded with
considerable inaccuracy to suggest that 'a good word' from
her had helped promote his brother Alec Waugh's book,
Island in the Sun which, she claimed, had dwarfed Evelyn
Waugh's total first edition sales.

The case is most memorable for what Evelyn Waugh
wrote about it. To his literary agent, A D Peters, he wrote
that day:

> I have waited a long time to catch the *Express* in libel ...
> There should be no difficulty in proving malice. Will you
> please take legal opinion and if that is favourable issue a
> writ? ...

To his brother, Alec, he wrote on 24 March:

> I hope to earn a nice tax-free sum which will pay for
> Teresa's coming out. It is all very satisfactory. I think I
> can't lose. It is simply a question of how little or how much
> damages I get.

On 20 February 1957 the jury decided the article was
defamatory and awareded him £2,000 damages. It is
impossible to improve on Evelyn Waugh's description of the
action in his letter to Nancy Mitford on 5 March 1957:

> I had an exhilarating expedition into the Law Courts and
> came out two thousand pounds (tax free) to the good.

There were anxious moments. At the end of the first day I would have settled for a fiver. . . . The judge was a buffoon who invited the jury to laugh me out of court. But I had taken the precaution of telling the Dursley parish priest that he should have ten per cent of the damages. His prayers were dramatic, Old Testament style. A series of Egyptian plagues fell on Sir Hartley Shawcross [the defendant's counsel] from the moment he took up the case, culminating in a well-nigh fatal motor accident to his mother-in-law at the very moment he had me under cross-examination and was making me feel rather an ass. . . . He had to chuck the case and leave it to an understrapper whose heart was in the case next door, where a Bolivian millionaire was suing Lord Kemsley for saying he buggered his wife (the Bolivian's wife, not Lady Kemsley). I had a fine solid jury who were out to fine the *Express* for their impertinence to the Royal Family, quite irrespective of any rights or wrongs. They were not at all amused by the judge. . . . So Father Collins got £200 and a lot of chaps in White's got pop.

Nancy Spain's part in the proceedings was chronicled by Eric Newby who, after commenting on Evelyn Waugh's ear trumpet, wrote:

Spain herself was wearing one of the really full-length mink coats that the Beaverbrook press used to keep in moth balls for their female staff to wear when appearing on such occasions, but with trousers, which was eccentric then.

On 4 April 1957, Evelyn Waugh collected a further £3,000 from Beaverbrook Newspapers, who had unwisely published defamatory remarks that Rebecca West had made about him in *The Climate of Treason*. They quoted a passage where she suggested that 'for many years Mr Evelyn Waugh had been implying that the worthless and dissolute are more worthy than people who are in fact worthy and sober' and had spoken of 'a crackbrained confusion between virtues and vices, a climate in which the traitor flourishes'.

Rebecca West and Pan Books had in December 1956 apologized and acknowledged in the curious language of such statements in open court that it was 'unfair to suggest that over many years Mr Evelyn Waugh had encouraged a hagiography of debauchery'. They paid his costs, but he waived damages against a fellow author. He had no such feelings about Lord Beaverbrook.

Four

The Pitfalls of Libel

People tend to think of litigants receiving enormous damages in libel cases, but there have been a number of cases in which the result has been disastrous for the parties involved. To fight a libel action and lose may well cause considerably more damage to your reputation than suffering in silence. This is particularly so if you lose the action on technical grounds such as failing to prove the article could refer to you. The result of the trial may be reported in such a way as to suggest that what was said was true.

There are two classic examples of the perils of libel actions. In the first, the plaintiff sued for slander when he was called a highwayman. He lost and was arrested when he was leaving the court, tried on a charge of being a highwayman and hanged at Newgate. In the second Oscar Wilde sued the Marquess of Queensberry (Lord Alfred Douglas's father) for his notice about Oscar Wilde 'posing as a sodomite' – or 'somdomite' as he spelt it in the heat of the moment. Wilde prosecuted, lost and was later tried himself and sent to prison for two years.

In this chapter four cases are considered where a libel action has been particularly disastrous for the parties. Three concerned plaintiffs and one a defendant.

The most spectacular fall from grace of a plaintiff was that of Sir William Gordon-Cumming. He owned two estates in Scotland, Altyre and Gordonstoun, with some 40,000 acres as well as a town house in London. He was the fourth baronet, a close friend of the Prince of Wales, and a Lieutenant-Colonel in the Scots Guards, much-decorated as a result of his exploits against the Zulus and the Egyptians and in the Nile Campaigns in such exotic reaches as Tel-El-Kebir, Korti-Gabut and Ulundi.

In September 1890 he joined a house party given by the nouveau-riche shipowners Mr and Mrs Arthur Wilson at Doncaster. The Prince of Wales was the principal guest. Gordon-Cumming had not originally been invited, but he was included at the request of the Prince and was accompanied by a subaltern in his regiment, Berkeley Levett.

On the first night the Prince proposed a game of baccarat, then generally considered a somewhat doubtful occupation. Like most games of chance, it was thought fairer if the participants staked their money before rather than after the fall of the cards was known. This was not the way Gordon-Cumming appeared to be playing. He was reckoned to be cheating by increasing his bet when the cards produced a winning score and withdrawing his counters when he lost – a dastardly trick known by the suitably Gallic name of *la poussette*. This was apparently spotted by the son of the house, Stanley Wilson, who whispered to Lieutenant Berkeley Levett: 'My God, Berkeley, this is too hot.'

After considerable discussion, it was decided to put the matter to the test the following night by chalking a white line on the green baize over which the players had to push their stakes. This merely confirmed their suspicions about Gordon-Cumming, who had won £228, principally from the Prince of Wales. He was accused of cheating by two other members of the house party, General Owen Williams and the Earl of Coventry. Despite his protests of innocence, Gordon-Cumming was persuaded to sign a solemn undertaking never to play cards again so long as he lived. This he did to avoid a scandal involving the Prince of Wales, in itself a somewhat uphill task. (As it was, Gordon-Cumming subpoenaed the Prince as a witness at the subsequent trial.)

Gordon-Cumming left the house party the next day, but his secret undertaking soon became the subject of considerable gossip. Eventually he received, two days after Christmas, an anonymous letter written from Paris signed by 'Someone who pities you' who clearly had heard most of the details of the scandal. Gordon-Cumming felt he had to sue and he issued proceedings for slander against Levett, Mr and Mrs Wilson and Mr and Mrs Lycett Green, his less blue-blooded accusers.

Much has been written of the proceedings before the Lord Chief Justice, Lord Coleridge. Certainly the way the case was conducted left much to be desired. Admission to the courtroom was by ticket signed by the Lord Chief Justice, who had appropriated half of them for his friends who came to court with their opera glasses. His family played an important role in the trial, his daughter sketching the scene and his wife periodically prodding the dozing septuagenarian judge.

The number of witnesses against Gordon-Cumming, the undertaking he had signed, the amount he had won and the evidence of his erstwhile friend the Prince of Wales made the result inevitable. The Prince was asked by a juryman:

What was your Royal Highness's opinion at the time as to the charges made against Sir William Gordon-Cumming?

To which the Prince replied:

The charges appeared to be so unanimous that it was the proper course – no other course was open to me – than to believe them.

The jury took only thirteen minutes to find against Gordon-Cumming. The result was, however, greeted with jeers and there were those who believed in his innocence. Sir Edward Clarke QC, his counsel and the Solicitor General, was to write in his memoirs: 'I believe the verdict was wrong and Sir William Gordon-Cumming was innocent of the offence charged against him'. Gordon-Cumming's wife was convinced that the accusation was engineered by the Prince of Wales to settle a score with Gordon-Cumming over his affair with the Prince's mistress, Lady Frances Brooke.

The evidence against Gordon-Cumming was however extremely strong. (He was a man who once boasted that he had broken every commandment except that against murder.) In any event his ruin was swift and complete. He had to resign from the army, leave Court and he was expelled from the Carlton, Turf, Marlborough and Guards Clubs. He did not again grace London or the racecourse, the hunting field or any of the fashionable resorts of the era. For the remaining forty years of his life he lived outside society at Altyre, dying in 1930, still protesting his innocence. The seal had been put upon his ruin by his libel action.

For a defendant, a libel action can mean going out of business and in the 1930s it could also carry the threat of imprisonment. This was the fate which befell the distinguished magazine, *Night and Day*, and which might have ended with Graham Greene going to prison.

Night and Day was a magazine somewhat along the lines of the *New Yorker*. Amongst its backers were Ian and Peter Fleming and Graham Greene. Books were reviewed by Evelyn Waugh, architecture by Hugh Casson, art by Osbert Lancaster and films and plays by Graham Greene. It was a particularly spirited review of the film *Wee Willie Winkie*, starring the child star Shirley Temple, which was its undoing and caused it to cease publication in December 1937.

Considerable latitude is given to the expression of comment in the law of libel, provided that it reflects the honestly held opinion of the critic and that it is not a cover for allegations of fact. Graham Greene's review, for all its fine writing, appears to have transgressed that second proviso. Godfrey Winn called the review 'a queer one, because it was not a criticism of Shirley's clever acting at all, but one which introduced potential audience reactions – reactions which were entirely alien to Shirley's lovable and innocent humour'.

The topic raised by the reviewer was, as Winn suggested, male audience reaction to child actresses and it was forbidden territory in the 1930s. When Greene wrote of 'the gasp of excited expectation from the antique audience', he had something rather different in mind from the normal adulation of cinemagoers; when he referred to the trousers she wore in *Captain January* and the short kilts she wore in

Wee Willie Winkie, he was not thinking of her costumier. Standards change and it is doubtful whether such an action would be brought today, unless it was being suggested that an actress was taking part in a pornographic film. Greene never suggested anything of the kind.

Of its genre, Graham Greene seems to have considered the film a reasonable specimen, although his enthusiasm was lukewarm:

> It is not hard to stay to the last prattle and the last sob. The story – about an Afghan robber converted by Wee Willie Winkie to the British Raj – is a long way after Kipling. Both stories are awful, but on the whole Hollywood's is the better.

The review might still be defamatory of the film company for its suggestion that it exploited its child stars, but it is doubtful whether they would now bring such an action.

Libel was admitted. Damages totalling £3,500 were awarded to Shirley Temple and the film companies. They were agreed at a modest level with the money being paid to charity. The publisher and printer had to meet the legal costs. The plaintiff's counsel, Sir Patrick Hastings KC, referred to it as 'one of the most horrible libels that one could imagine'. Obviously he would not read 'this beastly publication' in open court. The defendants made their deepest apologies praying in aid the fact that the magazine had ceased publication.

As the statement was read in open court, the Lord Chief Justice, Lord Hewart ominously asked:

> 'Who is the author of this piece?'
> 'Mr Graham Greene', counsel for the defendants, Valentine Holmes, replied.
> 'Is he within the jurisdiction?'
> 'I am afraid I do not know.' (Graham Greene was prudently in Mexico at the time.)
> 'The libel is simply a gross outrage and I will take care to see that suitable attention is drawn to it.'

The Lord Chief Justice's performance led Anthony Powell, himself a contributor to *Night and Day*, to observe that the judge gave the impression of a man for whom Freud appeared to have lived in vain.

When Graham Greene's collected criticism for the years 1935-40 was published in 1972, his review of *Wee Willie Winkie* was conspicuously absent. It was made clear to Greene that even thirtyfive years after the event any repetition of the libel would be unwelcome to the, by then, ambassadress.

Lord Hewart clearly had in mind a criminal prosecution of Greene. In fact no such action was taken. The judge had no doubt as to the role of criminal law in such matters. In 1935 the Duchess of Marlborough had brought an action in respect of a somewhat suggestive drawing of two rose trees (recognizable as the Duchess of Marlborough and the Rev F Page Roberts varieties) with its risqué but incorrect caption: 'I guess we shouldn't have planted the Duchess of Marlborough and the Rev H Robertson Page in the same bed.'

This not terribly grave action was proceeding, until Lord Hewart turned to counsel for the plaintiffs and asked: 'Have you considered the wisdom of prosecuting in this case?' That was enough to persuade the defendants to settle the case hastily. The judge congratulated the Duchess on her magnanimity in the face of this 'foul emanation from the printing press'.

An example in more recent times of the serious consequences that a libel action may have is to be found in the case that Tommy Docherty brought against Willie Morgan and Granada Television Ltd.

In June 1977 Docherty was manager of Manchester United and one of his former players, Willie Morgan, in a footballing preview programme called 'Kick Off' made a number of disparaging remarks about Docherty. He was 'about the worst manager there has ever been' and 'When he goes, I think the rejoicing in Manchester will be like winning the cup again and, when that happens, it will be a good club again'.

It was strong stuff but Morgan had left Manchester United following an eye injury and it was something that might have passed in the rough and tumble of professional football. It did not. Docherty sued and the gloves were off. He alleged that Morgan was motivated by malice after being relieved of the team captaincy. Morgan made a number of serious implications about Docherty's behaviour of which one of the milder was that Docherty had sung a dirty ditty about Morgan at the annual Catholic sportsmen's dinner in Manchester which was attended by priests, nuns and a bishop.

With allegations and counter-allegations, what originally had appeared to be a straightforward footballing libel case, was now scheduled to take five weeks. However, after three and a half days Docherty wilted under cross-examination from John Wilmers QC. He gave conflicting answers about whether or not Dennis Law knew that he was to be placed on a free transfer to Manchester City and, when asked:

'You told a pack of lies to the jury about this, didn't you?'

'Yes, it turned out that way', Docherty surprisingly replied. At that point he had earnest discussions with his lawyers and his case collapsed. He withdrew the action and paid Morgan's costs. Nearly three years later he found himself on trial at the Central Criminal Court on two charges of perjury alleging he had lied about the circumstances of Dennis Law's transfer and about the terms of a contract whereby Ted McDougall was transferred to Manchester United from Bournemouth Football Club at a price which was adjusted according to the number of goals he scored.

At the criminal trial Docherty was able to explain that he had not done justice to himself in the civil action and that the admissions were extracted from him under ferocious cross-examination. They were not evidence of any intention to lie to or mislead the jury. He was duly acquitted, but he had become a further victim of the pitfalls of libel.

If not actually a disaster, one of the more unsuccessful libel actions in recent years must have been that brought by Rolf Schild, an industrialist, against the *Sunday Express*.

Rolf Schild, his wife and his fourteen year old daughter
were kidnapped in Sardinia in August 1979 and a £3 million
ransom was demanded. After protracted negotiations first
Mr Schild was freed, then his wife in January 1980 and his
daughter two months later, in return for a ransom of
£300,000. His plutocratic-sounding name with its suggestion
of a link with the Rothschild family had scarcely helped in
the negotiations with the Sardinian captors.

While Mr Schild was still in the hands of his kidnappers,
insult was added to injury when Sir John Junor in his
Current Events column in the *Sunday Express* on 2
September 1979 appeared to link the ransom demand with a
debt owed by Schild to the merchant bankers Keyser
Ullman.

Sir John Junor wrote quite gratuitously:

> Is it not an extraordinary coincidence that the reported
> ransom of £3 million demanded by Sardinian bandits for
> the release of Mr Rolf Schild, his wife and child is exactly
> the amount, including interest, which Mr Schild is said to
> owe the London merchant bank of Keyser Ullman? It
> could not possibly be, could it, that the man responsible
> for taking on the loan, Mr Edward du Cann MP, is
> spending the parliamentary recess leading a debt-
> collecting bandit gang in Sardinia?

It was, as the trial judge, Mr Justice Mars-Jones observed, a
joking remark 'in the worst possible taste'. It was
undoubtedly defamatory of Edward du Cann and his bank.
In fact the claim was in excess of £3 million but was
ultimately settled for a smaller sum.

Understandably it outraged Rolf Schild and he issued
libel proceedings, claiming that the *Sunday Express* article
had branded the kidnapping a sham which had been
arranged by him in the hope of being able to exploit it to
avoid paying the £3 million he owed to Keyser Ullman. He
also claimed that the article depicted him as hypocritical,
dishonest and prepared to exploit his wife and daughter. At
the trial it was made absolutely clear than no such allegation

was intended and that Mr Schild was the entirely innocent victim of the kidnapping plot. The sole issue was what the words meant and what any reasonable reader of Sir John Junor's column would think he was driving at.

On the face of it, Schild stood a very good chance of recovering enormous damages. The article, although somewhat obscure, was snide and offensive and hinted at some sort of disreputable conduct on the part of Rolf Schild. Furthermore there was considerable public sympathy for Schild, who, ominously from the newspaper's point of view, was known to be £300,000 out of pocket after paying the ransom.

However, after two and a half days Mr Justice Mars-Jones stopped the trial, having decided that the interpretation which the plaintiff sought to put on the words was quite unreasonable. He therefore ruled that the words complained of by Schild were not capable of bearing a defamatory meaning. That was the end of the case and meant victory for the *Sunday Express*.

Rolf Schild was left with a bill for legal costs of not less than £50,000 and with the galling experience of having rejected the sum of £10,000 damages which had been paid into court before the trial by the *Sunday Express*.

His appeal against the judge's ruling was turned down by the Court of Appeal in October 1982.

All in all it is difficult to improve on the comment made by Samson Fox, following his libel action against Jerome K. Jerome. Jerome in his magazine *Today* criticized Fox, a Leeds company promoter for his dubious claim that he could make gas from water. After a thirty day case the judge decided that it remained to be seen if gas could be made from water and awarded Fox a farthing damages, leaving each side to bear their own costs, in Fox's case £11,000 and in Jerome's £9,000.

As Jerome shook hands with Fox, Fox told him he was going back to Leeds to strangle his solicitor and suggested he do the same to his. Jerome regretfully concluded that it seemed too late to do so. He had to sell out his interest in *Today*.

Five

A Doctor, Docker and Solicitor and the smallest coin of the realm

It will be apparent that it is a relatively simple matter to commit a libel. Much that is written can be technically defamatory, but it can be published either because it is very unlikely that action will be taken or because it is substantially true.

Unfortunately, plaintiffs do sue when discretion might have dictated restraint. Juries can deal with such cases by awarding contemptuous or derisory damages. The defendant can pay into court a token sum such as £5 so that, if the plaintiff receives less than £5, his delight at winning is tempered by having to pay the legal costs. Even this course is not without its difficulties, as an unmeritorious plaintiff can straightaway accept the £5, claim his legal costs from the defendant and request leave from a judge to read a statement in open court, reminding the world of his exemplary character.

Cases where derisory damages are awarded fall into two distinct categories: those, such as the cases of Dr Dering and Gordon Goody, where the plaintiff's complaint appears to be wholly without any merit, and those, such as Lady Docker's and John Elliott Brooks's, where the jury felt the storm should have stayed in its teacup.

In June 1959 Leon Uris's novel *Exodus* was published in England by William Kimber. The book traced the sufferings of the Jewish people in Europe and the Middle East in the twentieth century. Tucked away on page 155 was a short passage:

Here in Block X, Dr Wirthe used women as guinea pigs and Dr Schumann sterilized by castration and X-ray and Clauberg removed ovaries and Dr Dehring performed 17,000 experiments in surgery without anaesthetic.

It was, in fact, a passage borrowed from an earlier book, *Underground, the Story of a People*, published in New York by Joseph Tenenbaum. Dr Wirths's name was mis-spelt and Dering had dropped the 'h' from his name after the war. In all probability the passage caused little worry to the author's libel lawyers. Clauberg, a former SS general and the reputed gynaecologist of Frau Heinrich Himmler, had died in a West German prison in 1956 after ten years in a Russian prison. Dr Edward Wirths, a garrison doctor at Auschwitz from 1942 to 1945, had committed suicide while in prison in 1945. Dr Schumann had fled to West Africa. No one had heard anything of Dr Dehring.

However, in April 1962 a letter arrived at the publisher's offices from an English firm of solicitors acting on behalf of Dr Wladislaw Alexander Dering, a fiftynine year old doctor practising in Seven Sisters Road, North London. It appeared that he considered that his patients might have understood this passage to refer to him despite the different spelling of his name. He demanded substantial damages and an apology in open court.

The career of Dr Dering had followed a somewhat different course from those of the other persons mentioned in the passage in the book and, for that matter, from those of the two other doctors whose names were to feature in his libel action, Captain Dr Rohde and Dr Entress. They had both been hanged. In contrast Dr Dering had been awarded the OBE for his ten years in the Colonial Medical Service in Somaliland, 'a somewhat strange decoration for a "war criminal"', his counsel, Colin Duncan QC, commented at the trial with a greater sense of irony than he intended. He had even received a lump sum compensation payment from the West German Government for injuries to his health during his four years at Auschwitz.

Dr Dering had qualified in Warsaw in 1928 and

specialized in gynaecology and obstetrics. In 1939 he became
a member of the underground resistance army in Poland. In
July 1940 he had been arrested by the Gestapo and was a
prisoner at Auschwitz from August 1940 to January 1944.
There he was a medical orderly until July 1941 when he
became a prison doctor. In July 1944 he was released from
Auschwitz to help Dr Clauberg. Thereafter his fortunes
fluctuated. The Russians captured him in April 1945 when
they overran Poland. They locked him up, but he was
released after eight days and made his way from Warsaw to
join General Anders's army in Italy. He went to England
when the war ended and worked at the Polish General
Hospital in Huntingdon. In the meantime his name
appeared on three lists of war criminals prepared by the
United Nations War Crimes Commission and he was wanted
by the Polish, the French and the Czech governments.
France and Czechoslovakia conceded Poland's prior claim.
Dr Dering was called for an interview in London in January
1947, which resulted in him spending nineteen months in
Brixton prison until, following a dramatic identity parade
held before the Chief Metropolitan Magistrate at Bow Street
Magistrates' court, where he was not picked out by ex-
inmates of Auschwitz, he was released. On 20 August 1948
he received a copy of the letter from the Home Secretary
which secured his release - although it did not contain the
most handsome of exonerations: 'There is not sufficient
evidence to support a prima facie case for the surrender of
Dr Dering to the Polish Government as a war criminal'.
Dering untruthfully told a reporter, 'No operations were
performed anywhere near me. It was all slander and lies.'

Had the evidence which was available to the jury in the
libel action been seen by the authorities in 1948, the result
might have been different. In 1964 the jury was able to see the
neatly tabulated records written in Dr Dering's distinctive
handwriting in the Auschwitz prison hospital operations'
register which after being in private hands after the war was
then preserved in the Polish National Museum at Oswiecim.
Its significance was that it enabled an unparalleled form of
identification to take place for, even if a 'patient' could not

recognize Dr Dering as the surgeon, he could by raising his left sleeve reveal a tattooed concentration camp number which corresponded with the number recorded in Dr Dering's handwriting in the register.

When the author and publisher received Dering's solicitor's letter, they had to discover precisely who Dering was and what he had done. It was no easy task some twenty years after the event. Joseph Tenenbaum was by then dead. Enquiries made of the West German war crimes prosecutor who was conducting an Auschwitz trial at Frankfurt put William Kimber in touch with Dr Alina Brewda who was also living in North London. Thereafter, through the combined efforts of his publishers, William Kimber, their solicitors Rubenstein Nash and Leon Uris's solicitor, Solomon Kaufmann, a witness was traced to Greece, another to Los Angeles and a number to Israel. The advice received from Gerald Gardiner QC, who happened to have been one of the first British officers to enter Belsen, was that it was the public duty of the author and the publisher to fight the case.

No apology was given. Dering issued a writ, claiming damages for libel against the author, the publisher and the printer. On the advice of their lawyers the publisher paid forty shillings into court to ensure that, if the jury awarded contemptuous damages, Dering would have to pay their legal costs. The author refused to take even this modest step. The printer settled for £500 damages, an amount described in court as 'a substantial sum by way of damages' and an apology that came from the wallet rather than the heart.

In their defence to Dr Dering's claim for damages for libel, the remaining defendants, namely the publisher and the author, admitted the passage was libellous but asserted that it was true. They conceded that the number of 17,000 experimental operations was wrong; they would rely on a figure between 100 and 200.

The figure of 17,000 seems to have originated with Dr Alina Brewda. She had seen Dering perform experimental operations on ten Greek girls at Auschwitz and had concluded that when he had spoken of his 17,000 abdominal operations, they too were experimental. This was the figure

she had supplied to the UN War Crimes Commission. The
defendants further agreed that it was incorrect to say that
there was no anaesthetic. In fact, spinal anaesthetics were
given, but the defence case was that these were needlessly
painful and wholly inappropriate. The defendants also
conceded that Dering's operations took place in Block 21,
the operating theatre, and not Block 10, the experimental
unit.

On the face of it, these concessions appeared to indicate
that the defendants would fall far short of proving that the
allegations they had made against Dr Dering were true or
substantially true. The defendants had to prove the
substance of their allegations. These concessions made their
task considerably more difficult. However, as defence
witnesses came to London and were seen by the solicitors, it
became apparent that the evidence they could give was
stronger than had originally been thought. Normally the
plaintiff in a libel action will know the strength of the
defendant's case, as the defendant has to produce a written
defence before the trial. This will set out the principal facts
on which he will rely to prove the truth of what he wrote.
These are called the particulars of justification and the
general rule is that the defendant cannot go beyond the
particulars given before the trial. In the exceptional
circumstances of this case, the judge permitted this
additional evidence to be given subject to Dr Dering's right
to recall his witnesses.

Dering's case was that he had never carried out any
experimental operations, that what he did was done under
the threat of being 'liquidated', that he never failed to use a
proper anaesthetic and that what he did was for the best for
the wretched victims of Auschwitz. The defendants contended that Dering was a conscious tool in the hands of the
Nazis for their policy of mass sterilization. The purpose of
this 'policy' was to devise an acceptable way of eliminating
over a couple of generations those with partly Jewish blood,
whom it might be inexpedient to murder.

These were the issues that an English jury of ten men and
two women had to decide in the trial which was presided

over by Mr Justice Lawton and lasted eighteen days between 13 April and 6 May 1964.

That Dering was subjected to duress was beyond question. His wife was imprisoned by the Nazis in Warsaw and threatened with execution. He saw the inmates of Auschwitz being exterminated in their thousands. He and a number of his colleagues were convinced that disobedience to orders would result in their execution and would not help the prisoners. His health suffered; he had a hernia and large varicose veins; he had lost some teeth through beatings and had a very bad chest condition and fibrositis.

The jury had to decide under what conditions Dr Dering had worked. His case was that to refuse to remove ovaries required for further exploration would be sabotage punishable by death. Twenty to twentyfive Polish doctors had been executed, Dr Dering said. The defence denied that this was so; the only doctor sent to the gas chambers was a Dr Samuel who was sent prematurely senile by the horror of working at Auschwitz. Two doctors who had been at Auschwitz supported Dr Dering, Dr Mezyk and Dr Grabczynski, maintaining that a straight refusal of an order was unthinkable. Dr Grabczynski did, however, say that, if Dr Dering had refused to carry out the operations, he probably would also have refused. Dr Dering also contended that if he had refused to perform an operation, it would probably have been done by an unskilled SS corporal.

It seems that the jury found the defence witnesses more compelling. Dr Lorska, a Polish doctor who had been a member of the French Resistance, was asked what her reaction would have been if she had been asked to take out an ovary. 'I think I would have committed suicide.' Dr Alina Brewda, a Polish-Jewish doctor, of whom many of the victims of the experimental operations (though not Dr Dering) were to speak warmly said: 'If a surgeon had refused to do the operation, I very much doubt if it would have been carried out by someone else'. Dr Adelaine Hautval, had found herself in Auschwitz, because she had protested to the Gestapo about their treatment of Jews in France. They called her 'amie des juifs'. Mr Justice Lawton described her as 'one of the most impressive and courageous women ever to have given evidence in the courts of this country'. She told how she had been requested by Dr Clauberg to help him:

> 'Did you in fact take part in any of Clauberg's experiments?' Gardiner asked.
> 'No.'
> 'As a result were you shot?'
> 'No.'
> 'Were you punished in any way?'
> 'No, not in any way.'

Later she had been asked by Dr Wirths to give anaesthetic to a Greek girl to enable an ovarectomy to take place. She refused and Dr Wirths had asked her:

> 'Can't you see these people are different from you?'
> 'I answered there were several other people different from me, starting with him.'

In his summing up Mr Justice Lawton described that as a devastating answer.

Dr Hautval's advice to Dr Lorska had been that they would probably be executed in the end to prevent them telling the world what happened. 'So the only thing that is left to us is to behave for the rest of the short time that remains to us as human beings.'

In deciding where the truth lay the jury were perhaps assisted by the lack of remorse of Dr Dering and the surprising answers he gave. One of his counsel's final questions to him was:

> 'So far as you and your conscience are concerned, would you do the same today?'
> 'I would do just the same today. Maybe it would be done better, due to experience.'
> 'Do you think they had chosen Jews for these experiments because they were Jews or simply because there were more Jews than any others in the camp?'

'That was just bad luck for them. We were sorry for them. I would not have hesitated for the same reason to castrate Polish officers.'

The jury heard of operations too appalling and tragic to recount here. A number of witnesses spoke of Dering's anti-semitism – when he was a student no Jewish medical student was allowed to join the Polish Medical Association. One of the Greek girls recounted how Dering had hit her saying, 'You damned Jewess, keep still until I have finished'. One of the men had been told, 'Stop barking like a dog. You will die anyway.' Gardiner was to put one of the most damaging questions ever asked in cross-examination, a question that he claimed went to Dering's credibility:

'Do you remember saying "look closely at this tobacco pouch and see what is special about it? Can you see it is seamless? Do you know what it is? It is made from a tanned scrotum".'
'It is not true. I have heard about the allegation. It is absolutely wrong.'

Dr Dering had denied to the Home Office after the war that he carried out any operations of sterilization or castration. That was something he sought to qualify, rather un-convincingly at the libel trial. He was asked:

'You knew even at the time that Dr Schumann was engaging in experiments with a view to seeing how far after the war people in large numbers could be sterilized?'
'It was my and my colleagues' guess why these silly experiments were carried out.'

At the trial he initially denied that he had carried out experimental operations. This claim was skilfully demolished by Gardiner. He agreed he had sterilized a woman because of 'some crime against morality', and had castrated a German gypsy because of some 'hereditary disease'.

'Was it done against the patient's will?' he was asked.

'I did not ask because it was not my duty to ask.'

'Did the operation do the man any good?'

'No.'

'Was this done with or without his consent?'

'It was done on court orders.'

'With or without his consent?'

'He was not asked for his consent.'

'Was there any medical reason for it?'

'The diagnosis and sentence were based on his medical disability. I accepted this against my will and wish.'

'Well, Dr Dering, who wanted these operations performed, Dr Schumann or the patient?'

'Dr Schumann.'

'If you knew Dr Schumann wanted them for his experiments, they were experimental were they not?'

'Yes.'

'Should not a doctor always think of the welfare of his patient?'

'It was not always possible.'

Although the case raised many moral issues, it was ultimately to be decided on the facts. Was the passage in the book a near miss or not on the target area, the judge asked the jury. At one point in his evidence Dr Grabczynski had said that disobedience could result in death. Gardiner commented that that defence was rejected at Nuremberg. The judge intervened to say that the case was being heard according to common law in the Royal Courts of Justice. In his summing up the judge observed that two moral questions arose, first what should a doctor do if he is in fear of his life or of serious injury and secondly, what should he do if he thought that if he refused to do an operation it would be done by someone unskilled. Mr Justice Lawton commented that he took some comfort from the fact that, although the jury had to take the law from him, they would not have to take his views on moral problems. The dilemma was comparable, he suggested, to the position of the early Christians suffering persecution during the reign of Emperor Decius.

There were those who spoke highly of Dr Dering. Dr Jan Grabczynski, a Polish doctor, was one. Dr Mezyk testified as to Dering's operating skills. A number of Polish prisoners were called to speak of Dering's kindness until the judge asked his counsel, Colin Duncan QC, if he 'wanted to go on asking whether Dr Dering was kind to people. No doubt he was kind to certain people.' The defence witnesses spoke of his crude surgery, the severe scarring on the surviving victims, the use of spinal rather than general anaesthetics on terrified young girls, the unnecessary speed and lack of prophylactic sterilization that attended his operations.

Above all, evidence emerged of the specious justifications of the operations – to reduce the risk of cancer in irradiated patients – and of the privileged status of Dering: occasional trips to the cinema, being smartly dressed, clean shaven and one of only two doctors released from Auschwitz. When Dr Dering had told the Home Office after the war that he had been kept in solitary confinement and had been sent back to the concentration camp, what he had meant, he explained to the jury, was that he had had to stay in his block and could not go out for fourteen days and that, although he had not been sent back to the camp, he had been kept on the concentration camp list.

Twentytwo witnesses gave evidence for the defence including eight out of the ten women who had ovarectomies on 10 November 1943 and six of the young men who had their testes removed in 1943. 'Why are you operating on me? I am fit, not sick,' one had asked Dr Dering. In vain Dr Dering's counsel tried to establish that the girls were confused at the time of the operation and cheerful thereafter. 'I remember and shall till I die.' 'How could I have been cheerful? I had strong pain', were the unshakeable replies they gave.

After a retirement of two and a half hours the jury decided that the book was defamatory, but awarded no more than one halfpenny damages – the smallest coin of the realm.

Dr Dering was ordered to pay the defence costs which amounted to £20,000. He returned to his practice in Holloway, but he still owed £17,000 when he died the following year. The defence had fought the case on principal

but William Kimber, the book's publisher, has calculated
that the legal costs ultimately borne by the publisher were
about ten times what it would have cost to settle out of court
and apologize to Dr Dering. Despite the vindication of the
publisher's decision, the financial consequences, even of
victory, would scarcely encourage publishers to contest such
cases.

Why did Dr Dering sue? By issuing his writ, he reopened a
chapter of his life that was best left closed. It ruined him
financially and destroyed his health. Although he originally
wanted damages of £7,000, this was later dropped to £2,000
and one imagines the case was not brought just for money. It
appears he firmly believed that he had done nothing
reprehensible.

It is difficult to see why Dr Dering felt it necessary to bring
a libel action for such a passing reference, particularly when
his name was not even spelt right. He should have thought
rather more carefully whether his patients in the Seven
Sisters Road would ever have associated this with him and
how his behaviour would appear to others. Instead he
launched into libel proceedings without properly assessing
the prospects of the case being fought to the bitter end. As
often happens, he let the fact that he had been technically
libelled cloud his judgment. He failed to weigh up the
evidence that could be brought against him to prove some of
the allegations.

The majority of cases where contemptuous damages are
awarded do not involve such sombre facts. The usual reason
for such awards is that the jury find it difficult to take the
plaintiff or his complaint particularly seriously.

Lady Docker's love of publicity and controversial lifestyle
suited her for a libel action. She and her husband had
featured in a 1952 libel action arising out of a well-publicized
row the Dockers had had with the Monte Carlo Casino and
Sporting Club. Prince Jean Louis de Faucigny-Lucinge
successfully sued the *News Chronicle* for a headline
'Dockers' Prince Quits Casino' when it suggested that he was
involved in what was described as 'a very unpleasant incident

involving the Dockers at the Monte Carlo Sporting Club'.

Norah Docker's flamboyant lifestyle in the austere 1950s successively intrigued and scandalized such of the population who bothered to follow her exploits. It spilled over into her husband's business career. She could be seen in her furs in her husband's company's gold-plated Daimler. Although she confessed it was only gold leaf on brass, it had nevertheless cost the staggering sum of £10,000 in 1951. Eventually the shareholders took a dim view of the car and of her touring the production line swathed in mink. Sir Bernard was fired in 1956 after a row about the £7,910 expenses he was claiming from his company (BSA) for his wife's furs and clothing, and he had to repay the money.

Lady Docker was herself no stranger to controversy. She was refused entry to the Royal Enclosure at Ascot in 1953. She was banned from Monaco in 1958 after stepping ashore from her 833-ton yacht *Shemara* (itself subsequently to be the subject of litigation over broker's commission when sold to Harry Hyams) and proceeding none too inconspicuously to tear up the Monégasque flag in her rage at her son not being invited to a christening party given by Prince Rainier. Not until 1982 was she removed from the Monaco blacklist.

In July 1958 she had despatched two QCs to defend her in Naples against a charge of insulting a Capri customs official, one Benito Pellegrino, by knocking his cap off. There was little they could do as they were not qualified to address an Italian court. Notwithstanding, Lady Docker was acquitted. As a gesture of goodwill, Gilbert Beyfus QC's clerk did reduce the fee from 1,000 guineas to 750 guineas, as all he had done was to travel to Naples and back. Pellegrino's evidence that he had been called a son of a bitch by Lady Docker was rejected by the court owing to his lack of knowledge of the English language and the court's quaint belief that no English lady would speak that way.

In 1961 Lady Docker had successfully brought a libel action against Truth (New Zealand) Ltd for the suggestion that she had tried to sell her life story to Beaverbrook Newspapers for £30,000. By consent 'a substantial sum' was paid to charity.

It was against Beaverbrook Newspapers that she brought
a libel action in 1974. The case arose out of a story that
appeared in the *Sunday Express*, in May 1972 under the
headline 'Naughty words get Lady Docker thrown out of
Jersey hotel'. It was a drama that led to a three-day trial
before Mr Justice Melford Stevenson and a jury.

For reasons that were never altogether clear, Ross
Benson, a columnist employed by the *Sunday Express*,
decided in May 1972 to ask Lady Docker about a rather less
than memorable incident in October 1968 which led to the
Rozel Bay Hotel in Jersey joining the distinguished
company of the Royal Enclosure and Monaco as portals
barred to Lady Docker.

Lady Docker's conduct after receiving a parking ticket
had led to Bert Taylor, the manager of the Rozel Bay Hotel,
banning her from the hotel. 'I don't want Lady Docker in my
hotel ever again. I won't have her back,' he declared. She
vehemently denied she had used bad language.

It was, however, a serious allegation so far as Lady
Docker was concerned. 'You can get very touchy when you
live on an island twelve miles by six', she explained. She
brought the action, she said, to clear her name and if she had
lost she could not have returned to Jersey. Jersey was such a
small island and the story spread round in a flash. Her
concern with the attitude of right-thinking Jersey people
represented a shift from her remark in 1969 that they were
'the most frightfully boring, dreadful people that have ever
lived'.

When she had been asked about the incident by Benson
three and a half years after it occurred, she admitted she had
made 'a few stormy comments to the hotel keeper after
discovering she had received a parking ticket.'

At the trial Lady Docker explained to the jury that she had
made a jocular remark about a parking ticket to the
manager. It seems that this evidence was greeted with some
incredulity by the judge, Mr Justice Melford Stevenson.
Lady Docker explained she had said:

'What do you think Bert? We have got a ticket at last.'

'Is that all you said?'

'Yes.'

'You really invite the jury to believe that?' the judge asked.

'Yes.'

'If you had said no more than you have told the jury what conceivable reason could Mr Taylor have had for ordering you out? He is not a madman, is he?' the judge asked, somewhat rhetorically.

'I think he is.'

Benson came to give evidence in support of the newspaper's defence that the story was true or, improbably, that it was fair comment on a matter of public interest. 'Surely you must have asked her what the stormy comments were', he asked. The journalist with commendable reticence replied that he had not.

'Why not?' asked the judge.

'I accepted "stormy comments".'

At the trial it emerged that, although the story as written informed readers that this incident had taken place over three years ago, there was no mention of this in the edited story.

The jury found in Lady Docker's favour and awarded her one halfpenny damages, a sum which the judge described as contemptuous. He ordered her to pay her own costs. Worse was to follow, as he told the jury:

'I wish everyone in the community was as sensible as you. The lady was obviously after a banner headline. A sufficiently large headline would have healed her wounds.'

The reason for bringing the action was not apparent. Such stories are, even if untrue, soon forgotten.

Such damages are not normally paid to spare the plaintiff's feelings. Lady Docker was spirited to the last. She announced she planned to have the halfpenny framed in gold and stuck on the stern of her new yacht. A suitable halfpenny had to be found and was duly presented to Lady Docker.

The libel action that John Elliott Brooks brought against the *Sunday People* in 1972 brought him very unwelcome notoriety. He had been a successful wartime soldier, attaining the rank of Lieutenant-Colonel, and a Conservative parliamentary candidate for Faversham. He had been the Mayor of the Royal Borough of Kensington and Chelsea and remained an alderman of the borough. He was an eminent solicitor in his early sixties with a successful practice near the Law Courts. The writ for libel, however, was to acquire him a somewhat different reputation and even the *Daily Telegraph* was to refer to him as 'The self-confessed bottom-spanker of young girls, hunting squire and ex-mayor'.

The article which spawned this litigation appeared in the *Sunday People* on 8 October 1972 and was not a total surprise to Mr Brooks, for on learning of its existence the day before he had telephoned the night news editor and had told him that he would sue for libel if they published. Ironically he was the legal adviser to the *News of the World*, but that cut little ice with its rival the *Sunday People*. The article was published and on Monday morning a writ for libel was issued.

The newspaper story produced something of a dilemma, practical if not moral, for Brooks. Either he could leave these allegations of sordid and perhaps criminal conduct unchallenged, with the danger of disciplinary proceedings being taken against him by the Law Society, who in fact took no action, or he could seek to prove the allegations were untrue, but only at the cost of revealing rather unsavoury details of his private life. There are times, and this appeared to be one, when there is sufficient underlying truth in a story to merit overlooking its inaccuracies and innuendoes. There was little doubt that the newspaper had been overdramatic. Their headline, 'Exposed – the top lawyer who traps girls for sex', was defamatory and was not true.

However, this was a case where great reflection might have kept Brooks out of court. People's memories are remarkably short. Very occasionally, and it is much rarer than many people think, a writ for libel is not unwelcome to a newspaper. In this case the *Sunday People* had published a successful exposé and it could scarcely capitulate after the disagreeable experience of its female reporter.

It was presented with the opportunity of fighting a case which provided a field day for headline writers such as 'Hanky-spanky in the squire's cabin'. Indeed, at the conclusion of the trial, Mr Justice Bristow observed to the newspaper's counsel, Michael Eastham QC, that paying one penny into court would have meant that Mr Brooks would have paid the paper's legal costs, which were believed to total £12,000. The paper, counsel said, had decided as a matter of policy not to pay anything into court.

The case had its origins in a marginally ambiguous advertisement that appeared in *Private Eye* in January 1972:

> Good-natured young ladies required as crew for motor yacht on Thames. Weekends Easter to October. All found plus good pay. No technical knowledge required.

A nineteen year old Manchester University student answered the advertisement and was interviewed at Mr Brooks's solicitors' offices. No less than three female members of Mr Brooks's staff took some part in the interview: his sporting and social secretary, his fortyseven year old articled clerk and his secretary, who apparently left the room at the mention of flagellation. There was at the trial some dispute as to whether or not it was explained to the student why the ladies had to be good-natured. Brooks's contention was that it had been made quite clear to the student that the rates were £5 for domestic duties and £15 for other duties and that she had opted for the £15. She said she had no idea of what was in store and that when, following drinks in Brooks's flat and champagne in his chauffeur-driven Rolls, they had boarded his boat *Adelaide Cottage III*, she had no reason to suppose she was undertaking anything other than normal crewing duties.

The sordid details of what transpired need not be

recounted save that it involved some beating and a use of
whisky that was probably never in the mind of its distiller.
Brooks's case was that what took place was horseplay and
was consented to by the girl. He compared it to walking
across a pebbled beach, uncomfortable at first.

Evidently this was a most unpleasant experience for the
student. She was offered and accepted two £10 cheques from
Brooks. She also went out with his son on four or five
occasions. Brooks might have been forgiven for thinking
that this was the end of the matter, but the girl decided a few
weeks later that this was a matter that should be reported to
the press. The *Sunday People* took up her case. She was paid
£450 and was able to discharge a friend's £400 garage bill.

The newspaper sent a female reporter posing as a
respondent to his advertisement, an agent provocatrice to
confirm the girl's story. She too was taken to Brooks's office
and the Wig and Pen Club and was interviewed by Brooks
and his staff. This time there was no doubt as to the duties
she would be required to perform. 'Getting whipped' and
'flagellation' were mentioned. To make certainty more
certain, Brooks was induced to be indiscreet in a taped
telephone call about what he had in mind. Needless to say,
the reporter did not keep the assignation on *Adelaide
Cottage III.*

The reporter was to tell the jury that she had not come
through the ordeal entirely unscathed. She had been 'goosed'
in the Wig and Pen club. Brooks had earlier in the case
admitted in cross-examination his partiality for 'goosing'.
The judge had intervened to ask:

'Not all of us know what goosing is.'
'Pinching a girl's bottom, my Lord', Brooks replied.

The reporter describing her goosing to the jury said:

'No man ever did it before.'
'And presumably no woman?' the judge asked.
'No man or woman would ever have the chance again,
even if they tried', the reporter replied.

'Do you get danger money?' the judge asked solicitously.
'No, I'm afraid not.'

It was an incident about which the judge reminded the jury in
his summing up, adding for good measure: 'And this in the
Wig and Pen Club.'

At the trial Brooks's counsel, Roger Gray QC, sought to
portray Brooks's conduct as that of a rumbustious
eighteenth-century hunting squire. However, the propositions by which he sought to do so would perhaps have cut
more ice with an eighteenth rather than a twentieth-century
jury.

'I suppose every full-blooded healthy vigorous male is a
bottom slapper in mind if not deed.'
'The prettiest, most demure, the most butter-would-not-
melt-in-the-mouth types, are the girls who are the
naughtiest experimenters.'

Brooks's case was that what had happened in this case was
done, as it always was, with the other party's consent and
that the newspaper article, particularly with its headline, was
an unwarrantable slur on his reputation. 'I think spanking a
girl's bottom if she is willing and enjoys it is simply part of
the fun.' He denied he had ever 'trapped young girls for sex'.

The case continued amidst a blaze of publicity. A weekend
intervened in the middle of the trial and Mr Brooks's attempt
to relax with a quiet day's hunting with the Enfield Chace
was shattered by the anti-hunt demonstrators whose
placards had hardly any *double* to their *entendre*: 'Have a
spanking good hunt with the Enfield Chace', and for good
measure notes saying 'Hands off' were stuck on their
bottoms.

The newspaper claimed that the article was true and fair
comment on a matter of public interest. The issue the jury
had to decide was whether, as Michael Eastham QC
suggested, Brooks was a self-confessed sadist, or whether, as
his own counsel argued, he was the victim of 'a grubby little
trick which left him scarred for life'.

After a retirement of three hours, the jury of nine men and three women reached a verdict that was rather closer to Eastham's submissions than Gray's. Brooks had indeed been libelled but he should only receive one halfpenny damages, they decided.

Back at the Wig and Pen, Mr Brooks held an impromptu press conference, making the statements normally made by those who receive contemptuous damages: 'Of course this has been worth it. I've won.'

The Sunday People felt sufficiently emboldened to write a similar article on 3 June 1979 following another advertisement by Mr Brooks for crew in the *Evening Standard*, but he did not sue. While the original article had been defamatory of him, this was a case where clearly the newspaper had some evidence against him. If the newspaper defended the action the consequences were likely to be worse than letting the article pass.

It should be said that not all litigants who receive contemptuous damages were quite so sanguine as Mr Brooks. The unusually named Moses Fairchild Gohoho, a Ghanaian politican, author and publisher, brought two actions for libel against the distributors of an article about him in the *Ghana Evening News* in March 1959. The cases were heard in October 1963 with the result that he lost one case and was awarded a halfpenny in the other. When he lodged an appeal, the defendants, not unreasonably, wanted security for costs, that is to say an order that he should lodge some money in court to cover the likely cost of the hearing.

When the defendants' application was successful, Mr Gohoho felt sufficiently moved by the result to take off his raincoat, revealing that he was wearing nothing below the waist other than a pair of socks and shoes, a fact which it was a little difficult to miss when he lay down on the front bench of the court, announcing that he would remain there until the case was heard. When his raincoat was securely fastened by the police, he was sentenced to seven days' imprisonment for contempt of court.

The recent case brought by Mrs Hazel Pinder-White

against her Member of Parliament Jonathan Aitken showed
that the spirit of Lady Docker lives on. She complained of a
passage written by Jonathan Aitken in the *East Kent Critic*,
a paper with a circulation of no more than 1,200 in his
constituency. Aitken had given offence by suggesting in his
column that the television series 'Dallas' could be reset in
Thanet.

'Who is dreadful enough to play JR? Step forward Charles
Pinder-White and his lovely wife (don't you think Hazel
could play Sue Ellen beautifully?) as the perfect anti-hero
of Thanet Dallas comedy.'

Harmless enough stuff one might have thought but Mrs
Pinder-White issued a writ for libel claiming that Aitken was
suggesting she was an adulteress and an alcoholic. Aitken
denied it meant any such thing. Mr Pinder-White also sued
but his action lapsed as he had the good fortune to die before
the case came to trial.

When Mrs Pinder-White had complained, Jonathan
Aitken had apologized but it seems that he did not take the
matter sufficiently seriously for the liking of Mrs Pinder-
White. 'I thought you would be flattered, Sue Ellen is a very
beautiful woman,' he ventured.

'So was Lucretia Borgia but I would not like to be
compared with her, either,' Mrs Pinder-White replied.

Jonathan Aitken did not improve things by the tongue-in-
cheek apology he published in the following issue of the *East
Kent Critic* which praised Mr Charles 'Tiger' Pinder-White
as the 'Sage of Sewage, Scourge of Seaweed, close personal
friend of Ronald Reagan; intimate pen-pal of royalty and
the sparring partner of Mohammed Ali.' The *East Kent
Critic* had not redeemed itself either by a spoof report that
JR was consulting his solicitors over the comparison with
Mr Pinder-White.

It emerged during the trial that what Mrs Pinder-White
had in mind by way of apology was Jonathan Aitken going
down on his knees in the middle of the public beach in
Thanet and telling the entire population of East Thanet how

sorry he was he had caused so much distress.

The case ran for five days to the merriment of Fleet Street, which reported with delight the fact that she and her husband, a retired textiles company director, had at various times owned ten Rolls Royces and that he had assisted during election campaigns in a white Rolls Royce.

The jury decided that she had not been libelled and she had to bear the costs of the five day case estimated at between £20,000 and £30,000. Jonathan Aitken who had to devote considerable time, energy and money to the case, quoted Groucho Marx with some feeling after the trial, 'If I never see her again, it's too soon.'

Six

No Jesting in the Public Interest

The traditional test for libel used to be whether the words brought the plaintiff into hatred, ridicule or contempt. Actions brought on the grounds of ridicule or lampooning are fairly rare. Such cases have considerable perils for a plaintiff, win or lose. He may make himself appear more ridiculous even if he wins. If he loses, he may make the incredible appear credible. Nevertheless if such an action is brought, it may turn out to be difficult to defend. The only defence may be that the words were too far-fetched or absurd for people to think the worse of the plaintiff. If the lampooner intends to lower the plaintiff in the estimation of others, the jury may well conclude that the words do just that and find in favour of the plaintiff.

This was the issue that arose in the second of two cases that Miss Nora Beloff, the political and lobby correspondent of the *Observer*, brought against *Private Eye* in 1971. The first gave rise to an eight-day action for breach of copyright which Nora Beloff lost on a technicality despite establishing a breach of copyright, and the second of a two-day libel action which she won, receiving £3,000 damages.

Although the two actions arose out of different articles in the same issue of *Private Eye* and out of similar subject matter, the legal procedure for each was different. The first action being a copyright matter had to be heard by a High Court judge in the Chancery Division; the second, a libel action, was heard by a judge sitting with a jury in the Queen's Bench Division. It might have been thought that with the technical copyright point raised in the Chancery Division and the scurrilous lampoon in the libel action, Miss Beloff might have prospered with the Chancery judge and failed with the jury; the reverse proved to be the case.

The issues raised in both cases were not dissimilar. Indeed it was argued on behalf of *Private Eye* that the copyright action was a device whereby Nora Beloff hoped to obtain libel damages by 'a side wind', when she could not bring a libel action. Unlike a libel action, truth or fair comment are not a defence to a claim for breach of copyright. There is a defence of fair dealing but it is very limited in scope. If Nora Beloff could establish that it was her copyright which had been infringed, she had a virtually unanswerable case.

The event which gave rise to the litigation was the lift which William Whitelaw, then Leader of the House of Commons, gave Miss Beloff from lunch at the Carlton Club to the House of Commons. Conversation in the car turned gloomily to what would happen if the Prime Minister, Edward Heath, ran under a bus. Mr Whitelaw said that there was no doubt that Heath would be succeeded by Reggie Maudling. The interest of this lay in the fact that since 1969 Mr Maudling had featured in a less than flattering series of articles in *Private Eye* highlighting his business relationship with Jerome Hoffman, the President of the Real Estate Fund of America. This grand title had not prevented Hoffman being sentenced to two years' imprisonment and fined for fraud offences. These articles had questioned Mr Maudling's financial integrity.

As it happened, it was to be the miners in early 1974 rather than a bus which did for Mr Heath (although not terminally). Mr Maudling had by that time resigned from his post as Home Secretary owing to another unfortunate business connection, also well-chronicled in *Private Eye*, this time with John Poulson, an architect who was given a seven-year sentence for corruption.

Following her conversation with Mr Whitelaw Nora Beloff wrote a confidential memorandum on 17 February 1971 to her editor and six editorial colleagues suggesting she should write a profile on Maudling, investigating the allegations against him by *Private Eye*, and 'set it in the wider context of his political personality and morality'. This article appeared in the *Observer* on 28 February.

Not everyone at the *Observer* was delighted by her article. Anthony Bambridge, the editor of *Observer* Business News, already had a team working on the allegations against Reginald Maudling, including information supplied by *Private Eye*, to find out whether he was a greedy rogue or merely ill-advised in his business contacts. Bambridge did not write his article, but it seems he inclined to the greedy rogue theory. *Private Eye* felt that Miss Beloff took a view which was unduly sympathetic to Maudling and hostile to them. In this they were less than just to her. When Maudling heard what was in her article, he was on the telephone to David Astor, editor of the *Observer*, trying to stop it being published. Nora Beloff felt that Maudling was to some extent both ill-advised in his business contacts and a greedy rogue. Where she differed from Anthony Bambridge was that she wanted her article to reflect Maudling's political abilities.

By this time her scenario for the Prime Minister's demise had moved a little upmarket for the headline read: 'Make no mistake if Ted Heath falls off his yacht, Reggie will become P.M.' Below that was another headline: 'Optimist in the Wings'. The article was a strong defence of Maudling. 'He would be the man who could best offer a genuine alternative Conservative policy. The country may need him.' He was still regarded as the government's number two and was unlikely to be damaged by *Private Eye*'s 'smear campaign'. She had few kind things to say about *Private Eye*; she wrote of 'the fortnightly political comic' and its 'anti-Maudling campaign' and their 'familiar mix of genuine revelations, half-truths and pure fabrication strung together by damaging insinuations'.

This did not go unnoticed by *Private Eye*. Someone at the *Observer*, 'willing and anxious that they should publish it', telephoned them with the text of her confidential memorandum. *Private Eye* published it with some relish, because they felt that the article written about Maudling did not bear out her professed aim of looking carefully at the evidence against Maudling and confronting him with it. The information they had supplied to the *Observer* about Maudling's relationships with bankrupts and swindlers appeared to them to have been overlooked or dealt with very perfunctorily.

The result was that Auberon Waugh wrote a piece in his 'HP Sauce' column about 'Miss Nora Bailiff' and Paul Foot wrote an article in his 'Footnotes' column called 'The Ballsoff Memorandum', which Mr Justice Ungoed-Thomas said at the trial was written 'in language that does not appeal to my generation'. However, he did go on to observe that 'the press was not a gentleman's club' and that 'you cannot live in glasshouses in this sort of life'.

A libel action on Foot's article was not really a possibility, as it was based on the 17 February memorandum and so a defence of justification or fair comment would probably have succeeded. The action therefore had to be brought on the basis of breach of copyright in the memorandum.

There was a technical difficulty to be overcome in that, as Miss Beloff was the *Observer*'s employee, the copyright of the memorandum belonged to The Observer Ltd. To remove this obstacle David Astor, her editor, assigned the copyright to her on 26 March thus, so it was thought, leaving the field clear for her to bring an action against *Private Eye*. This she did on 31 March 1971 claiming exemplary, aggravated and statutory damages for breach of copyright. At the trial it emerged that Mr Astor had never, in his twentyfour years as editor of the *Observer*, found it necessary to assign such a copyright. Indeed there was some doubt as to whether the editor had authority to assign the copyright of such an article. In any case it was a rather curious affair for the *Observer* newspaper had a liberal reputation and had published the odd leaked memorandum themselves.

It was rather more the sort of case a government department might bring than a journalist to whom leaks were part of life. There was an element of the biter bit. The distinctions that were drawn on behalf of Nora Beloff between permissible leaks (ie from official sources) and impermissible leaks (ie by stealth or theft) were rejected by the judge. Such a line could not realistically by drawn in copyright, as opposed to cases of breach of confidence.

The *Observer* was underwriting Miss Beloff's legal expenses and eventually these were estimated at £10,000. While *The Observer* stood behind their political correspondent, their Business News editor gave evidence for *Private Eye*, albeit under a subpoena.

The judge reviewed the evidence he heard in the eight-day trial at some length and in such terms that it was difficult to see how such nice people found themselves locked in this litigation. Miss Beloff was described as having an 'exceptionally quick mind and fluent speech' and was 'sensitive to all around her' and 'very adaptable'. David Astor was 'clearly experienced, wise and most kindly, with the qualities to get strong-minded persons to work together and produce the happy atmosphere which the evidence shows generally prevails among *The Observer* staff'. The defendants, Richard Ingrams, editor of *Private Eye*, and Paul Foot 'were of the younger generation, very able and serious-minded, impatient with what they regarded as stuffiness or pomposity, sincere and truthful'. They were 'forthright and outspoken' and 'there was nothing devious or muffled about them'. Anthony Howard, the editor of the *New Statesman* and Anthony Bambridge, the editor of *Observer* Business News were 'objective, reliable and most helpful'.

Mr Justice Ungoed-Thomas held on the evidence that the editor did not have authority to assign the copyright. However, but for that, *Private Eye* would have had no defence to the claim. *Private Eye* therefore won a technical knockout. It was clear that there could be a breach of copyright in such a case. If The Observer Ltd themselves had thought it worth taking proceedings, they would have won. However, only in the most flagrant of cases would the plaintiff obtain more than purely nominal damages, because the article published in breach of copyright would have no monetary value. The suggestion in the Beloff case that the publication of the memorandum was in the public interest or that this was fair dealing, 'tit-for-tat', failed completely. There was, it seems, no such thing as a jest in the public interest.

Undaunted by this setback Nora Beloff proceeded to her

libel action in respect of Auberon Waugh's 'HP Sauce'
column. It was scarcely a column that set out to be taken
seriously and it is worth looking at other articles that
appeared in it. Auberon Waugh wrote of the editor of *The
Times* having finally gone round the twist as evidenced by his
paying Bernard Levin £24,000 a year for his column. He put
forward John Freeman, the former British Ambassador in
Washington, who was 'thought to be living in a cave in
Epping Forest, eating honey and leaves' and Sir Malby
Crofton, the leader of the Kensington and Chelsea council,
'a much-maligned forty-seven year old letter-writing baronet'
as possible successors to the editor.

Miss Beloff was referred to 'as delicious seventyeight years
old Nora Ballsoff, who sometimes wrote under the nom-de-
plume Nora Bailiff ... Miss Bailiff, sister of the late Sir Alec
Douglas-Home was frequently to be seen in bed with Mr
Harold Wislon and senior members of the previous
administration, though it is thought nothing improper
happened'. The article also suggested that Mr Maudling 'is
the only important politician left who will talk to her'.

Readers of the column would have known that Miss
Beloff could give Miss Bailiff over a quarter of a century, she
never wrote under the name Nora Bailiff and she was no
relation of Sir Alec Douglas-Home, who was alive and well.
The article was untrue and unashamedly scurrilous. It need
scarcely be added that there was no hint of a suggestion at
the trial that any of the other allegations were true.

Private Eye did not call any evidence. Their defence was
simply that the whole thing was in jest and so absurd and far-
fetched that no one could possibly take the article seriously
or think the worse of Nora Beloff. This was not the view of
the plaintiff whose counsel, Thomas Bingham QC, argued
that this was a vicious and despicable attack on her morals in
revenge for what she had written about them in the
Observer. His argument was that readers might think that
many a true word is spoken in jest. There was certainly some
force in his argument. People are all too ready to believe that
there is no smoke without fire. Certainly no one would have
a higher regard for Nora Beloff after reading the article,

particularly at the Houses of Parliament, where she was a lobby correspondent, Nora Beloff did not call any witnesses to give evidence of having understood the article to reflect on her moral character. However, the jury was satisfied that the article did indeed libel her and they were no doubt influenced by the nature of the attack on her.

Mr Justice O'Connor in summing up to the jury had told them:

> Lampooning the establishment is age old. It has been done in all civilized societies and it is the hallmark of a civilized society that there should be a good deal of satirical writing and taking the wind out of unnecessarily puffed sails.

However, he went on to point out that it was:

> the law that one who defamed a person as a jest did so at his peril.

The jury agreed and awarded Miss Beloff £3,000 damages. *Private Eye*, however, undermined her victory by launching the 'Ballsoff Fund', an appeal to its readers for assistance in meeting the liability. Furthermore, Bernard Levin, virtually republished the libel complained of in his *Times* article 'Eye for an Eye'. He wrote:

> If Miss Beloff's copyright action had succeeded, it would have rendered almost impossible some of the most important and valuable contributions the press makes to public life ... As for her libel action, it has made even the wildest fantasies and jokes dangerous, if they are made about somebody with a seemingly underdeveloped sense of humour.

Miss Beloff saw matters very differently. In her reply to Bernard Levin's article she made the point that she was trying to distinguish between the truth and the distortions in the anti-Maudling campaign. One such distortion was *Private Eye*'s allegation that at one stage Maudling as Home

Secretary had instructed immigration officers to protect
Hoffman. In the copyright action her real objection was not
so much the leaking of the document, but the disclosure of
her confidential source. She brought the libel action
because, with the *Private Eye*'s mixture of fact and fiction,
mud might stick and people might believe that there was
some substance in what was written. For instance Auberon
Waugh's article did have an accurate account of an incident
about her and the parliamentary lobby. She wrote generally
of *Private Eye* mixing its filth with genuine revelation.

Honours remained about even, although, on the legal
issues, Miss Beloff came out ahead. There was too much
suspicion that *Private Eye* was trying to make a fool of Miss
Beloff and to have their own back for her article in the
Observer of 28 February for them to escape liability. They
faced, therefore, a bill of £3,000 damages and £2,000 costs. It
was a sum comfortably within their resources, as, by that
time, they had a circulation of about 100,000. The 'Ballsoff
Fund' raised no more than £1,200, but its main effect was to
perpetuate the libel and to discourage other would-be
litigants.

Despite winning the case and the argument, Miss Beloff
could be said to have come off worse in the litigation. An
inconsequential article was given a far greater importance
and degree of permanence than it deserved. By launching an
appeal to its readers accompanied by an unflattering
photograph of a grim-faced Miss Beloff, *Private Eye* was
able to extract the maximum capital from the case.
Somewhat unfairly, Miss Beloff emerged as totally lacking a
sense of humour. Perhaps if she had not lost the copyright
action on a technical point, she might well have accepted an
apology and there would have been no libel action.

This rather unpromising precedent was followed by Clive
Jenkins, General Secretary of ASTMS, when he sued the
Socialist Worker, a Trotskyist newspaper, for its article, 'Fly
me, I'm Clive', in 1977. It was full of abysmal left-wing
humour attacking Jenkins for his union's decision to assist
its members to take their holidays in Spain, while it was

governed by Franco. If you laughed at the references to Franco Chappelli (the electricians' union leader, Frank Chapple) you were presumably convulsed by the references to ringside seats at the garrottings of Spanish militants. In any event, for this bizarre article Jenkins recovered £1,000 libel damages and, interestingly, £1,000 copyright damages for the use of his facsimile signature. ASTMS likewise received £100 libel damages and £1,000 copyright damages.

It clearly was most unpleasant for a leading trade unionist to have his left-wing credentials undermined in this way. However, it also had the disagreeable consequence, as with the Beloff and *Private Eye* action, that Clive Jenkins found that an appeal fund was launched within his trade union and the Labour Party to help raise the damages and costs that had been awarded to him (and a few others) against the *Socialist Worker*.

The lampooner is likely to come a cropper in a libel action. When the article has been read out a few times in the Royal Courts of Justice, it will have lost most of its original humour. As Richard Ingrams has pointed out, cases do not tend to get laughed out of court. Occasionally, however, a plaintiff does pay the penalty for a lack of sense of humour.

Recently a jury found it difficult to take too seriously a light-hearted caption 'Marine Thief' to a photograph in the *Yachting World* of a respectable dentist repairing his outboard motor. They awarded him a halfpenny, leaving him to pay the costs of the action.

Cases do sometimes get laughed out of court. Such a case was that brought against the *Daily Sketch* by Mrs Quinn, wife of the impresario Paul Raymond. She was a director, with her husband, of Paul Raymond Productions Ltd. She objected to the headline 'Mother takes nude's place in lion show'. Her complaint was that her predecessor, despite appearances to the contrary, had not been nude, but wore a strategically located 'V-shaped garment'. She herself was more decorously dressed wearing a brassière with sequins.

The article did not show her in a particularly good light. What had happened was that, following an unfortunate

accident to the lion-tamer Nikolai in the lion cage at
Nottingham, the near-nude, Miss Zelda Lamone, had
decided to leg it. Mrs Quinn had stepped Daniel-like into the
lion's cage in the best tradition that the show must go on. The
suggestion that she appeared in the show in a state of near-
nudity was particularly unfair and unmerited. Nevertheless,
her case was destroyed by a few music hall turns by the judge,
Mr Justice Hilbery.

When W A Fearnley-Whittingstall QC, her counsel, was
explaining about his client's bikini, there was the inevitable
question 'What is a bikini?' and the judge suggested to
counsel that he should show the jury how it is worn. 'My
Lord, it would not fit me,' was the reply.

All was not quite what it seemed; the plaintiff admitted
that she had no connection with Brazil despite having
appeared in 1953 at the Theatre Royal, Margate as Zsa-Zsa,
the Brazilian Bombshell. Equally in this show all the Nues de
Paris were English and had no particularly noticeable
connection with Paris.

In his summing up, the judge observed: 'It has been said
that a nude was a girl who wore a large hat and a G-string.
All I knew about a G-string was that it was the lowest note on
a violin'.

The jokes may not have been original, but they ensured
that the plaintiff's claim failed.

The lampooner did however win in the case brought in
February 1984 by Derek Jameson against the BBC for their
satirical sketch about him in the Radio 4 programme *Week
Ending*. He was the former editor of three tabloid
newspapers and did not find to his liking the programme
which suggested that he went to the *Daily Express*
uncluttered by taste or talent and took to his new role like a
duck to orange sauce and had an editorial policy of all the
nudes fit to print and all the news printed to fit. He was
described as the archetypal East End boy made bad and the
programme was full of doubtful jokes suggesting that he
thought erudite was a kind of glue. In any event he issued a
writ alleging that the programme made him out to be stupid
and illiterate.

The BBC denied that the words would be understood to be libellous and claimed that viewed as a whole, the programme fell within the permissible bounds of fair comment. After a lengthy trial and an examination of the tit and bum press the jury agreed and Mr Jameson was left with a bill for legal costs reported to total £75,000.

Seven

Libel and the Criminal Classes

It has been said that the Law Courts like the Ritz are open to all. Money is an essential ingredient in both, particularly in libel cases, where legal aid is not available. One noticeable difference between the two is that those who are enjoying Her Majesty's hospitality in prison can use the Law Courts, even though the Ritz is barred to them.

A number of libel actions have been brought by prisoners. The most well-known is that brought by Alfred Hinds against the police officer who arrested him. With the assistance of James Comyn QC, he was able to prove that he was not guilty of the offence for which he had been gaoled. Harold Loughans was not so lucky: with the assistance of Sydney Silverman MP, he was able to show that he had been wrongly acquitted of a charge of murder.

In the 1960s various attempts were made by convicted prisoners to establish their innocence in front of civil juries because of a curious legal ruling that a conviction was not necessarily proof of guilt in a civil case. This device was used by a number of the Great Train Robbers, including Gordon Goody, with the result that the law was changed in 1968.

Another feature of cases brought by prisoners was that prison made them sensitive on matters that would scarcely have troubled those outside. This was exemplified by the actions brought by Francis Fraser and Jack Day.

The strangling of Mrs Rose Robinson, the licensee of the John Barleycorn public house in Portsmouth on 28 November 1943 may have seemed a routine crime to the police. There was one odd feature in that she had been strangled with one hand – the right hand. The case was to have a number of curious consequences. A man was tried twice for the murder and acquitted at the second trial. A retired judge who had been the prosecuting counsel at both trials found himself sued for libel eighteen years later for suggesting in a Sunday newspaper that a man called Harold Loughans had been lucky to get away with it. The jury in the libel action decided that the original juries were wrong and that Loughans was guilty of murder. Loughans appealed against their verdict but forestalled the appeal by confessing to the paper that he had committed the murder.

The unfortunate Mrs Robinson was murdered at her public house in the course of a burglary in which £400 was stolen. The police had no idea who had done it until three weeks later they arrested a middle-aged lag called Harold Loughans for trying to sell a pair of stolen boots in London. To their amazement he promptly confessed to the Portsmouth murder in these remarkable terms:

'The yard wants me for things far more serious than this. It's the trapdoor for me now. I am glad you picked me up.'

and subsequently:

'She must have had a weak heart, poor old girl.'

Loughans not only told this to the incredulous police officer, but he signed a confession. Nevertheless at his trial at the Winchester Assizes he ran an alibi defence that he had been in Warren Street tube station at the time of the murder with sufficient skill to ensure that the jury failed to agree. He claimed he was an inveterate liar given to making false confessions. In the fortnight before his retrial at the Old Bailey he altered the main thrust of his defence. He claimed that a childhood accident to his right hand, which left him with only a thumb and a little finger and three stumps, meant that he could not physically have strangled Mrs Robinson with that hand. This defence was supported by Sir Bernard Spilsbury and the man known inside as 'Fingers' Loughans was acquitted. His forensic triumph was lessened by being

arrested on a charge of robbery at the door of the Central
Criminal Court and jailed for five years. This and other
matters kept Loughans in prison for most of the time until
1963.

Prosecuting counsel at his trial had been Joshua David
Casswell QC, who was subsequently appointed to the High
Court post of Official Referee. When he retired, he wrote his
memoirs entitled *Lance for Liberty*. These dealt in suitably
judicial terms with the Loughans case. He made the point
that Mr Justice Atkinson at the Winchester Assizes had not
permitted the prosecution to call evidence of a dummy run
carried out by police officers to demonstrate that Loughans
could have returned to Portsmouth to commit the murder
despite having earlier been at Warren Street tube station.
The suggestion was that Loughans would probably have
been convicted if the jury had heard about these tests.
However, to avoid any legal difficulties, he concluded his
account, 'Not for one moment do I wish to impugn the
complete and utter vindication of Loughans's entire
innocence'.

Not even Loughans could have taken issue with such a
handsome exoneration. Unfortunately the judge's publisher,
George Harrap, sent a copy of the manuscript to the *People*,
who decided to serialize the book. They felt that they needed
a ghost-writer to 'jazz-up' or, as Harrap's editor, Joseph
Gaute, helpfully explained to the judge, 'rewrite it to suit the
particular market for which they cater'. The judge endorsed
the serialization but probably gave it no more than a cursory
glance. What was written in the *People* in December 1960
was more sensational in tone:

THE CASE OF THE CONFESSION AND THE CAST-IRON ALIBI

'This was the perfect murder', said the judge. He shook his
head in sheer bewilderment. A full confession and an
unshakeable alibi. Mr Justice Atkinson could do nothing
but order a retrial. By Joshua Casswell QC. Today this
famous barrister reveals the secrets of the strangest and
most baffling murder trial of his career, a case which the
judge called the perfect crime.'

By this time Loughans was well into a ten-year stretch of preventive detention in Wormwood Scrubs. He had to make do with the version in the *People* rather than in *Lance for Liberty*. He sought advice and, as he later recounted, a prison officer suggested that 'I should do something about it. He said that, as I had not been found guilty of the murder, I should sue the *People* for libel. He suggested I should write to Mr Sydney Silverman MP and ask him if he would take up my case.'

Silverman did take up his case and a writ for libel was issued against the editor and publisher of the *People* and Mr Casswell, the ghost-writer having remained too ethereal for any process-server. The case was heard before Mr Justice Gorman and a jury in January 1963.

Loughans was not an impressive witness. Defence counsel, Joseph Molony QC, accused him of being 'artful, cunning, treacherous and deceitful'. In cross-examination it was suggested that he was a man of violence. He angrily denied this.

> 'Listen to me; if you were not in the position you are, I should tell you something.'

On the question of his veracity, he was asked:

> 'You have been spending your whole life telling lies?'
> 'Not my whole life.'

He was asked about his motives in bringing the case:

> 'No doubt you enjoyed the publicity you were getting?'
> 'Oh yes, I love it.'

His counsel, Patrick O'Connor QC, produced a forceful argument that this was a gross libel even of a man of his client's bad reputation. It had been open to the defence to plead in mitigation of damage, to reduce the sum they might have to pay, that Loughans was of bad character, but they had chosen not do so so. His client might be a thief and a housebreaker and (in an unfortunate choice of phrase) a man who could not keep his fingers off other people's property, but he was not a murderer.

There were alternative lines of defence which might appear contradictory to ordinary mortals but are standard form to libel lawyers. These were that the article did not mean Loughans was guilty of the murder or, if it did, he was. After a retirement of three hours five minutes, the jury decided that the words did mean that Loughans was guilty of the murder of Rose Ada Robinson and that the article was true in substance and in fact.

The jury in the 1963 libel action had only to be satisfied that Loughans was guilty on the balance of probabilities as opposed to proof beyond reasonable doubt in criminal cases. Furthermore no one was going to hang Loughans in 1963, as they certainly would have done in 1944. It was a most unusual result, particularly in the light of the limited evidence that was available to the 1963 jury. Undaunted by this setback, Mr Silverman immediately announced that an appeal was under consideration. Before it could be heard and as soon as he was free to do so, Loughans visited the offices of the *People* and confessed that he had indeed strangled Mrs Robinson. With a commendable sense of fair play, the *People* 'gave him a few pounds to help him on his way'. Loughans having been acquitted could not be re-tried and in any event he had terminal cancer.

It seems he had no more substantial reason for bringing the action than to help while away his time in prison and to gain the publicity of which he was so fond. Money does not appear to have been the motive. He had originally written from prison to the paper's solicitors, saying that he would be happy with £150 plus costs. The newspaper paid £250 into court which Loughans could have accepted but he chose to fight on.

Loughans was foolish not to let matters rest in 1944. The defence by 1963 had the advantage of knowing what Loughans had said at the trial and why the prosecution had failed. What they had to do in the civil action was to prove that it was more probable than not that Loughans committed the murder. All Loughans had succeeded in doing was underlining his good fortune in being acquitted and avoiding the hangman.

The most successful libel action brought by a person convicted of a crime to clear his name was unquestionably that brought by Alfred Hinds against Detective Superintendent Herbert Sparks, the officer who arrested him. He was awarded £1,300 damages. The case was the culmination of an eleven-year struggle to obtain a retrial.

Hinds had been convicted at the Old Bailey of involvement in the robbery on 24 September 1953 at Maples's store in Tottenham Court Road, London in which some £34,000 in cash and jewellery was stolen. His original trial lasted two days, whereas the libel action in June and July 1964 took six weeks.

Sparks had told Hinds that one of the two 'inside' men at Maples had named him as being involved in the robbery. Allegedly Hinds, although he always denied it, had incriminated himself by replying to Sparks's questioning:

'How did you know? I suppose the missing watchman is the grass. I would like to know who shopped us.'

Such verbal admissions carried much more weight with juries at that time. With the aid of one of the robbers who turned Queen's evidence and some not very impressive forensic evidence about the dust on his shoes, Hinds was convicted. His alibi defence that he was at home watching television and his claim that the main prosecution witness against him was giving false evidence to reduce his sentence were rejected. The fact that two of his co-accused had given evidence for him did not assist him. It did not help them either. They each received ten years' preventive detention despite pleading guilty. By contrast the robber, who pleaded guilty but did not give evidence for Hinds, got six years and the one who gave evidence for the prosecution received a mere twelve months.

In sentencing Hinds to twelve years' preventive detention,

Lord Goddard had told him that he was satisfied that he was
a most dangerous criminal and that he was the person
mainly responsible for the safe-blowing carried out in the
course of the robbery. Sparks was congratulated by the
judge 'on bringing to book a very dangerous gang of
warehouse breakers'. On 10 May 1954 Hinds's appeal to the
Court of Criminal Appeal was turned down.

Hinds had made no secret of the fact that he was a man
with a criminal record. He had eight previous convictions,
but he said that he had given up his life of crime in 1945 and
that he ran a successful, legitimate business as a demolition
contractor.

Many of those who feel they have been wrongly convicted
face up to the inevitable after the dismissal of their appeal,
but not Hinds. He remained in prison until 26 November
1955 when he made the first of his three escapes. This was
from Nottingham Prison and he was out for two hundred
and fortynine days until he was recaptured in the cottage he
had bought near Dublin.

He had bombarded the Home Office, MPs and newspapers with letters and leaflets protesting his innocence. He
attended law lectures at Trinity College, Dublin during his
period of freedom and this helped him achieve the first of his
legal successes. He was acquitted at Nottingham Assizes on a
charge of breaking out of prison on the basis he had merely
followed others through a breach in the wall. He was
convicted of the lesser charge of escaping from lawful
custody. This point of law earned him a mention in the 1957
Criminal Appeal Law Reports.

He started a number of legal actions which led to his
appearing twelve times in the High Court and three times in
the House of Lords. Among those who received writs from
him were the police officer who brought him back from
Ireland, the Attorney General and the Prison Commissioners.

In the course of his litigation with the Prison Commissioners for failing to afford him his statutory rights in the
conduct of other litigation, he devised his second escape
plan. Master Diamond, a High Court Master, had

adjourned the attempt to strike out Hinds's proceedings against the Prison Commissioners. Hinds noticed that the Master's room in the High Court was ill-equipped to deal with maximum security prisoners. On the adjourned hearing, he arranged for a friend to leave £5 and an air ticket to Dublin at an agreed spot in the Law Courts, together with a key to lock his prison escort in the gents. On 25 June 1957, with the assistance of his brother and one Anthony Maffia, he casually strolled unescorted past the Prison Commissioners' lawyers and escaped from the courts. He was taken off the Dublin plane just before it took off at Bristol. His brother and Maffia both received twelve months' imprisonment for their pains.

His next escape was on 1 June 1958 from Chelmsford Prison. This time he was free for twenty months. Following his recapture in Eire, an English magistrate refused to hear a charge of escaping from lawful custody in order to avoid giving Hinds a platform to state his grievances. Thereafter his protestations of innocence took the form of more litigation and a twentysix day hunger strike at Pentonville.

In 1962, while still in prison, he learned that Detective Superintendent Sparks, upon his retirement, had sold his story to the *Sunday Pictorial*. Two articles were published on 19 and 26 August under the heading. 'They called me the Iron Man'.

The Iron Man and his ghost writer had some fairly forthright things to say about Alfred Hinds.

His widespread protests of innocence are completely bogus. I say on the contrary justice was done. He should have taken his medicine like a man.

He alleged Hinds was a fraud and a perjurer and quoted a telegram he said he had received on his retirement but which Hinds denied sending.

So you go out before me after all, you basterd [sic]. Alfie Hinds.

Hinds had already looked into the possibility of bringing a

libel action to prove his innocence, as he had been advising 'Fingers' Loughans about his claim against the *People*.

Hinds issued a writ for libel against Detective Superintendent Sparks (who had retired with twentyfive commendations, and now worked in the security section of Barclays Bank). The case was heard in 1964 before Mr Justice Edmund-Davies and a jury. Desmond Ackner QC and David Hirst appeared for Sparks and James Comyn QC and Bryan Anns for Hinds. Sparks, who had received no more than sixty per cent of the £4,000 fee for the articles, was not assisted in meeting his own legal costs and had little prospect of recovering them, if he was successful, against a man in prison.

Hinds's case was that the robbery had taken place some hours earlier than the police alleged. This enabled him to call further alibi evidence. He contended that he would hardly have reported his Land Rover missing to the police, as he had done on the night of the robbery, if it was to be used in the crime. Furthermore nothing had been found in his bungalow to link him with the crime and the forensic evidence of mahogany dust on his shoes was inconclusive. The verbal admissions, he suggested, were unreliable and in certain cases untrue.

The case lasted twentysix days. Hinds was in the witness box six days and cross-examined for four days. His witnesses were severely questioned by Desmond Ackner QC who suggested that Hinds was 'a plausible rogue who could tell a superficially attractive story' and that his alleged 'accomplice', Frank Martin, was 'an inventor of improbabilities' and that Hinds's brother was not to be outdone by Martin's 'inventive genius'. One witness called on behalf of Hinds said that the fifth man in the robbery was not Hinds but one 'Monkey' Lewis. As 'Monkey' had by then fallen off his perch, this could not be proved.

The prosecution evidence was more carefully scrutinized than it had been at the trial. Whether policemen had changed between 1953 and 1964 is a matter of conjecture, but certainly the way a jury looked at police evidence had altered. The 1964 jury was surprised to hear police officers deny they ever used certain well-known Anglo-Saxon swear words. The detective constable who said he did not know what 'verbals' were was viewed with a somewhat more jaundiced eye than in 1953.

In his book *Contempt of Court*, Hinds recorded his admiration for the way James Comyn QC cross-examined Sparks and his concern at the strain the hard work Comyn was putting into the case might be having upon his health. It was a striking tribute from a person who had a very low opinion of lawyers, particularly those who had hitherto defended him.

The judge had the daunting task of summing up the two wholly conflicting accounts of Hinds's involvement. It was a case of tremendous gravity, he told the jury, commenting that 'the most shattering observation he had ever heard in a Court of Law was that made by Mr Comyn when he said Mr Hinds was innocent of the crime and Mr Sparks knew it'. They had to decide whether Hinds was an innocent man with a burning sense of injustice or, as Desmond Ackner QC had suggested, 'a wily, wriggling liar, furious at being brought to book in 1953'. The judge pointed out to the jury that they had to consider the allegations made against Sparks, who had had a long and honourable career in the police force and who held in retirement a position of trust and responsibility. An adverse verdict, as his counsel suggested, could spell 'red ruin and the break-up of all'. As he pointed out, they should put aside all feelings of sympathy and administer strictly impartial justice.

After a retirement of five hours the jury found that Hinds had been libelled and awarded him £1,300 damages against Sparks.

Nevertheless, after drinking his champagne he had to return to Pentonville by 10 pm to comply with the terms of his parole. Shortly afterwards the parole was lifted and he became a free man. On 15 November 1965 his attempt to have his conviction quashed was rejected by the Court of Criminal Appeal. The Lord Chief Justice, Lord Parker, said that it was fruitless for the court to speculate why the two juries had reached different conclusions. The result was that

Hinds had cleared his name but his conviction remained.

Hinds became a successful businessman living in Jersey and a figure in Mensa, the organization for those with IQs over 150, lecturing one year at its annual general meeting on 'The Sub-Culture of the Criminal Mind'.

Alfred Hinds was to find himself the victim of a libel a few years later, but in circumstances where he could seek no redress as the mention of his name was covered by the absolute privilege which attaches to what is said in court cases. This arose out of the trial of the man alleged to have murdered Anthony Maffia – an ill-starred name for a small-time villain: he met his end by being shot in a marina and dumped in a car park.

Hinds had no involvement whatsoever in these matters, but he had the misfortune to have his name mentioned in a police interview and to find that most newspapers chose to report that aspect of the trial, as he was 'good copy'. The only remedy was to apply to the trial judge for leave to make a statement through counsel at the end of the case. The judge gave leave and Hinds was able to exonerate himself. There was some irony in the fact that the man who was libelled had been wrongfully imprisoned but had cleared his name, while the police officer, Detective Superintendent Kenneth Drury (later commander of the Flying Squad, with thirtytwo commendations), who recorded the allegation, was subsequently sentenced to eight years for corruption.

Libel damages are assessed upon the jury's estimate of the injury to the plaintiff's reputation. It was therefore something of a disadvantage to Douglas Gordon Goody to have to bring his claim in a court ringed by police armed with rifles and revolvers. The court at Leicester Assizes had been selected because of its proximity to the maximum security wing at Leicester Prison. The Royal Courts of Justice in the Strand, where such actions are normally heard, was considered too insecure for this plaintiff. The reason for these unusual precautions was that Gordon Goody, a Putney hairdresser by occupation, was serving a thirty-year prison sentence for his part in the Great Train Robbery. Two of those convicted with him had already escaped and Alfred Hinds had shown how it was possible to escape from the Royal Courts of Justice.

To someone like Goody a libel action might appear something of an indulgence. It was made possible by an unsatisfactory rule of law that a criminal conviction was not by itself proof of guilt in a civil case. This dated back to a decision of Lord Justice Goddard in 1943 in the case of Hollington v Hewthorn & Co Ltd. where, despite the powerful arguments of A T Denning KC (later Lord Denning), it was held that the fact that a person had been convicted of careless driving did not itself prove in civil proceedings that the driver had been negligent. This meant that, despite the fact that Goody had been found guilty beyond reasonable doubt after a fiftyone-day trial, a newspaper sued for libel could not rely on the conviction to prove he was guilty. They had to call evidence to establish his guilt.

It was a rule which gave those convicted of serious crimes the opportunity to have their case reheard often on less compelling evidence than at the trial and thus to obtain a technical acquittal. It was an opportunity that Gordon Goody and his fellow train robbers, James Hussey, Robert Welch and Thomas Wisbey had seized when the *People* carried a story in their issue of 26 July 1964 headlined: 'A suburban housewife reveals how she was caught up in the great mail bag plot.'

In the article, Mrs Karen Field, whose husband had a few months before been imprisoned for his part in the conspiracy as a bent solicitor's clerk, described how the gang had congregated at her house two days after the robbery and how she had been forced to help them dispose of the loot. She referred to Goody's participation in the robbery and explained how he had used the proceeds of a robbery at London Airport, of which he had been acquitted, to finance the Great Train Robbery, of which he had been convicted.

On the face of it there appeared to be nothing objectionable in this in view of the fact that Goody had been found guilty of robbery with aggravation and conspiracy to stop the mail train with intent to rob. The libel writ would impose an intolerable burden on the newspaper, if it had to re-establish Goody's guilt.

Leonard Lewis, Goody's counsel at the libel action, commented to the jury:

> 'You may think it amazing that a man who has been convicted of participation in a crime should then bring a libel action, because someone has accused him of doing it.'

However, as he pointed out, that was a perfectly proper course for Goody to take and they should treat him as an innocent man who had 'the misfortune to be convicted'.

Sir Joseph Molony QC, counsel for the newspaper, suggested that to do so involved an exercise in 'mental gymnastics'.

> 'Here is a man with no reputation at all who has been at pains to destroy his reputation throughout his adult life claiming damages for injury to his reputation.'

Having obtained a ruling from the Court of Appeal that they could rely on Goody's list of convictions dating back to 1948, the newspaper wisely decided not to reopen the question of Goody's guilt. The case against Goody depended upon the forensic evidence that the yellow and khaki paint which disguised the Austin truck and Land Rover used by the train robbers at Leatherslade Farm was also found on his suède shoes. If Goody's case had been heard alone by the jury in the civil case the result might have been different. Whatever the verdict it would have been a costly and difficult affair. It was scarcely the role of newspapers to retry aggrieved criminals. The newspaper therefore admitted that the article was defamatory but asked the jury to concentrate on Goody's bad reputation and to award contemptuous damages.

It was a risky course for the paper to take and it would only work where there was a man of evident bad character. It would also lead to the absurd result that Goody had technically been libelled by the suggestion that he was guilty of participating in the Great Train Robbery, when another court had arranged that he should spend the greater part of the next thirty years in Parkhurst for that very reason.

As it turned out, Goody declined the opportunity to give his version of events, Mr Justice Widgery wryly observing: 'quite understandable'. The judge then summed up to the jury suggesting that if they considered there really was no injury to Goody's reputation or feelings they should award him a nominal sum and conventionally that would not be more than forty shillings.

After a retirement of thirtytwo minutes, the jury awarded exactly that sum, leaving the newspaper which, to protect itself against such a result, had paid £25 into court, with a valueless order for costs against Mr Goody. Wisbey, Hussey and Welch made even less impression on the jury that tried their case, for they received no damages at all.

These cases cost the newspaper a considerably sum in legal fees. They had published a perfectly proper article only to find themselves confronted by a forensic exercise on the part of Goody to establish his innocence. Fortunately, immediately after the case, Parliament changed the law by what became Section 13, Civil Evidence Act 1968. This means that in libel proceedings a person is now taken to have committed an offence of which he has been convicted unless the contrary is proved. The result of the 1968 Act has put an end on such libel actions. Goody himself was released on parole in 1975 after twelve years in prison.

That prisoners have their own special feelings was illustrated by the case which Francis Davidson Fraser brought in 1959 against Kemsley Newspapers. He was at the time doing seven years for his part in a razor attack on 'Jack Spot' Comer, and was upset by the suggestion in a newspaper that while in Stafford Prison he had assisted the police in further enquiries which could have led to other persons being charged. No one in his position should be seen to be helping the police.

Fraser was asked by the defendants' counsel, Helenus Milmo:

'Do you seriously suggest that an honest law-abiding

citizen would think one whit the worse of you because you
gave information to the police?'

To this he very frankly replied.

'I do not know what would be in an honest person's mind.'
'I appreciate your difficulty,' observed Mr Milmo.

He did not enhance his reputation in the eyes of the jury,
when he was asked in a little detail what he had done to Jack
Spot.

'And he was pretty badly cut up? – a pretty ugly business?'
'A pretty ugly man,' Fraser replied darkly.

It took the jury twentyfive minutes to decide he had not been
libelled.

Even more curious was a case brought by Jack Day in
1961. His complaint arose out of a letter written to *The
Spectator* by Harvey Cole (a London journalist and
opponent of capital punishment) which, it was claimed, said
that Day had been found guilty of murder and subsequently
executed. At that time Day had been convicted of the
shooting of Keith Arthur and was sufficiently alive to issue a
writ for libel claiming that Cole's article suggested that his
crime was so heinous as not to warrant a reprieve. It was an
interesting point for lawyers, but it was cut short three days
later by Day's execution. As a libel action is a personal
action which does not survive the death of either party, that
was that.

However, some cases brought by prisoners do restore
faith in human nature. In 1960, Christopher Craig was
falsely accused by a newspaper of taking and driving away
other people's motor cars, while working at an out-hostel
prior to his release. Not only was he able to vindicate his
reputation and preserve his release date, but for good
measure he gave the damages to charity.

The fact that a man is in prison does not, of course, mean
that he has no reputation which he cannot sue to preserve.

There are obviously problems for a prisoner who wishes to take action to clear his name, but it can be done. This is illustrated by the case brought by Denys Bower against the *Sunday Pictorial* in 1962. He was serving a life sentence for attempted murder. However, it was clear that his crime was committed in the heat of the moment. He was the owner of a stately home, Chiddingstone Castle, which contained a large collection of ancient weapons. He had had a row with his fiancée, a Miss White, which arose out of the fact that she turned out not to be the Countess d'Estanville as he had thought, but a dental nurse from New Cross. Despite his Buddhist views, he had picked up a conveniently handy nineteenth-century pistol and shot her. He had tried unsuccessfully to commit suicide. Since these unfortunate events, he had been a model prisoner and was by then being considered for parole. For reasons best known to itself, the *Sunday Pictorial* chose to publish an article suggesting that he had had a mental breakdown while in prison and that, rather than being imprisoned as a first offender at Wormwood Scrubs, he had been moved to Parkhurst, a prison for hardened criminals.

Although it might have been thought that his reputation was not of great value, the jury, having heard that these allegations were untrue, concluded that this was tantamount to kicking a man when he was down and they awarded the princely sum of £7,250.

Eight

Libel and the Politicians

As is apparent in this book, libel actions cover practically
every field of endeavour or the lack of it. Politics are
however its most recurring theme. This comes about as a
result of the persons who enter politics, the issues with which
they deal and a certain sensitivity that manifests itself among
politicians, particularly at election times. Both the cases
examined in this chapter concern politics.

On 16 June 1945, some three weeks before the General
Election, Professor Harold Laski, then Chairman of the
National Executive Committee of the Labour Party and
Professor of Political Science at the London School of
Economics, addressed some 1,500 of the electorate of
Newark from an open lorry in Market Place. The Socialist
candidate, Air Vice-Marshal Hugh Vivian Champion de
Crespigny, had said what he had to say in fifteen minutes.
Professor Laski had been speaking for fortyfive minutes, by
which time, as his counsel at the subsequent trial said, people
were beginning to leave, when a man dressed in plus-fours
strode forward. He was James Wentworth Day, a former
publicity manager and feature writer for Beaverbrook
Newspapers and a former editor of *The Field*, but at that
time publicity adviser to the conservative candidate, Lt Col
Sidney Shepherd. He had attended the meeting for the
purpose of heckling rather than instruction and was armed
with the Conservative Party's booklet *Notes for Speakers
and Writers*, which included extracts from a couple of
Laski's earlier speeches, on which he could possibly be
tripped up.

Day's question was straightforward enough, if a trifle biased and wordy. He asked why the bloodthirsty professor advocated revolution by violence when speaking at Bishop's Stortford and Bournemouth during the war, while most Englishmen were either fighting or being bombed at home, and why had he spent the greater part of the last war lecturing in America. There then followed what one witness was to call 'an exchange of incivilities'. With some justification Laski called these questions insolent, impudent and insulting, but they were undoubtedly the high spot of the evening. It seems that when Day called Laski 'the sort of bloodthirsty little man who had never smelled a bullet, but was always the first to stir up violence in peace', the professor's sense of humour was strained to breaking point. 'Judging by the temper you display, you would be naturally one of the objects of violence when it does come', he snapped at Day.

When these comments were reported, the Labour Party put out a statement complaining of 'barefaced misrepresentation'. Nevertheless, no less than four writs were issued against the papers that reported the meeting. Beaverbrook Newspapers, whom Day had telephoned 'for propaganda not payment', received two: one for the *Daily Express* ('Laski unleashes another General Election Broadside: Socialism even if it means violence') and the other for the *Evening Standard*. The *Nottingham Guardian* received another for the letter it had published from Councillor Carlton, who had been at the meeting. The last to be sued were the proprietor, publisher, printer and editor of the *Newark Advertiser and South Nottingham Gazette*, a weekly publication with a circulation of 10,000 and a staff of sixteen. Although the last to publish, on 20 June, the *Newark Advertiser*'s case was the first to be tried. If Professor Laski hoped to pick off the weakest defendant and to split their ranks, he underestimated Beaverbrook Newspapers, who helped pay the *Newark Advertiser*'s legal costs.

This spate of writs led the Lord Chancellor, Viscount Simon, into a remarkable indiscretion. As Lord High

Chancellor of Great Britain he issued the command on the writ to every defendant to enter an appearance to the writ or to face the legal consequences. Yet he commented in the course of the election campaign about these writs: 'If you want to stop people's mouths, the way is to issue a writ. I'll bet you as soon as this election is over, you won't hear anything more about these writs'. It was a remark for which he had to issue a public apology long before any question of his losing his bet arose.

The report of the meeting in the *Newark Advertiser* that led to the five-day libel action was as follows:

REVOLUTION BY VIOLENCE
PROFESSOR LASKI QUESTIONED
There were some lively exchanges between Mr Wentworth Day and Professor Laski following the latter's speech in Newark Market Place on Saturday night.

The article then referred to questions put by Mr Day, including the question 'why had he openly advocated a revolution by violence during the war' and set out Laski's reply:

REFERENCES TO VIOLENCE
'As for violence', he continued, 'if Labour could not obtain what it needed by general consent we shall have to use violence, even if it means revolution. When people felt it was the moment for great experiment, for innovation, because when the war was over, people so easily forget – especially those who had the power in their hands – was the time for experiment. Great changes were so urgent in this country and if they were not made by consent, they would be made by violence, and judging by the temper this questioner had displayed, he would be perfectly naturally one of the objects of violence when it came.'

This account of Laski's speech no doubt lost something in the reporting; it was no doubt more fluent and coherent when delivered. However, Sir Patrick Hastings KC, for the newspaper, was rather nearer the mark when he suggested to the jury that people would think 'old Laski's been at it again' than Laski's counsel, Gerald Slade KC, who called it 'one of the most serious libel actions to come before the court for many a long day.'

Indeed it is difficult to know precisely why Laski did bring the action. As he was to be reminded by Sir Patrick Hastings, he had written a passage that was tactless but prophetic.

'A London jury is fairly certain to award damages for libel to a Tory Member of Parliament, but it is fairly certain to assume a Labour sympathizer cannot be libelled.'
'Is not that unfair, stupid and offensive?' he was asked.
'No, I think it is an accurate summary of the history of political libel actions in London between 1794 and 1924.'
[A date presumably chosen as being the year Hastings became Attorney General.]

It was on the face of it a libel action Laski should have won. The questioner was clearly motivated by malice. Not only was Day's heckling highly loaded, but he had gone even further in his then unpublished book *Harvest Adventures* where he referred to 'that urban-minded and garrulous little petrel of socialist politics ... dressed in a tight-fitting, hip-slinky overcoat of the sort dance band leaders wear'. His sneer at Laski's absence of war record (in fact due to ill-health) had already been the subject of an apology by Wing Commander James MP in the House of Commons. Furthermore considerable doubt had been raised as to the accuracy of the reports of Laski's speeches at Bishop's Stortford and Bournemouth. In addition there were questions as to the correctness of the newspaper's accounts of Laski's remarks at Newark. Their shorthand writer James Opie had not recorded the all-important phrase 'we shall have to use violence, even if it means revolution'. This was included in the article because Day had been 'so astonished' by Laski's reply about violence that he had written it out on a pad when he stayed for the night at the Conservative candidate's house, Elston Hall. A Nottingham town councillor, Henry Carlton, alerted the local press by telephoning a reporter early the next day with his detailed comments on Laski's behaviour. The editor Cyril Everard Parlby, asked Day to produce his note and was convinced from what he himself had heard at the meeting that Laski had used the word 'revolution' in conjunction with 'violence'. Professor Laski was to call ten witnesses who were to say that he had not advocated revolution by violence.

However, Professor Laski's ability to lose the case was not to be underestimated. He clearly had been provoked and had lost his temper. He admitted using the words 'revolution' and 'violence' but in entirely different contexts. He was talking theoretically of revolutionary change, of the choice that faced the people between revolution by general consent, or revolution by violence if they did not consent. He had never, he said, advocated revolution by violence in his speeches or writings.

The Lord Chief Justice, Lord Goddard, who presided over the trial before a special jury, was to observe in his summing up that 'heckling at political meetings was all part of the fun ... A person should not be thinskinned at election times'. Sir Patrick Hastings KC was to call the case a storm in a teacup. That was not the way that Professor Laski saw matters. He was represented by Gerald Slade KC, Sir Valentine Holmes KC and Peter Bristow. The newspaper was represented by Sir Patrick Hastings KC, Holroyd Pearce KC, Arthian Davies and Anthony Gordon. *The Daily Herald* which, as a socialist newspaper, was not being sued, nevertheless found it necessary to instruct junior counsel to keep a watching brief.

Professor Laski's statement of claim asserted that the words meant he intended to commit and had declared his intention to commit crimes of treason, – felony, sedition, riot and breach of the peace, – if the policy of the Labour Party could not be put into operation by constitutional means. These alarming meanings were nicely deflated by Sir Patrick Hastings who suggested that Laski looked in the witness box rather more like a Professor of Economics than a treasonable felon. Indeed Lord Goddard ruled that the words could not be taken to be imputing treason and that they could mean no more than that Laski was a stirrer up of sedition and breaches of the peace.

The defence was that this was a fair and accurate newspaper report of matters of public concern at a public meeting. If it was a fair and accurate report, it mattered not that it might otherwise be defamatory. Alternatively, the defence argued that the report was substantially true in that Laski had spoken the words and had said similar things on other occasions.

The case was won and lost in the cross-examination of Professor Laski by Sir Patrick Hastings. Hastings had read some thirty to forty of Laski's books and he sought to prove that what Laski was alleged to have said at Newark did not greatly differ from what he had written. Sir Patrick initially set out the propositions he sought to prove.

'Mr Laski, do you believe that the use of violence to achieve your political ends is practically inevitable?'
'No.'
'Have you ever believed that which I put to you?'
'No.'
'Do you believe that if achievement of political aims cannot be arrived at without the use of violence, then violence is justifiable?'
'Not in all circumstances. In circumstances where a burden is intolerable, violence may be inevitable, because the burden is intolerable, but not otherwise.'
'Did you on 16 June 1945 think that if the aims of the proletariat could not be achieved without the use of violence then violence was justified?'
'No.'
'Have you preached that doctrine for twenty years?'
'No, if I have preached to the proletariat the inevitability of violence for twenty years, I certainly would be a public danger.'
'Do you agree that a man can advocate violence in his

writings without actually using those words?'
'Yes.'
'Have you preached consistently that the time is ripe for
revolution?'
'No, for great change, for revolution in the sense of a great
transformation forward.'

By constant references to Laski's writings, Hastings was able
to establish, despite Laski's complaints that the quotations
were taken out of context, that Laski's views were closer to
these propositions than he cared to admit. Laski's answers
became increasingly wordy, the distinctions he sought to
draw more obtuse. He complained at having to answer
questions 'Yes' or 'No'. He was told by Lord Goddard that he
could explain his answers but the case was not to turn 'into a
history of the Socialist creed'. He agreed that in 1934 he had
written in his book *The State in Theory and Practice* of 'the
inevitability of revolution' and 'the resort to force as the
ultimate arbiter of destiny', but his views had since changed.
   The somewhat theoretical tone of the cross-examination
was altered when Professor Laski was thought by Sir Patrick
to be answering back. It took on an altogether more
ferocious form, and led to a number of questions that
probably discredited Laski further in the eyes of the
burghers on the special jury.

   'Are there any privileged people in the Labour Party?'
   'Indeed, Sir Patrick, when you were a member of the
Socialist party.'
   'No, Mr Laski,' Lord Goddard intervened.
   'Don't be rude,' Sir Patrick retorted.
   'That is the last thing in the world I wish to be.'
   'It may be difficult for you to be courteous, but don't be
rude. You are rude to everyone are you not?'
   'I don't think so.'
   'When you are rude to other people you think that is
argument, but when people say something about you, you
bring actions for libel. Is that your view of fairness? I will
now put to you a question I was not proposing to put, the

most offensive thing you have ever said. It is in your book *Threat to the Constitution* or something of that sort.'

He then read what Laski had written about Wesley 'inducing the masses in England to accept the grim discipline of the new factories in return for the dubious consolation of an unproved and unprovable eternal bliss'.

> 'Did you not mean by that, Wesley blackmailed workmen to go into the factories?'
> 'That is fantastic rhetorical exaggeration. Wesley deflected the sense of the masses' indignation to religion as a consolation.'

These were scarcely answers to endear Laski to the jury, if they understood them. Nor was his reason for attacking Churchill in the war.

> 'I regretted Mr Churchill's decision not to take advantage of the war to make a great renovation by consent.'

The knife was to be further turned in Sir Patrick's closing speech.

> 'I don't suppose anyone cares tuppence for Mr Laski. Rude as he is, if anyone says one word about him, he flees to the tribunal of justice which he despises ... You might think that he was not a dangerous person at all, more (and I do not wish to be rude) in the nature of someone troublesome or tiresome ... It must not be thought that anyone in this court on this side is suggesting that the socialist party believes in the rubbish of Mr Laski. He might be as much of a nuisance to the Labour Party as to everyone else.'

Hastings was able to deal with Laski's witnesses as to what was said at the meeting by establishing that they had not heard certain parts of Laski's answers which he admitted. As often happens where too many witnesses are called, one gave an unsatisfactory answer. He was asked if Laski had said 'as for violence, if the Labour Party could not obtain what it needed by general consent, we shall have to use violence even if it means revolution'.

'No,' he replied.
'Or words similar?' Laski's counsel rashly persisted.
'Similar, but the word Labour Party was never used.'

As against this, the defence witnesses were able to produce unimpeachable independent witnesses who could positively assert that they had heard Laski utter these words. Evidence was even taken in Turkey from the acting British Consul in Trebizond, Major Richard Breene. He recollected Laski saying at Newark amidst 'a well-designed heckling calculated to get Laski's dander up':

'If the Labour Party does not obtain the reforms desired, it may be necessary to use violence, even if it means revolution',

a remark which apparently caused him to turn to Mrs Breene and say: 'My God, Laski has slipped here. That's a pretty serious statement'.

The jury found that the report was a fair and accurate one and accordingly did not have to decide whether or not the words were true.

Professor Laski was left after the trial with a bill for legal costs of the order of £13,000. However, Morgan Phillips as Secretary of the Labour Party opened an appeal fund and the costs were paid. In some respects, Laski had been unlucky to lose the case. Certainly, he had been unwise to bring it. Sir Patrick Hastings wrote of the case in his book *Cases in Court*: 'It was a battle of huge importance fought about nothing at all'.

Laski was shattered by the verdict and dropped all his other libel actions. He resigned from the National Executive Committee of the Labour Party in 1949 and died in 1950 aged fiftynine. Fenton Bresler in his biography of Lord

Goddard has recounted how the result troubled the judge
and how he did not agree with the jury's verdict. Air Vice-
Marshal de Crespigny lost the election for Newark, but
became the Regional Commissioner of Schleswig-Holstein
instead.

One lasting effect of the case was that it hastened the
abolition of special juries by the Juries Act 1949. The
qualification for being a special juror was that the person
should be an esquire, banker or merchant and should live in
a house with a rateable value of £100. A common juror's
house needed only to have a rateable value of £30 and his
occupation was of no consequence. (Owing, it seems, to their
different stations in life, a common juror received only one
shilling a day for sitting on a jury, whereas the special juror
received a guinea for precisely the same task.) Until then libel
actions were normally heard by special juries.

'A General Election campaign which has Mr Randolph
Churchill issuing writs within the first three days has
certainly got away to a classic start', the *Financial Times*
observed on 11 September 1959. On that occasion he was
alleging that a Labour Party pamphlet called *The Tory
Swindle* in breach of copyright had lifted material from his
book *The Rise and Fall of Sir Anthony Eden*.

Although Randolph Churchill's political career lacked the
essential ingredient of success at the polls, it was in some
measure compensated for by success elsewhere – in the law
courts.

He started inauspiciously but in a manner that reflected
his fiercely independent and individualistic views. In
February 1935 he was sent as a journalist by the *Daily Mail*
to report the Wavertree by-election in Liverpool. He found
he did not greatly care for the answers given him by the
Conservative candidate on India and national defence. He
promptly decided to jump into the ring as an independent
Conservative. This was to provide him with his first brush
with the law of libel. He wrote an article in the *Sunday
Dispatch* suggesting that Sir Thomas White, one of the
leading Conservatives in the city, had improperly influenced

the promotion of the Socialist lord mayor. In the ensuing libel action, damages of £1,000 were awarded to Sir Thomas.

Churchill lost at Wavertree but, despite his sin of having stood against the Conservative candidate, he was adopted later in the same year as the official Conservative candidate at West Toxteth. He reduced the Labour majority but lost again. In 1936 he lost in Ross and Cromarty when he stood against the National Government candidate. He was elected in 1940 for Preston when he stood unopposed, but was seldom able to sit in Parliament owing to his war service. In 1945, he contested Preston and lost. In 1950 and 1951 he was no more successful, being twice defeated by Michael Foot at Devonport. After these results he decided not to stand for the 1955 General Election. He took a keen interest in the campaign and on 12 May 1955 launched a fierce attack in the *Evening Standard* on Cyril Lord for his forecast that the Conservatives would lose every marginal seat in Lancashire. Under the title 'They are talking a lot of rot in Lancashire', he dismissed Cyril Lord's 'loud-mouthed vapourings' as 'nonsense'. In the event he was proved correct, as the only Lancashire marginal to change hands was gained by the Conservatives.

The Sunday following his article, the *People* sprang to the defence of Cyril Lord with a vigorous attack on Randolph Churchill.

VOTERS BEWARE

In eleven days' time you will have to make up your mind. Most of all, beware of party propagandists – those who haven't seen fit to fight openly for a seat but prefer to be paid hacks to write biased accounts of the campaign.

Chief among these – as usual – is Randolph Churchill, that slightly comic son of our greatest statesman, who poses as a political expert, but whose offer to serve as an MP was rejected time and time again.

Yet this egregious failure has the impertinence to refer to the views of Mr Cyril Lord the textile expert who has done more for Lancashire than any other man of his generation as 'loud-mouthed vapourings'. Mr Lord has protested against the Government's handling of the cotton crisis. The ignorant Randolph, who is an expert at nothing except word-spinning dismisses this as 'nonsense'. If the Tories are hoping to win votes on the wild blatherings of the younger Churchill and his kidney, then it will be better for politics if the electors turn the other way.

Man o' the People

The strident terms of this attack on Randolph Churchill can be explained by the campaign he had been waging since 1953 against what he termed 'pornography on Sundays'. He had recently attacked the *People* and its editor Harry Ainsworth for 'four cretinous articles' including one entitled 'I was the spoils of war' by a woman in Berlin. The *People* ranked near the bottom of Randolph Churchill's scale of degradation. 'The lowest mongrel curs' he called them, although he explained in court this was a purely canine metaphor deriving from the Fleet Street rule that 'dog does not eat dog'.

In its evident irritation at Randolph Churchill, the newspaper allowed itself to be carried away. They failed to realize he was offensive to a great many other people as well. They chose to attack him on two grounds that could not be sustained. Whatever failings Churchill may have had, they certainly did not include writing to the dictates of his employer or a reluctance to fight in the open. When Churchill worked for the *Evening Standard*, Lord Beaverbrook had from time to time found it necessary to publish disclaimers of what hc had written. When in 1953 Randolph Churchill found that *The Times* had not published his strictures on the gutter press and pornography, he had the speech which he had given at a Foyle's Literary Lunch published in a pamphlet entitled *What I said about the Press*. The allegation that he was a paid hack engaged to write biased accounts of the election campaign was clearly defamatory and the suggestion that he had as usual failed to stand for Parliament was not sustainable.

With some good humour Randolph Churchill was to

concede in the subsequent libel action that the reference 'this
egregious failure' was 'purely a matter of opinion. I do not
agree with it but I see what the fellow has in mind'. So far as
the reference to that 'slightly comic son of our greatest
statesman' was concerned, he commented: 'I think the word
slightly is rather offensive. I try and entertain my readers.'
The allegation of being a paid hack was however, 'a libel and
a lie'.

Five days after the article had been published, Randolph
Churchill wrote a letter to the editor setting out the facts and
seeking a full retraction. As W A Fearnley-Whittingstall QC
his counsel commented, it was a 'good-tempered, dignified
and restrained letter'. It offered the paper the chance to
avoid proceedings but they found themselves unable to
publish a paragraph which stated that Churchill had been
advised by counsel that he had strong grounds for bringing
an action for libel. It is difficult to see what harm this could
possibly have done appearing in the correspondence
column. Instead the paper published the letter without its
final paragraph and somewhat gratuitously added an
editorial comment:

> We apologize to Mr Churchill for any reflection on his
> record as a consistently losing Conservative candidate, a
> record only relieved by his success at Preston in 1940.

This act of petulance concerning a passage about which he
had not complained no doubt contributed to what was in the
1950s a very high award of damages.

On 8 and 9 October 1956 the case was heard before Mr
Justice Jones and a jury. Randolph Churchill was asked by
his counsel to give details of his career in politics and
journalism and to give details of his relations with the *People*
and its editor Harry Ainsworth. The case came to life when
he was cross-examined by Gilbert Paull QC, one of the
foremost advocates of the day. He faced the problem that his
clients were most reluctant to apologize to Churchill. Yet
they had no real defence. They admitted the words were
defamatory but contended that they were fair comment.

They faced the difficulty that the facts on which the comment was based could not be proved to be true and the terms in which Churchill was attacked indicated a fair degree of malice.

The approach Paull adopted was that the jury should consider Churchill's conduct as a whole and the respect he had shown for the feelings of others. He spoke of Randolph Churchill behaving like 'a wounded angel'. 'If a prize fighter hits you, it is not malice to hit him back.'

Paull extracted the admission from Churchill that it was he who had first brought Ainsworth into public scandal, odium and contempt rather than the other way round. Randolph Churchill admitted, not without some relish, that he had written very disparagingly of Sir David Eccles, the Minister of Works at the time of the Coronation, for having said that in the Queen, he had 'the perfect leading lady'.

'Sir David Eccles went whining round, complaining about it something terrible. As a matter of fact he has spoken more respectfully of Her Majesty ever since.'

Sir William Haley, the editor of *The Times*, he had called an 'automatic suppressor of the truth', but that was a joke, he said. Attlee was 'a tardy little marionette' – that was 'rather a good phrase'. Sir Anthony Eden was afflicted by 'exceptional vanity'. John Gordon, the editor of the *Sunday Express* was 'an unctuous humbug'. Charles Eade, the editor of the *Sunday Dispatch* he had called 'an old hack' (a phrase uncomfortably close to the one he was complaining of).

'So would you, if you read the *Sunday Dispatch*. I suppose if Mr Eade thought "old hack" was a lie or libel he would have written to me.'

He did later qualify this to say he was merely using 'a metaphor of the racecourse'.

He agreed he did say outrageous things but only regarding those he considered were acting contrary to the public interest. He conceded he did enjoy a spot of mischief but he

did not think he was a malicious person. To the suggestion
by Paull that he might try to be reasonably polite to the
people he wrote about, he replied: 'It is too late to start
taking lessons in journalism at my time of life'.

An impressive array of witnesses gave evidence of
Randolph Churchill's complete independence. It was absurd
to suggest that he was a hack. Michael Foot as a former
editor of the *Evening Standard* was able to testify that
working for that newspaper did not require one to be a hack.
Charles Wintour, the deputy editor of the *Evening Standard*
spoke of Randolph Churchill as a journalist of marked
courage and independence. He was asked in cross-
examination whether he would call John Gordon an
'unctuous humbug'. 'That is a matter of opinion', although
he did later feel it prudent to add of the editor, 'I am not
myself using it of Mr Gordon'. Similar evidence was given by
Ian Gilmour, the proprietor of *The Spectator*, and Henry
James Hopkinson, the former editor of the *Picture Post*. The
defence called no evidence to support their plea of fair
comment. They had to rely on the skill of Paull in his closing
address to the jury. However, Churchill had successfully
parried the cross-examination and it was scarcely a surprise
when the jury took no more than fortyfive minutes to return
a verdict of £5,000 damages for Churchill.

Two years later, on 6 December 1958, Churchill found he
had been libelled again, or strictly speaking slandered, as it
occurred during a speech by Sir Gerald Nabarro, MP for
Kidderminster, at the Conservative Club at Halesowen. In
referring to Churchill's attack on Sir Anthony Eden in his
book *The Rise and Fall of Sir Anthony Eden*, Sir Gerald
said: 'That is a pernicious, cowardly and uncalled-for attack
in the present circumstances. This was the action of a
coward'. By this he meant that Churchill was attacking
someone who could not answer back without revealing
Cabinet secrets. However, as Gerald Gardiner QC, Churchill's
counsel at the subsequent libel action, commented, that did
not appear to be an insurmountable difficulty, as Eden had
put his version of events in his autobiography *Full Circle*, for
which he was receiving the not inconsiderable sum of
£100,000.

When Randolph Churchill heard of the speech, he sent a telegram to Sir Gerald requiring an apology, failing which he would issue a writ for libel. For good measure, the text of the telegram was sent to the Press Association. This elicited a reply from Nabarro's solicitor that: 'Our client asks us to say that he does not buy expensive dogs and bark himself'. They then proceeded to write a letter of such obscurity that Gardiner had to read it twice to the jury for it to be understood.

This lent a somewhat canine tone to the proceedings. In one of his many clashes with defence counsel, Geoffrey Lawrence QC, Churchill replied to a question about what he had written about Sir Anthony Eden:

'I was setting out to write the truth as God has given me to see it, which is not what happens to every lawyer.'
'Was that meant to be offensive to me, Mr Churchill?' Lawrence snapped.
'I was thinking of your profession in general. Lawyers, after all, are expensive dogs, as your client describes them, paid to answer a case in which they have no personal stake. That is a perfectly fair comment on a matter of public interest.'

The jury found that Nabarro's speech went beyond mere comment, and, as the facts could not be justified, they awarded £1,500 damages. After the case, Churchill sent his counsel, Gerald Gardiner QC, a memento in the form of a leather dog's collar with a gold disc appropriately inscribed 'Good Dog'.

The following year, 1961, Randolph Churchill found himself on the losing side in that he had to pay 'substantial damages' to Douglas Clark, the political editor of the *Daily Express*, for a comment in an article entitled 'Political Talking Point' suggested that Clark was a hack whose opinions were dictated by his employers. It was curiously reminiscent of his 1956 libel action.

The libellous permutations of being a hack were not yet exhausted. In February 1963 *Private Eye*, then in its infancy, published a strip cartoon entitled 'Great Dying Englishmen'.

It showed Randolph in a less than flattering light directing other authors to write his book on the life of Winston Churchill and the caption: 'It's not me that's the hack, it's the people who are writing the book'.

Within days, an irate letter was received from Churchill. Unfortunately, the recipient of the letter, Christopher Booker, was preoccupied with affairs of the heart and the letter remained unanswered. The result was the issue of twelve writs for libel. The names on the masthead of *Private Eye* were rounded up and sued. The leading libel QCs were retained on behalf of Randolph Churchill, thus reducing the talent available to *Private Eye*. In fact, he used Gerald Gardiner QC again. The writs even adopted Mrs Ingrams's nickname, 'O'Morgo', and the knighthood *Private Eye* had conferred on John Harness, who puzzlingly had become 'Sir Charles' Harness.

The writs led *Private Eye* to exhibit in their front window three cartoons of a Suffolk boar, clearly recognizable as Randolph Churchill, peacefully defecating.

On 1 March 1963 Mr Justice Paull, in a fortyfive seconds' hearing, granted an injunction by consent preventing the repetition of the libels in the original article and ordering 'the removal forthwith from public view of three documents of which complaint was made and which were exhibited in the window of the defendants' premises in Greek Street, Soho'. It was the first time that such an order had been made before the evidence was heard. In their place a notice went up in the window, 'Killjoy was here'. In those days *Private Eye* were less agile in libel actions. They managed to mislay their file about the action. It was returned via Randolph Churchill with a note: 'Yours, I think. R C'.

The litigation was shortly thereafter settled upon the basis that Randolph Churchill's original letter of complaint was published in a full-page advertisement in the *Evening Standard* paid for by *Private Eye* at the cost of £1,200. This was accompanied by a withdrawal signed by the defendants, including Mrs 'O'Morgo' Ingrams and 'Sir Charles' Harness, who felt it prudent to sign with their writ names. It was the first time that a libel action was settled by an advertisement of this sort.

Randolph Churchill claimed the litigation had cost *Private Eye* £3,000 in all. Although he had been advised he could obtain substantial damages, he said he did not want to close the magazine down. 'I think it's quite amusing so long as it leaves me alone'. That was a view that many others were to form of *Private Eye*. Their stories were fine so long as they were about other people.

With the injunctions he had obtained, he remained well protected against *Private Eye* and no one was unwise enough to call him a hack again during his lifetime.

Nine

Libelling the Fictitious

It is one thing to libel a person by deliberately attacking them. It is another to find that in a work of fiction you have inadvertently libelled a stranger. The consequences can be severe and involve the book being pulped and abandoned altogether or withdrawn from sale just at the time it is being reviewed, quite apart from any question of damages and legal costs.

In the law of libel it is not the intention of the writer which matters, but what a reader of the material reasonably thought the words meant. Thus film-makers, novelists and even advertising copywriters have been caught by a plaintiff of whose existence they were unaware.

In the 1920s and 1930s there were a number of gold-digging cases where mysteriously an expensive array of legal talent materialized for not particularly wealthy plaintiffs. On occasions the cause of the litigation was no more than an injured sense of self-importance coupled with a lack of sense of humour. In other cases the argument arose because of a failure to take obvious precautions in the selection of names of such people as clergymen or lawyers or because the author was engaging in a private joke or settling an old score, when he chose to name one of his particularly disreputable characters.

The author of a well-known recent novel which borrowed heavily from his childhood gave a graphic account of a clearly identifiable factory. 'There was a fire at the works almost every year. It seemed a way of balancing the books. When we got to the fire, we found it a particularly good one.' It never occurred to the author that this would be considered anything other than pure fiction. However the factory owner found his insurance company distinctly unamused and felt compelled to take action to clear his name.

There was another author who chose the name for a peer in his book by selecting an appropriately aristocratic-sounding river on an ordnance survey map. The name sounded right, but unfortunately it coincided with that of a highly respectable aristocrat with a wholly different sexual appetite from his fictitious namesake. The book had to be pulped and libel damages paid. The fictitious peer was given a new name.

The most successful action brought in such circumstances was that brought by Princess Irena Alexandrovna Youssoupoff. In December 1916 her husband Prince Felix Youssoupoff, with the very best of motives, had killed Gregory Rasputin. In the early 1930s Metro-Goldwyn-Mayer produced a film called *Rasputin – the Mad Monk*. The fact that Youssoupoff had killed Rasputin was a matter of common knowledge. There was little difficulty in the moderately well-informed filmgoer identifying the film's characters Prince Paul and Princess Natasha Chegodieff as the Youssoupoffs. Unfortunately, the film contained a sequence which suggested that Rasputin was doing more than just hearing Princess Chegodieff's confessions.

Princess Youssoupoff sued and was awarded by the standards of the day the enormous sum of £25,000. Such was the size of the award that MGM soon heard from an actual Prince and Princess Chegodieff. Not surprisingly, MGM did not want another court case and so they agreed to pay them an undisclosed amount of libel damages – although, of course the whole basis of the Youssoupoffs' claim was that anyone seeing the film must have concluded that the Chegodieffs were in fact the Youssoupoffs.

Such actions divide into cases where an inadvertent or, sometimes, not so inadvertent injury is done to a living person, and those where there is an unduly sensitive plaintiff too ready to detect an insult. William Lewis Rowland Paul Sebastian Blennerhassett, a stock-broker, definitely fell into the latter category.

A seemingly innocuous advertisement appeared in the *Evening Standard* of 26 May 1932:

BEWARE OF THE YO-YO. IT STARTS AS A HOBBY AND ENDS AS A HABIT

Take warning by the fate of Mr Blennerhassett, as worthy a citizen as any that ever ate lobster at Pimm's or holed a putt at Walton Heath. 'Sound man, Blennerhassett', they said on Throgmorton Street, 'Nice people, the Blennerhassetts' was the verdict over the teacups and in the local tennis clubs. But Yo-Yo got him ... and today he is happy in a quiet place in the country and under sympathetic surveillance he practises Yo-Yo tricks having succumbed to the fascination of Yo-Yos. So beware of Yo-Yos which start as a hobby and end as a habit.

The advertisement had been commissioned by Novelty Sales Services Ltd, to promote the sale of their Cheerio 99 Yo-Yo, a child's toy. They had asked a copywriter, Joseph McNulty, for some suitable copy. This, and more, was what he produced. The reason he chose the name Blennerhassett became a matter of some importance at the trial. The answer lay in the rather horrific details of the McNulty levée. When he awoke each morning, his daughter would come into his bedroom asking 'Will Mr Blennerhassett have his trousers this morning?' It was a game apparently with a number of permutations.

All this was unknown on 26 May 1932 to William Blennerhassett who had enjoyed an agreeable, if lengthy, luncheon when he met Sir Stephen Killick, an alderman of the City of London and a member of the Council of the Stock Exchange. Sir Stephen had read his *Evening Standard* as, apparently, had a number of other stockbrokers for, when Blennerhassett entered the floor of the Stock Exchange, he was met with jeers and ribald laughter. Poor Blennerhassett could do no work that afternoon. He followed Sir Stephen's advice and consulted solicitors. A solicitor's letter was written. The *Evening Standard* responded by publishing an apology. Blennerhassett was not satisfied: what may have been harmless fun to some was a serious matter for him and he sued for libel.

It was a case that really belonged to the world of the late Sir Alan Herbert. Had Mr Haddock been on the job, the issue no doubt would have been 'Do stockbrokers have a sense of humour?'

On 18 May 1933 the trial opened before Mr Justice Branson sitting with a special jury. Mr Blennerhassett was represented by J F Eales KC and the defendants by Sir Patrick Hastings. The case was outlined in suitably ponderous terms by Eales.

'The advertisement might appear partly humorous, but it was only when one reflected on the effect that it might have on a man of Blennerhassett's position that the gravity became apparent.'

Blennerhassett had to prove that there were sufficient similarities between the fictitious character and himself for people reasonably to associate the two. The way in which he sought to do so was rather tenuous. He was in the habit of lunching at Pimm's restaurant, named after the well-known Pimm's drinks, but he had not done so very often since 1928. However, he was the only stockbroker of the name Blennerhassett and the only person of that name associated with Throgmorton Street. He was also, it seems, fond of lobster.

His attempt to prove that the reference to the Blennerhassett in the advertisement was to William Blennerhassett the stockbroker was to result in some devastating cross-examination by Sir Patrick Hastings. He was in consequence subjected to greater and more long-lasting ridicule than if he had let the advertisement pass.

In cross-examination Blennerhassett had to admit that he did not play golf and therefore had not holed a putt at Walton Heath or elsewhere. He did not play with Yo-Yos. He agreed that the two children in the advertisement, whom Sir Patrick described as particularly unprepossessing, were aged five or six, whereas he had one son aged twentyone. He

conceded that the name Blennerhassett did not appear in any
professional directory relating to stockbrokers which
McNulty might have consulted. If it had, he might have been
able to establish lack of care on the part of the copywriter.
He agreed that the name Blennerhassett had been used for
humorous characters by W S Gilbert in the *Bab Ballads* and
by Mark Twain. For good measure Sir Patrick observed that
Blennerhassett had a good head of hair, whereas it appeared
that mice had had a go at the head of the character in the
advertisement. He further agreed with counsel that he had
never been in a lunatic asylum. The inconsequential nature
of his case was also established by a few further questions.

'Have you any sense of humour?'
'You must ask other people about that', he replied to
general laughter.
'Are you suggesting that people could have thought that
you had been taken away to what the Americans called the
funny house?'
'No.'

He agreed that the Stock Exchange was the home of
practical jokes such as creeping up behind people and setting
alight the *Financial Times* tucked under their arms.

'Do you agree that funny scenes sometimes take place on
the Stock Exchange?'
'When times are good and the Stock Exchange is in a
pleasant mood there is any amount of ragging, but the
Stock Exchange was very depressed and very little joking
had taken place of late.'
'You must have cheered them up?'
'I was the first joke that had happened for a long time.'

Somewhat unwisely Blennerhassett then called one of his
partners to prove what was thought to be the defamatory
innuendo in the advertisement. The stockbroker suggested
that people might think that this was an attempt on the part
of Blennerhassett to advertise his name to the public. Such

conduct would involve disciplinary action from the Council of the Stock Exchange, as advertising was strictly prohibited. It may have seemed a good point until he was asked by Sir Patrick:

> 'If you wanted to advertise yourself as a member of the Stock Exchange would you select a picture of yourself being escorted into a madhouse with a Yo-Yo?'

Sir Stephen Killick, perhaps feeling in some measure responsible for the débâcle, then gave his evidence of the serious consequences of this advertisement for Blennerhassett. By this stage it became apparent that the judge had had enough and he took over the cross-examination.

> 'Did you think he had gone mad with a Yo-Yo?'
> 'No.'
> 'Or that he had been taken to a lunatic asylum?'
> 'I knew he had not.'
> 'Or that he had gone into this to advertise his business as a stockbroker?'
> 'No.'

After McNulty had told the jury what happened to his trousers each morning, the judge took the unusual step of stopping the case and not sending the jury out.

Since Fox's Libel Act of 1792 each side in a libel action has been entitled to ask for trial by jury except in certain circumstances where cases are of unusual complexity. The judge rules on whether the words are capable of bearing a defamatory meaning and the jury then decides whether these are in fact defamatory. Judges normally leave the question for the jury to decide. In any event, where a specialist libel barrister has drafted the plaintiff's claim, there are relatively few cases which cannot be said to be capable of being defamatory. That was not the view of Mr Justice Branson.

> 'No reasonable being would after reading the advertisement have thought it referred to a living person. Even if

they did, it is not capable of bearing a defamatory meaning and there is no case to go to the jury.'

It was a view with which it would be difficult to disagree, and it was an appropriately robust way of dealing with the wounded pride of those who feel hurt by fiction.

Mr Blennerhassett was not the only stockbroker in the 1930s to lack a sense of humour and to launch into an ill-advised libel action. His example was followed by John Duffy Canning of Hove, who found a book entitled *People in Cages*, written by Helen Ashton and published by William Collins, more than he could endure.

The cause of the trouble was a character called Captain John Canning, 'a financial crook, a criminal, a cad, a seducer of women and a person without any sense of morality'. There was no evidence to suggest that any of these descriptions particularly fitted the Hove stockbroker. Nevertheless, he found himself being teased by his friends and acquaintances. This, it seems, was the unpromising basis for his libel action.

The book centred on London Zoo. It recounted the experiences of various characters one afternoon at the zoo. A Captain John Canning appeared in the book as a City financier wanted by the police, running panic-stricken from cage to cage. It was published in 1937 and enjoyed a modest success. Mr Canning did not read it. Indeed he had not heard of it until in the latter part of the year he started receiving telephone calls consisting of growling and quacking noises which he was 'quite at a loss to understand'. Later he was 'completely baffled' when an anonymous postcard came through his letter-box saying 'Get back to your ruddy cage'.

He soon learnt that the cause of these annoyances was the book *People in Cages*. On reading it he found a number of similarities between himself and the fictitious Captain Canning. He, too, had been a captain in the war although he no longer used the rank. He was engaged in finance in the City. He also had a sister called Mary. He was a member of the Zoological Society in London. He was about the same age as the fictitious Captain Canning. He, too, had broad shoulders and 'he was dark-haired not very long ago, although recently time had removed portions of it.'

He did not know the author and the case was at most one of accidental libel. On this evidence he retained the services of Lord Reading KC and Valentine Holmes. Despite their efforts, the case was lost in the cross-examination of Canning by W N Stable KC, whose junior was H C Leon (the author Henry Cecil).

Canning was asked by Stable:

'I have never been to the Stock Exchange, but I have heard that in times when business is slack the members have a rather reprehensible habit of ragging people?'
'Yes.'
'Are the reasonable people who, we have been told, thought the book referred to you, the people who rang up at midnight and made growling and quacking noises down the telephone?'
'I do not know who they were.'
'Is not the position that your friends in the Stock Exchange seized upon a heaven-sent opportunity for a little harmless banter?'
'I do not call it that.'
'Captain Canning in the book was making love to the doctor's wife and kissing her parlourmaid when he came to call at the doctor's house. No one would think that was you?'
'No one who knew me, but I am continuously making new acquaintances and it might be by some people with whom I might seek to do business.'

He was asked about the reference to the sister called Mary. He replied that he had not seen his sister Mary for fifteen years.

'So for fifteen years, no friend or business acquaintance of yours can have known that you had a sister called Mary?'

At this point even the judge, Lord Hewart, the Lord Chief

Justice, joined in the levity.

> 'She was the lady who "walked like that",' he reminded the
> jury amid laughter.

There was further laughter when the author, Miss Ashton,
told them that she had got the name Canning out of a history
book. John, she said, was 'as about as common a name as I
could find'. She had checked in the London telephone
directory and could not find any John Cannings.

The evidence upon which it could be said that people
might reasonably have supposed the book to be referring to
Mr Canning was very weak. Stable suggested to the jury that
if Canning were to recover damages in these circumstances
there would be no novels at all or they would have to deal
with exemplary characters only.

The facts were for the jury to decide, but in his summing
up of the law and the evidence Lord Hewart gave more than
a hint of what his own view was:

> 'The question of damages may not arise – in any event you
> may think there is no coin of the realm sufficiently small to
> indicate the damage that this man has suffered. The
> question is whether an intelligent reader with a rational
> mind could draw the inference that the person referred to
> in this book was Mr Canning.'

The jury was of the same opinion and Canning's claim was
dismissed, leaving him to bear the costs of these proceedings
which he had been so foolish to bring.

In 1952 a book entitled *The Sugar House* was published by
Eyre and Spottiswoode. It was written by Eirene Antonia
Hopkinson under her pen-name, Antonia White. The book
seemed fairly innocuous, so much so that it had not been
read for libel risks before publication. This was scarcely
surprising because it concerned a theatrical company in
York in 1920 and 1921. However, there appeared on four
pages a character called June Sylvaine. As the judge in the
subsequent libel action, Mr Justice Ormerod, observed 'the

character of June Sylvaine was only introduced in a very minor way and apparently only for the purpose of adding colour to the life of a theatrical company on tour'. She did not appear in the most flattering light; she was described as:

> a voluptuous redhead who called herself June Sylvaine. June was only twenty and had an extraordinarily pretty face and had hoped to play the leading ingénue but being decidedly fat had been cast as the comic elderly cook.

A character called Maidie, whom June Sylvaine referred to as 'that skinny has-been', was sharing a room with June and she complained to the leading man:

> 'Pardon me, Mr Lister. I'm such a small thing. I might get rolled on in my sleep.'

Later she makes a remark which Mr Justice Ormerod was to call 'an extremely unpleasant thing to say about anyone':

> 'All the women in the company are RC, thank God, except that bloody bitch, Sylvaine.'

It so happened that the book was read by George Bernard Shaw's secretary, Blanche Patch. She was struck by the similarities between the fictional character and the June Sylvaine she knew, the daughter of her friend, Vernon Sylvaine, the writer of farces. She was to tell the court that it was 'a very unkind description of June and a very wrong one'.

The resemblances were very striking. From September 1947 to July 1948 June Sylvaine had had a place at the York Repertory Theatre as leading ingénue. She had been twenty at the time. Her hair was then similar in colour. At York it had been its original auburn, although by the time of the trial in 1956 it was blonde. The names were identically spelt. At York her leading man had been Lister Skelton. In the book it was Mr Lister. In both the book and real life, Lister was a Roman Catholic, whereas she was not. However, she was not fat, but she did have to keep her weight under control and her evidence was that it was highly damaging for an ingénue to be thought to be fat.

As Gerald Gardiner QC her counsel at the trial pointed out, there were similarities of name, age, appearance, profession and religion. There were dissimilarities – Skelton did not consider her to be 'a voluptuous redhead' nor 'decidedly fat' – but, as the judge pointed out, 'if anyone wished to libel a person in a book they would not do it by faithfully representing details of that person's life and age'. He did not, therefore, think it particularly significant that the book was set in 1920 or that it claimed on its flyleaf to portray fictional events.

By the time the book was published June Sylvaine had acquired a considerable reputation as an actress. She had played the leading ingénue role in her father's play *One Wild Oat* opposite Robertson Hare and had appeared in a film and on television.

As Gerald Gardiner related, friends were 'not slow in drawing her attention to the book and some believed it was deliberately aimed at her'. She consulted solicitors and they wrote a letter of complaint on 13 March 1953. On 20 March the publisher's solicitors replied that they would be prepared to publish an announcement in the personal column of *The Times* stating that the book was fictitious. Not surprisingly that was rejected. It was not until 30 April 1953 that a formal offer of amends was made. This was rejected and proceedings claiming damages for libel were commenced against the author, the publisher and the printer. The plaintiff, by then married but still an actress, alleged that the words showed her to be of a jealous, spiteful and vindictive disposition and an undesirable person to engage as an actress.

Despite the striking similarities between the real and the fictitious June Sylvaines, it appeared that it was, as the author stated, a case of 'total coincidence'. She did agree in cross-examination by W A Fearnley-Whittingstall QC that there were 'unusual coincidences in the book'. Coincidence was a word that featured prominently in the trial, for when

Miss Sylvaine was asked by Gerald Gardiner QC if she thought the author had deliberately picked on her, she replied:

'I thought it a series of extraordinary coincidences.'

The case was treated by the judge as one of accidental libel.

Antonia White, the author, said that she did not know of June Sylvaine (although she had heard of her father) or of Lister Skelton's existence. Indeed, the author and the actress were of different generations. As it happened, the author had played one or two small parts on stage in a touring company. Skelton she thought was a 'pretty safe' name and right for the time and Lister was chosen because it did not 'sound obvious or commonplace'. She explained that she thought June Sylvaine was 'a good name for a person with this tiny part', but it seems that the remark was not meant as unkindly as it sounded. It seems that, having set the book in 1920, it never occurred to her that there was a risk of libel proceedings. A telephone call to the theatrical directory *Spotlight* would have revealed that there was a whole page devoted to a living actress called June Sylvaine.

As the trial proceeded, the somewhat artificial approach of the law to such cases emerged. The law of libel is less about hurt feelings than damage to reputation. Actual damage to reputation does not have to be proved, merely a tendency to damage. Yet the people whom a plaintiff can call to give such evidence will almost invariably say that they did not think any the worse of him or her. A plaintiff therefore has to rely on the possibility of unknown persons having a lower opinion of him or her as a result of reading the book, which itself involves two unprovable assumptions.

'Those who knew you would realize that the description in the book does not fit you?' she was asked by Fearnley-Whittingstall.
'Yes possibly they would – it is the people who do not know me I am worried about.'

She was asked if she had lost any theatrical engagements.

'That I may never know because one does not know what goes on in a theatrical manager's office. I have been in Australia until a few weeks ago. I am out of a job now.'

To the suggestion that this book could not have harmed her prospects in Australia, she retorted,

'I would not choose Australia. It is theatrical death.'

She went on to say she thought the book:

'had not done me any good at all. One gets a very unsavoury picture of the character and I am very worried about the reference to me being too fat. It is bad to be fat if one wants to play leading ingénue parts.'

The defence called a number of distinguished witnesses who dealt with the problem of libel in fiction. Graham Greene spoke of the author's high reputation and said that there was nothing in the book which made him feel that the book was other than a work of fiction. He did not see how one could libel a character in a novel.

Sir Compton Mackenzie told the judge that he had known the author fiftyfour years and that his father, grandfather and sister Fay Compton had all been on the stage. He said that he had never heard of June Sylvaine, for which he apologized, and that, as the novel in which the character appeared was set in 1920, the reference could hardly be to the charming young lady in court. He explained he had created two thousand characters in his forty novels. His solution for selecting names was to consult gentlemen's magazines of long ago and Old Bailey Sessions jury lists. He never looked up the names of his characters to see if there was any living person of the same name.

A defence of unintentional defamation was introduced by the Defamation Act 1952 in order to strike a balance between private reputation and the rights of novelists to select realistic names. June Sylvaine's case was the first and, as it happened, the only time this defence came before the courts. If a writer did not know of the circumstances which might cause his words to be understood to refer to that person and had exercised all reasonable care, he would have a defence under the statute, provided he made a suitable offer of amends as soon as practicable.

It was a defence with a number of hurdles, and its technicalities – the need to admit liability and to act with speed – have made it unpopular with lawyers and thus very rarely used.

The case was being heard by a judge alone; it is open to the parties to a case to agree, as they did here, to dispense with a jury. Mr Justice Ormerod decided that the author had not exercised reasonable care. She had failed to make any checks in any theatrical directory against the name Sylvaine. An advertisement in the personal column of *The Times* was not an offer of amends and the delay from 13 March (the date of the letter of complaint) to 30 April (the date of the formal offer of amends) was too long for it to be said that the offer was made as soon as practicable. The reason for the delay was not practicability but the reluctance of the defendants to admit liability.

The judge ruled that the passages in the book would be regarded by any reasonable person as references to the plaintiff. He considered that in view of the number of coincidences it was more likely than not that anyone who knew the plaintiff and of her career would think that it was referring to her. He decided it was not a case for heavy damages; the main purpose of the action had been to enable the plaintiff to bring the matter before the public so it could be cleared up to her satisfaction. He therefore awarded her £200 damages.

There was no reason to suppose that the use of June Sylvaine's name was other than accidental. It is often difficult to establish how such coincidences come about. Sometimes the reason is nothing more sinister than a half-remembered name lodged in the author's subconscious. The name of a clergyman may seem appropriate because of some long-forgotten encounter.

From the author's point of view the decision may have

seemed harsh. The work was clearly fictitious and set in the 1920s. The checks that might have been made were not carried out, because it never occurred to the writer that any living person could be identified as her fictional character.

From the victim's point of view, there was the possibility of ridicule, but more importantly there was the danger that some mud might stick and that an agent might have a vague recollection of reading something discreditable about June Sylvaine and choose someone else. She would never know why she was not engaged.

The balance that the law has tried to strike is well-intentioned, but extremely difficult to operate. At present the law is tilted against the author. It is bound to be extremely rare for a series of coincidences to arise such as in the Sylvaine case; normally the problem is a failure to consult the appropriate directories. Clearly a writer of fiction should not be entitled to borrow the name of an identifiable living person under the guise of fiction and make lurid allegations against him. However, the law at present does favour the living 'fictitious' plaintiff.

In a recent case which turned upon its special facts, such as the failure by the BBC to act upon a complaint before a broadcast, a highly reputable firm of solicitors recovered substantial damages because of a similarity between its name and that of a questionable but fictitious firm of solicitors who appeared in two radio plays. The resemblances other than in the name, were not particularly striking, with one firm practising in Birmingham and the other in the Home Counties; and no particular partner of the real firm was identifiable. However, a woman doing her ironing had thought that it must refer to the solicitors she knew with a similar name.

While any such association is obviously most disagreeable, it might be fairer in such instances to require more stringent proof that a reader or listener really thought that this was other than fiction and that there was a likelihood of significant damage.

Ten

Deceit in Venice

In February 1957 Aneurin Bevan, Morgan Phillips and Richard Crossman attended the National Congress of the Italian Socialist Party in Venice. In November 1957 they each trousered £2,500 in libel damages for suggestions in *The Spectator* that they had been drinking excessively at the congress. £2,500 was a substantial sum by the standards of the day but the plaintiffs who received the damages were themselves substantial figures. Aneurin Bevan was a Privy Councillor, Shadow Foreign Secretary and a very prominent figure in the Labour Party. He had gone as the party's delegate to the congress. Morgan Phillips was Secretary of the Labour Party. Richard Crossman was a member of the party's National Executive and a journalist of some distinction. He became a Cabinet Minister in the next Labour Government.

Yet only a few weeks later, when they met before appearing on the television programme 'What the Papers Say', Crossman told Brian Inglis the assistant editor of *The Spectator*, that Morgan Phillips and Aneurin Bevan had committed perjury: Morgan Phillips had been drunk and Bevan had been drinking heavily; he himself had been drinking wine but not whisky and had remained sober.

Crossman's entry in his diary for the first day of the trial described Morgan Phillip's performance in the witness box in these terms:

But, directly Morgan got into the box, it was clear he was a subnormal witness – shifty, fearful, sweating with panic (legitimately, for he'd been dead drunk for most of the conference).

The action itself was not particularly worthy of note. *The Spectator* had published a background article on the congress. They offered no real defence to the claim. It was the fact that the plaintiffs had been lying or at the very least condoning their colleagues' perjury that gave the case its interest.

Like many libel actions, it arose almost by accident. The article was nearly not written and then it was almost not published. Jenny Nicholson, the author of the article, was an occasional contributor to *The Spectator*. She was a descriptive writer rather than a political commentator or columnist. She happened to be in Venice for different reasons and had not intended to write a piece on the congress. Her account has been attacked on the basis that 'she was not even in Venice for the conference'. This has been thought to mean that she was not there at all. She was, and the way in which she came to write the article provides some indication of where the truth lies. She and her husband Patrick Crosse, then Reuter's correspondent in Rome, had lived in Italy for a number of years. They knew many of the leading Italian journalists. She first heard of the allegations about the behaviour of Bevan, Crossman and Phillips from complaints from a number of Italian journalists including Luigi Barzini. The Italians had attached considerable importance to the fact that such a high-ranking delegation had been sent by the British Labour Party.

The Italians felt that the congress raised critical issues. Would Nenni's Italian Socialist Party and Saragat's Democratic Socialist Party merge and would Nenni break away from his alliance with the Communists and turn to the West? The Italians thought that the fact that such a strong delegation had come from England was evidence of a desire to forge links between Nenni's Socialists and the West in the wake of the invasion of Hungary. In retrospect the Italians attached too great a significance to this congress and overestimated the importance of the British delegation, which in reality consisted of three eminent members of the Labour Party in Venice for different reasons.

With these expectations about the British delegation, the

Italians were particularly incensed by the arrogant way in which they considered they behaved. The British seemed uninterested in the congress. They did not attend many meetings. They did not bother to have translations made of what had been said. They did not talk to Italian journalists who could not speak English, although interpreters were available. One journalist, Luigi Barzini, who did speak excellent English, had tried to interview them, but he found they were interested only in discussing restaurants and what to do in Venice. The Italians complained to Jenny Nicholson of the time the British delegates had spent in the bars of their hotel and at the congress and of their boorish habit of swilling down large quantities of Italian coffee with their whisky.

It was Jenny Nicholson's description of their behaviour in her article entitled, 'Death in Venice', that gave rise to the libel action.

And there was the occasional appearance of Messrs Bevan, Morgan Phillips and Richard Crossman who puzzled the Italians by their capacity to fill themselves like tanks with whisky and coffee, while they (because of their livers and also because they are abstemious by nature) were keeping going on mineral water and an occasional coffee. Although the Italians were never sure if the British delegation was sober, they always attributed to them an immense political acumen.

The congress had taken place in the early part of February and Jenny Nicholson submitted her article a couple of weeks after the end of the congress. It was inserted at the last moment in the 1 March edition of *The Spectator*.

The question of whether the article was libellous was never really considered before publication by the editor or assistant editor. To them it was merely a background piece describing the atmosphere – black gondolas, straw hats and Nenni playing *scopone* – of a Socialist convention in Venice. They did not consider that the article accused the delegates of drunkenness. The writer was merely commenting on, amongst other things, the drinking habits of Bevan or Phillips and the effect their behaviour had on the Italian onlookers.

Nobody had given much thought to the implications of the article and no one had anticipated the possibility of a libel action. This as much as anything decided *The Spectator* against defending the action. They felt that, if they had wanted to accuse Bevan, Phillips and Crossman of drunkenness in a journal such as *The Spectator*, they should have written an article about it rather than making a passing reference. Having not spotted the libel, for libel it clearly was, they felt they should not justify an unintended allegation of insobriety. They were satisfied, however, from the time the plaintiffs complained of the article that what Jenny Nicholson had written was true.

As a young barrister Ian Gilmour (then proprietor of *The Spectator*) had learnt from his pupilmaster Quintin Hogg (later the Lord Chancellor, Lord Hailsham) the unwisdom of pleading justification, a view belonging to a more gentlemanly era. Despite this excellent grounding in the law, he was faced with an article in which the libel had not been spotted. He was also uncomfortably aware that the 1 March issue had in addition carried a piece by Randolph Churchill praising a jury's award of £20,000 libel damages to Mr Ortiz-Patino for vile allegations of matrimonial misconduct.

Gilmour and his counsel, W A Fearnley-Whittingstall QC, felt that it would be suicidal to run a defence before a British jury based on the word of a handful of Italian journalists and waiters against the sworn testimony of a Privy Councillor and two other leading British politicians. A jury would be most reluctant to decide that such persons would lie about a relatively minor allegation of excessive drinking.

Another thing that worried *The Spectator* was that, if they apologized in terms that completely disowned Jenny Nicholson, they could face a libel action from her. In 1954 the *Sunday Times* had to pay £3,000 libel damages to their journalist Honor Tracy, when they apologized for libelling the Doneraile parish priest without first obtaining her consent. She had criticized the expense of building a house for the priest in Doneraile in a community of that size and wealth and she had strongly resented the *Sunday Times* disowning the article.

It was decided to apologize and try to mitigate the damages. It was a perfectly reasonable decision as most libel cases are settled out of court for a fraction of the figure that the jury might award. Unfortunately, it played into the plaintiffs' hands, as they showed little inclination to settle.

Most of those at *The Spectator* involved in the action feel in retrospect that they should have justified the article. However, at the time their overwhelming thought was that the plaintiffs would not commit perjury for money and that the matter was best resolved by a suitable apology and modest financial terms. They knew that an unsuccessful plea of justification might result in a sufficiently large award of damages to put *The Spectator* out of business.

The moving spirit in the litigation appears to have been Aneurin Bevan. Not surprisingly, Morgan Phillips was involved against his will. Crossman, as a journalist, had misgivings as to whether he ought to be suing. Bevan approached the matter with considerably more enthusiasm. His motives in taking action seem to have been a mixture of factors. He wished to teach those he felt had been libelling him a lesson. He believed that an allegation of drunkenness was something a man of his position and standing in the Labour Party could not let go unchallenged. He is said to have discussed the action with Randolph Churchill who a few months previously had received £5,000 damages against *The People* (*see* chapter 8).

When the article was published, Bevan, Crossman and Phillips consulted Arnold Goodman, the solicitor to the Labour Party. A letter of complaint was sent on 5 March. The following day *The Spectator* stated that they would publish a mutually acceptable apology. The version they sent was immediately rejected by the politicians on the grounds that it did not make it clear that the story was 'untrue and baseless'. The first apology was a somewhat tortuous affair and scarcely contained the most generous of apologies, ending as it did:

> Whilst the article was published in good faith, we would
> like to express our regret for any inconvenience to which
> the paragraph might unwittingly have given rise.

While it is possible to see why this apology was rejected, it is
clear that Bevan, Phillips and Crossman would have known
before they started proceedings that *The Spectator* would
not seek to prove the truth of the allegations, as they had to,
if they were to defend the proceedings successfully. It was
simply a question of how much damages they would receive.

After meeting Ian Gilmour at a dinner party given by Roy
Jenkins, Richard Crossman drafted an apology. He required
The Spectator to grovel and to disown Jenny Nicholson. His
version was suitably uncompromising:

> These allegations were as absurd as they were offensive
> and we have since confirmed that there is no truth in them
> whatsoever. We and the author are both glad to withdraw
> them unreservedly and to offer our sincere apologies and
> to express our sincere regret that they were ever published
> in the columns of *The Spectator*.

This was watered down by *The Spectator*, who replied on 3
April that they would publish the following apology:

> These allegations if taken seriously would be absurd and
> offensive and we are assured and accept that there was no
> truth in them whatsoever. Whilst we had no intention of
> causing offence we and the author now realize that these
> remarks should not have appeared and we are both glad to
> withdraw them unreservedly, to offer our sincere
> apologies and to express our sincere regret that they were
> ever published in the columns of *The Spectator*.

This was an unequivocal withdrawal and apology and it is
difficult to see why it was rejected by the plaintiffs on the
grounds of the 'absence of some genuine kind of regret'.

The case, therefore, proceeded inexorably to trial. Some
two months before the case was heard. *The Spectator*,
having failed to agree the text of an apology, published its

own version. This unreservedly withdrew 'any suggestion
that the Italians might seriously have doubted their sobriety'
and 'hastened to take this opportunity of tendering to Mr
Aneurin Bevan, Mr Morgan Phillips and Mr Richard
Crossman our sincere apologies and of expressing our regret
for any inconvenience or annoyance they might have
suffered'.

At the same time *The Spectator* paid into court 500
guineas (£525) for each plaintiff. The effect of this was that
they could have taken this sum as damages and received their
legal costs up to the date of the payment into court plus a
public apology in court. This would have satisfied Richard
Crossman and Morgan Phillips, but not Aneurin Bevan who
wanted more money. The danger of not accepting the
payment into court was that if they recovered less than £525
each, they would have to pay *The Spectator*'s legal costs
from the time that the money had been paid into court. After
the trial Crossman told Gilmour that they were dissuaded
from settling by the promise of a Socialist millionaire, to pay
all their costs if they lost.

According to Richard Crossman, just before the trial
Aneurin Bevan was prepared to settle for £500 ('his old
pendulum-swinging self'), but after seeing his counsel,
Gilbert Beyfus QC, his resolve was stiffened and £1,000
became his minimum settlement figure. *The Spectator* did
offer £1,000 at lunchtime on the first day of the trial: Beyfus,
seeing the way the case was going, advised the plaintiffs to
reject the offer and they did. The plaintiffs had agreed to
present a united front.

The Spectator had nevertheless thought it worthwhile to
ask Jenny Nicholson to return to Venice before the trial to
see what evidence could be produced. Her impression was
that the decision not to justify had already been taken and
that this was something of an afterthought. She spoke to the
barman at their hotel and a couple of waiters at the bar at the
congress who were prepared to come to England to give
evidence, although their English was very limited. Luigi
Barzini, the journalist, was also prepared to give evidence of
seeing Bevan and Phillips drinking heavily and as to their

conversations. The incident (described later) of Morgan Phillips having been drunk at the British Consulate was not then known to *The Spectator*. This only emerged when the story was later disclosed by a foreign diplomat. In any event it would have presented a thorny diplomatic problem for a diplomat of one country to give evidence that the Shadow Foreign Minister of his host's country was committing perjury and had, in fact, been drunk and incapable.

The attempts to settle the matter had failed and the case came on for trial on 21 November 1957. There was little doubt that the plaintiffs would win; the real question was how much would they get. Beyfus, who had done much to stiffen the resolve of the plaintiffs, set about *The Spectator* with relish. Their various apologies were 'sly and slippery', 'a mock apology' and 'a contempt of court'. It was not long before he realized that in Lord Goddard he had a formidable wind behind him. It was, Beyfus told the jury, 'a grave libel on these three men who were not in Venice enjoying themselves'. They should award damages that would make an example of *The Spectator* and not surprisingly he commended to them Randolph Churchill's praise of the jury's £20,000 award in the Ortiz-Patino case.

The plaintiffs all sounded suitably aggrieved and distressed at *The Spectator*'s article. They had the advantage of knowing that the magazine had chosen not to justify the article and, therefore, could not assert in court that the three had indeed been drinking heavily.

Aneurin Bevan said that the article made him 'exceedingly angry and indignant' and the apologies appeared to make the position worse. On the question of what they had had to drink, Bevan's evidence was that he had had 'no more than one whisky and some wine'. 'No one could have been in doubt about my sobriety. Whisky is not the alcoholic refreshment generally taken at an Italian conference.' At this Lord Goddard helpfully pointed out that whisky was an expensive drink and Bevan smiled for the only time in the case.

Morgan Phillips stated that the piece had made him 'very angry because it suggested I had neglected my duties for consuming large quantities of whisky'. Morgan Phillips said he had had 'one whisky with a French colleague, paid for by him'. He was 'never the worse for drink while at Venice'.

Richard Crossman said that his view was that if we 'didn't sue and get an apology, normal readers would think that we had gone round tiddly at Venice and behaved in an outrageous way where every delegate could see and that we had not done our jobs properly'. It is difficult to believe that Crossman can have supposed he was telling the truth when he gave that evidence. He had said just the opposite in his diary; Phillips 'got tiddly by midday' were the words he used. Richard Crossman said he drank 'no whisky at all'. 'At no stage was I in a state of insobriety or doubtful sobriety.'

In his evidence at the libel action, Ian Gilmour said that, had he read the article to mean any of the plaintiffs were drunk in Venice, it would not have been published. He understood the article merely to mean that they enjoyed themselves in the normal way. It was an explanation which was met by some scorn on the part of the plaintiffs' counsel, Gilbert Beyfus QC, and the Lord Chief Justice, Lord Goddard, but it was *The Spectator*'s view of the matter.

Many felt that Beyfus overstepped the mark of legal proprieties when he accused Gilmour of lying by suppressing the existence of without prejudice negotiations. (Such dealings between the parties are never revealed to the court so as to enable parties to explore the ground for negotiating a settlement.) His cross-examination of Gilmour exploited the difficulty that faced *The Spectator* on the question of what a reader would think the article meant. When Gilmour denied that the article cast a slur on the plaintiffs, he was asked where he was educated. When he replied 'Eton and Balliol', Beyfus asked:

'With that education behind you, do you say you do not think that to say of three leaders of the Labour Party on official missions to Venice that they filled themselves like tanks with whisky, obviously in public, casts any sort of slur on them?'

'Yes,' Mr Gilmour replied.

One of the features of the trial was the very strong stance taken by Lord Goddard against *The Spectator*. It bordered on the injudicial and certainly encouraged the plaintiffs not to settle for the £1,000 they were offered. After the trial *The Spectator*'s counsel, W A Fearnley-Whittingstall QC, wrote in reply to a letter from Ian Gilmour:

> Goddard was quite shocking and, having ranged himself on Beyfus's side, the latter needed no courage to be as offensive as he was irrelevant.

It was an unusual way for a Queen's Counsel to write of a Lord Chief Justice and for that matter of another Silk.

Fearnley-Whittingstall's handling of the case was itself criticized, but he was in ill-health and he was to die within two years at the age of fiftysix. He argued that the article meant no more than that the plaintiffs were 'on a convivial busman's holiday, while at the same time retaining the utmost political sagacity'. It was curiously expressed and cut little ice with the jury.

Fearnley-Whittingstall's view of Goddard was in some measure supported by Crossman in his diaries:

> Even after half an hour it was clear that this astonishing monster of eighty had made up his mind that we were in the right and that *The Spectator* had behaved outrageously.

When Richard Crossman was giving his evidence, Lord Goddard leant across and whispered helpfully, 'Do remember you're not in the House of Commons'.

The Spectator had not endeared itself to Lord Goddard by its attack on his robust views on hanging, as expressed in the debates on the abolition of capital punishment. They particularly criticized Lord Goddard's enthusiasm for hanging insane murderers. Capital punishment was a subject on which Lord Goddard had very strong views, as appears even from the index of the biography of Lord Goddard by Fenton Bresler, which refers specifically to twentyone pages on capital punishment, and *passim*.

When, most unusually, Lord Goddard after his retirement was interviewed by Iain Adamson, Gilbert Beyfus's biographer, he firmly denied the suggestion of any bias at this trial, although it was clear that it did trouble him.

However, the force of his views was such that he found himself being accused of entering the arena. After Ian Gilmour had given his evidence in reply to his counsel, he was subjected to a virtual cross-examination by Lord Goddard. Ian Gilmour said that as soon as he had heard from Crossman at Roy Jenkins's dinner party, he had tried to get in touch with Jenny Nicholson:

'Why did you do that?' Lord Goddard asked.
'To find out about the reference.'
'To see if it was true?'
'Yes.'
'What was wrong with Mr Crossman's draft?'
'Nothing my Lord.'
'Then why not publish it? You were saying all along you wanted to apologize. Why didn't you?'
'We took it for granted that an apology acceptable to the other side would be better than one they did not approve. I was under the impression it was universal practice to agree an apology.'

Beyfus was then able to do some cross-examination as to what Gilmour thought the article meant before Lord Goddard intervened again and these were some of the questions he asked:

'Then what do you think it meant?'
'This libel [this was a matter for the jury to decide] is not "inconvenient". It is intensely annoying. What do you mean by "good faith"?'
'I suppose you might have considered what a gentleman should do in these circumstances quite apart from lawyers?'
'But you recognize they [the words] are offensive?'

'You know what the English language is. Do you say these
words are not offensive – to say a man is filling himself up
with whisky like a tank?'

Lord Goddard did not seem to think much of the title of the
article, 'Death in Venice'. When Richard Crossman gave
evidence, he was asked by the judge to explain what the title
meant and who it was who had died in Venice. Crossman
tactfully answered that he thought it was a reference to one
of Thomas Mann's short stories, 'a literary joke'. When Ian
Gilmour gave evidence he was also asked by the judge to
explain the reference and he said that it was to the death of
the hopes of the two Socialist parties in Italy uniting. Even
so, when Lord Goddard summed the case up to the jury, he
said:

'You might have thought you were going to read a thriller
by Agatha Christie. Instead you have one of the dullest
articles you have ever read and I should have thought one
of the most difficult to understand.'

Observing the proceedings, Richard Crossman was not
particularly impressed by the closing address to the jury of
either counsel.

But the Lord Chief Justice changed all that by making the
speech on our behalf which I had hoped Beyfus would
make.

Lord Goddard ruled that he had no hesitation in saying the
words could be defamatory and suggested that whether they
were defamatory ought not to cause the jury much trouble.
The article was 'a spicy item in an otherwise extremely
uninteresting article'. He cautioned them against awarding
extravagant damages. After a retirement of twentyeight
minutes the jury awarded £2,500 to each plaintiff.

The case was most striking for what happened after the
trial. A number of those present at the trial had watched
these politicians lying from the witness box with some

amazement, but there had been no evidence at the trial to prove that they had been drinking heavily. Of the three, Crossman's part was the least culpable, but he was nevertheless a party to an action based on false testimony and some of his evidence was false.

After the trial Jenny Nicholson, having heard all the evidence and spoken to the potential witnesses, believed that Crossman was telling the truth in court about his part but that Bevan and Phillips had been lying. She was sufficiently convinced of this and outraged by what she had heard to tell Brian Inglis after the trial that she had placed a curse on Bevan and Phillips. It seems this was done in reaction to their testimony rather than any firm belief in its efficacy, although, as it happened, Bevan was dead within three years and Phillips within six. She told Inglis she had been convinced by something Crossman said in the witness box that he was telling the truth. In the original article she had made no distinction between the three.

The first positive indication that the plaintiffs had been committing perjury had come with the conversation between Brian Inglis and Richard Crossman before the television programme 'What the Papers Say' a few weeks after the trial. Crossman told Inglis that Morgan Phillips was drunk and Bevan had been drinking heavily.

The next time the matter was raised was when Iain Adamson was preparing his biography of Gilbert Beyfus QC. This was published in 1963, but significantly it was written before Phillips's death. Bevan had already died by then. Adamson saw Crossman at the House of Commons in 1962. Crossman spoke freely to him and said that Bevan and Phillips had been drunk and had committed perjury, but that he had been sober. He also said that Morgan Phillips had not wanted to sue but Bevan had insisted. 'I've been libelled too often. I can get them on this', Bevan had told Crossman. Iain Adamson sent the first draft of his chapter to Crossman who replied that what he had said was off the record and that if ever publicly questioned he would deny that Bevan and Phillips had committed perjury. This, of course, conflicted with what he had written in his diary about Phillips.

Following the publication of Adamson's book, Crossman did issue a short statement to the *South Wales Echo* regarding the allegations of perjury. 'It is quite untrue. I do not want to argue the case and give them the opportunity of continuing the attack.'

The next occasion the matter was raised was in 1972 at a *Private Eye* lunch. Crossman was asked by Auberon Waugh in the presence of Patrick Marnham, Richard Ingrams, Richard West and Geoffrey Wheatcroft whether the plaintiffs in *The Spectator* action had been drunk. Crossman replied that they certainly were, a reply which Auberon Waugh was to paraphrase as an admission that 'they were all pissed as newts'. It seems that Crossman's earlier and more considered versions to Brian Inglis and Iain Adamson are more likely to be accurate, given Crossman's tendency to embroider stories.

In 1978 Auberon Waugh wrote an article in *The Spectator* about the trial. By this time all three politicians were dead and the matter could be discussed without the danger of being sued for libel. The matter was further revived by the posthumous publication of Richard Crossman's diaries in 1981. This contained the passage about Morgan Phillips already quoted.

What then was the truth about the politicians' drinking? Morgan Phillips had a considerable reputation for drinking to excess and he had left a number of conferences the worse for wear. To have had only one whisky would have been well below par. Richard Crossman referred to him in his diary as 'dead drunk for most of the conference. He drank steadily – I think mainly to avoid conversation – with the result he got tiddly by midday and soaked by dinner-time.' Even when one allows for an element of hyperbole, it suggests considerably more than one whisky. Crossman also spoke of Phillips being scared stiff of fighting the case and of being 'shifty, fearful and sweating with panic' in the witness box. Certainly a number of those who saw Phillips give his evidence suspected he was not telling the truth. In fact not only had Phillips been drinking excessively at the bar but he had been so drunk at a dinner given by the British Consul in

Venice and attended by a number of foreign diplomats that his head had fallen into the soup and he had to be taken back to his hotel.

Word of this incident had reached the two Italian Socialist leaders. Saragat was shocked by it. Nenni appeared indifferent to the news.

By all accounts Bevan was a man who liked his drink, but he had a high tolerance of alcohol. There was no evidence of his being in a drunken state, but the Italian journalists and the bar staff did tell Jenny Nicholson that Bevan had been drinking whisky in large quantities. Crossman accused both Bevan and Phillips of excessive drinking on the three occasions in 1957, 1962 and 1972 and he had written about Phillips's drunkenness in his diary in 1957.

The charge of perjury made by Iain Adamson has been severely criticized by Michael Foot in the second volume of his biography of Bevan. He speaks of Bevan's 'extremely strong head' and says that the charge was 'a most improbable one'. 'No one could ever call him abstemious, but hardly anyone ever saw him drunk. He rarely "drank" when he was working, never when he had to make a speech.'

This is not necessarily inconsistent with what Richard Crossman told Brian Inglis a few weeks after the trial and was to repeat to Iain Adamson in 1962 and to Auberon Waugh at the 1972 *Private Eye* lunch. There is some conflict as to whether Crossman's view was that Bevan had been drinking very heavily or was actually drunk, but there was little doubt he had considerably more than the one whisky he claimed.

Iain Adamson's account (which, when published, did not name Crossman as his source) has been attacked by Michael Foot on the basis that it is not supported by any evidence. The fact that Bevan had been drinking very large amounts and that those who did not know the strength of his head may have doubted his sobriety is supported by Richard Crossman's verbal accounts and by the Italian bar staff and journalists.

The position regarding Crossman appears to be that the evidence he gave to the court was substantially true. He did not normally drink whisky and had consumed only a small amount of wine. This was consistent with what he told Brian Inglis and Iain Adamson, and with his reputation of being a moderate drinker. As against this is his answer to Auberon Waugh's question at the 1972 *Private Eye* lunch, where he is recorded as having admitted that they certainly were all drunk.

The point has been made on behalf of Morgan Phillips and Aneurin Bevan that it is inconceivable if they were lying that they would run the risk of *The Spectator* justifying its article. It is on the face of it surprising that these politicians did lie about what was not a particularly serious libel. Committing perjury is a dangerous business, but the risk that *The Spectator* would try to prove the article was true was a small one. The magazine's article was inaccurate. They had not *all* been drinking whisky. Furthermore they did not have long to wait before they received *The Spectator*'s reply to the initial letter of complaint to see that they had no intention of proving that the article was true. They knew this at the outset.

Those who accused Bevan and Phillips of lying at the trial found themselves attacked in vigorous terms on three grounds. The first was that the charge of excessive drinking against Bevan was highly improbable in view of his strong head. This was principally propounded by Michael Foot who declared that, having examined the then unpublished Crossman *Diaries*, 'nowhere was it suggested or hinted that *The Spectator* libel against Aneurin Bevan was true, rather there were extensive paragraphs which told powerfully in the opposite sense'. Crossman did not say in his diaries Bevan was drunk or even drinking heavily; he was silent on the matter. He did, however, say Phillips was dead drunk for most of the congress and that Bevan was the moving spirit behind this litigation. Morgan Phillips's widow, Baroness Phillips, wrote that her husband had told her that they had drunk Vichy water throughout the congress – making the point that it was not his favourite drink.

The second argument was the unreliability of Crossman. Michael Foot referred to his 'marvellous gift of hyperbolic expression in light-hearted moments'. Lord Goodman wrote of this 'immensely talented, quick-witted and at times even great man' but said it was 'clear that he possessed a streak of mischief and irresponsibility'. Gwyneth Dunwoody MP, Morgan Phillips's daughter, was even more forthright – showing that speaking ill of the dead was not confined to the *Spectator* camp, spoke of Crossman as 'one of the most unstable men in politics, a man who continually told lies'. She had 'long ago ceased to be surprised by anything he said. He was always called Double Crossman in the Party. He owed my father a great deal.'

Crossman no doubt was a man whose stories lost nothing in the telling, but that does not mean that he would make false allegations of perjury against his Socialist colleagues. If he was given to uttering such falsehoods against them, it is surprising he attained the position he did in politics. There is no other incident of this gravity in his political life about which Crossman is said not to have told the truth.

Thirdly, the point is made by his legal advisers, counsel and solicitors, that at no stage during the proceedings or their lifetime did any of the three suggest to them that the evidence given by any of the three was untrue. To be fair, no such suggestion has ever been made. That scarcely carries the argument further, as they would have declined to act for them if they had been told by their clients that the story they proposed to tell in court under oath was untrue.

Whether it was the love of money or the desire to settle political scores that influenced Bevan will probably never be known. It is clear, however, that the plaintiffs' case was an untrue one. It would be an odd streak of mischief and irresponsibility that led Crossman to tell three different people whom he scarcely knew that their evidence at the trial had been untrue, particularly when that evidence corresponded with what the Italians said they saw and with the way Bevan and Phillips were prone to behave.

Crossman's own verdict was that 'it seems to me the more I reflect on it to have been the kind of gamble which no one should responsibly have taken, even though we did win in the end'. It is a view with which few would disagree, although some might put it more strongly.

Much has been written of the injustice of reopening this matter after the death of the three politicians, but against this must be set the fact the principal evidence of perjury emerged when Crossman's backbench *Diaries* were published in 1981. By then all three were dead. Some thought should also be given to *The Spectator* which had to pay substantial damages and costs and could have been put out of business by an award of the size that Bevan may have been hoping for. Jenny Nicholson herself was deeply upset by the case and gave up journalism out of a feeling of responsibility for the damage she had caused to *The Spectator*.

Another case where the facts presented to the court in a libel action were subsequently called into question also comes from the political field. It concerned actions for libel brought in 1963 by Jack Profumo MP, then Minister for War, against two foreign magazines, *Tempo Illustrato* and *Paris Match*.

In early 1963 rumours were circulating regarding the Cabinet Minister's relationship with Christine Keeler. Added spice was given to the newspapers' fascination with this politician's extra-marital affair by the belief that those sharing Miss Keeler's favours included a singer due to face serious criminal charges at the Central Criminal Court and a Russian diplomat.

The laws of libel imposed the need for extreme discretion upon the English press, even though the allegations were subsequently considered grave enough for the Master of the Rolls, Lord Denning, to investigate. Continental magazines and papers were under no such constraints in their own countries. Two such magazines, *Tempo Illustrato* and *Paris Match* published articles which clearly cast doubt on Profumo's statement to the House of Commons on 22 March 1963 that he had not been guilty by an impropriety with Miss Keeler. Writs were immediately issued against their distributors. In view of the Minister's unequivocal denial and their small circulation in this country they had little alternative but to settle the action on the best terms possible.

Distributors of such foreign news magazines consider they perform a useful service in informing English readers of what is being published abroad. It is however, difficult for them to justify the expense of defending libel proceedings and they are on occasions compelled to withdraw what was perfectly fit and proper for European readers.

In this case they were faced with a categorical denial by a Minister of the Crown. The layout of the articles was such that it could not be said that they were distributing the magazines in ignorance of their libellous content. Accordingly they agreed to withdraw the magazines in the face of the Minister's action and to agree to a public apology.

On 10 April 1963 a statement in open court was read on behalf of *Tempo Illustrato* before Mr Justice Hinchcliffe.

At the end of last week, it had been drawn to Mr Profumo's attention that the article in question repeated an alleged rumour that Mr Profumo had in some way been involved in the failure of Miss Christine Keeler to appear at the Central Criminal Court at which she had been bound over to give evidence. The article also contained suggestions that Mr Profumo had been or may have been in some improper relationship with Miss Keeler. The attention of the defendants [the distributors of *Tempo Illustrato*] had been immediately drawn to the gravity of the libel contained in the publication and the defendants appeared by their counsel to state that they recognized that any such allegations were unjustifiable and without foundation.

(Accordingly, the publication had been withdrawn and Profumo had been indemnified as to his legal costs.)

Mr Profumo, recognizing that the defendants were not the originators of these defamatory allegations and the propriety of their prompt action in preventing further publications, has agreed to accept in this particular case a token sum which he proposes to give to an army charity.

Suitable expressions of regret were then made on behalf of

the distributors who pointed out that a number of other publications had been withheld from distribution. The *Paris Match* case was settled on similar terms.

The allegation that Profumo had in any way influenced proceedings at the Central Criminal Court was manifestly untrue, but his denial of an improper relationship with Christine Keeler was not.

On 6 June 1963 Profumo admitted that his statement in the House of Commons on 22 March 1963 had been untrue and he resigned.

Armed with this new information the solicitors for the distributors of *Tempo Illustrato* announced on 13 July 1963 that, following further discussions regarding the terms on which the litigation had originally been settled, the case had now been resolved on mutually satisfactory terms, which were not disclosed.

Such cases of lack of candour were eclipsed by the case that Edwina Mountbatten brought against Odhams Newspapers in 1932. She had become friendly with the black American actor, Paul Robeson, following his success in London in the role of Othello. Robeson was frequently to be seen at the Mountbattens's parties at Brook House. It was at the time most unusual to see a black person in fashionable society and his friendship with Edwina became well known.

However, it was one thing for this association to be discussed in polite society. It was apparently quite another for it to be commented upon in the popular press. In May 1932 *The People* published an article in its gossip column:

SOCIETY SHAKEN BY TERRIBLE SCANDAL
I am able to reveal today the sequel to a scandal which has shaken society to the very depths. It concerns one of the leading hostesses in the country, a woman highly connected and immensely rich.
Associations with a coloured man became so marked that they were the talk of the West End. Then one day the couple were caught in compromising circumstances.
The sequel is that the society woman has been given the

hint to clear out of England for a couple of years to let the affair blow over, and the hint comes from a quarter which cannot be ignored.

The quarter which could not be ignored was a none too oblique reference to Buckingham Palace. Edwina was compelled to sue to deny that she had an association with a coloured man and that she had been ordered to live abroad.

It was a shameful betrayal of her friendship with Paul Robeson, but the case duly came on before the Lord Chief Justice, Lord Hewart in July 1932.

Her counsel, Norman Birkett, told the judge, 'It is not too much to say that it is the most monstrous and most atrocious libel of which I have ever heard.' Patrick Hastings offered the newspaper 'genuine and deep regrets'. The newspaper publicly apologized and Edwina declined to accept any damages.

The case did however have two unusual features, firstly that it was heard at 9.30 am one hour before the court normally opened, so that it was over before the press knew about it and secondly, although the case was uncontested, Edwina was permitted to go into the witness box and to testify to the surprise of her friends that she had never in her life met the man in question.

Eleven

Unfair Comment

On 25 September 1956 Wladziu Valentini Liberace came to play in England. He had travelled from New York to Southampton on the *Queen Mary* and the last leg of his well-orchestrated journey was by a special six-carriage train to Waterloo. As his counsel, Gilbert Beyfus QC, put it at the libel action against the *Daily Mirror* two and a half years later, there was 'a tremendous hullabaloo at Southampton and Waterloo stations'. Women stood on the railway tracks to get a glimpse of Liberace and threw themselves forward to kiss the train windows. One reporter wrote of the scene at Waterloo that there were 'squealing women, weeping women, screaming women and fainting women'. Even *The Times* wrote of 3,000 women at Waterloo and of girls pressing against Mr Liberace's coach and crying 'swoon'.

This, together with the widely reported press conference at Cherbourg, where Liberace was surrounded by forty-eight discreetly positioned candelabra, was too much for William Neil Connor, the columnist 'Cassandra' of the *Daily Mirror*. He wrote comparing Liberace to a German drink called *windstärke fünf*, which he described as 'the most deadly concoction of alcohol that the Haus Vaterland could produce'. He continued:

I have to report that Mr Liberace, like *windstärke fünf*, is about the most that a man can take. But he is not a drink. He is yearning wind-strength five. He is the summit of sex, the pinnacle of Masculine, Feminine and Neuter. Everything that He, She and It can ever want. I spoke to sad but kindly men at this newspaper who have met every celebrity arriving from the United States for the past thirty years. They all say that this deadly, winking, sniggering, chromium-plated, scent-impregnated, luminous, quivering, giggling, fruit-flavoured, mincing, ice-covered heap of Mother Love has had the biggest reception and impact since Charlie Chaplin arrived at the same station, Waterloo, on September 12th 1921.

This appalling man, and I use the word appalling in no other than its true sense of 'terrifying', has hit this country in a way that is as violent as Churchill receiving the cheers on VE day. He reeks with emetic language that can only make grown men long for a quiet corner, an aspidistra, a handkerchief and the old heave-ho. Without doubt he is the biggest sentimental vomit of all time. Slobbering over his mother, winking at his brother and counting the cash at every second, this superb piece of calculating candyfloss has an answer for every situation.

The article went on to quote Liberace on religion:

'I feel I can bring people closer to God through my appearance. I happen to be a religious man and I want my marriage to be blessed with my faith.'

On mother love:

'I think it is my mother love which so many of them [middle-aged women] do not get from their children.'

The article continued in similar vein and concluded with two further thrusts:

Nobody anywhere ever made so much money out of high-speed piano playing with the ghost of Chopin gibbering at every note. There must be something wrong with us that our teenagers longing for sex, and our middle-aged matrons fed up with sex, alike should fall for such a sugary mountain of jingling claptrap wrapped up in such a preposterous clown.

On 18 October 1956 this was followed by an article where 'Cassandra' commented under the heading 'Calling all Cussers' that the column 'Today's Arrangements' in *The Times* showed the newspaper 'at its impassive unsmiling best'. After listing the times and details of services in the leading London churches, it added 'Albert Hall: Liberace 7.30'. 'Rarely', 'Cassandra' commented , 'has the sacred been so well marshalled alongside the profane.'

These two articles led to a seven-day action brought by Liberace against William Connor and Daily Mirror Newspapers Ltd. The case attracted enormous publicity. The trial raised the issue of how far a critic could go in his criticism. If these words were merely an expression of 'Cassandra's' honestly held beliefs however prejudiced, the defence had an answer to the claim. If they were no more than a mask for making false allegations of homosexuality against Liberace or the comments were made maliciously, the plaintiff would succeed.

Liberace's libel action called to mind Ruskin's controversial criticism of James McNeill Whistler, the American Impressionist painter, after seeing the exhibition of his paintings at the Grosvenor Gallery in 1877:

> For Mr Whistler's sake, no less than for the protection of the purchaser, Sir Coutts Lindsay [the exhibition organizer] ought not to have admitted works into the gallery in which the ill-educated conceit of the artist so nearly approached the aspect of wilful imposture. I have seen, and heard, much of cockney impudence before now; but never expected to hear a coxcomb ask two hundred guineas for flinging a pot of paint in the public's face.

Whistler won his case, but he received a paltry one farthing's damages.

With this inauspicious precedent, the case opened on 8 June 1959. Liberace was represented by Gilbert Beyfus QC supported by two junior counsel, of whom the more senior was Helenus Milmo. On receiving his brief to represent Liberace, Gilbert Beyfus had had to refer to his more worldly clerk to discover who this Liberace might be. The lack of initial admiration turned out to be mutual. On seeing Beyfus in his crumpled suit, aged seventyfour, grey-faced and with a marked twitch in one eye, one of the Liberace entourage remarked, 'We wanted the best lawyer not the oldest. We might as well fly back straight away.' Of the more youthful and distinguished-looking Gerald Gardiner QC for the defendants, he remarked, 'that's the lawyer we should have gotten'. However, things improved after this unpromising start with Beyfus breaking the habit of a lifetime and inviting a client to his house in Haslemere and Liberace after the trial, publicly thanking his very wonderful lawyer, who was in the audience, from the stage of the Chiswick Empire theatre.

The *Daily Mirror* was represented by Gerald Gardiner QC supported by another leading counsel, Neville Faulks QC and one junior counsel.

Liberace had been born in Milwaukee, Wisconsin in 1919. In cross-examination he agreed that some of his publicity gave his date of birth as 1920, but he explained it was thought desirable by his public relations men to make it a round date. His father, Salvatore, was an Italian immigrant who gave up playing the French horn for an ice cream parlour in order to make ends meet. His mother, who remained prominently in the background during his trial, was a Polish concert pianist. She had taught the infant Wladziu to play the piano and dissuaded his father from sending him into the undertaking business. She even brought the composer Paderewski to see the four-year-old Wladziu. It was apparently Paderewski who suggested that Wladziu cease to play under the name Lee Liberace and adopt the style Liberace. It was said by one of Liberace's biographers that Paderewski had said of the young Liberace, 'When I have gone you will take my place'. A more cynical observer commented that great pianists are not necessarily great prophets. His mother had nursed Liberace through a near fatal attack of pneumonia and successfully rejected a doctor's advice that Liberace's poisoned finger was best cured by amputation.

Liberace became a successful nightclub performer, but his huge fame could be traced to a 1951 television appearance. From this he went on in July 1952 to appear before an audience of 22,000 in the Hollywood Bowl. By the time of the trial he was earning $1 million per year from his concerts and TV shows alone, before taking into account record sales, his real estate transactions and his company giving piano instruction – a sum which it has been observed was then more than sufficient to pay all the judges in England. His career became inseparable from the lifestyle he presented with such enthusiasm to the public.

His success was rooted in his intimate nightclub style where he treated his audience to impromptu patter in which he chatted about his mother and his brother George and anything which came into his head. Critics hated it, but Liberace asserted 'nobody loves me except my public' and so it seemed. He had two hundred fan clubs in America, a mailbag of 6,000–10,000 letters a week and 27,000 Valentine cards a year. He told the somewhat bemused jury that he had sixty suits, eighty pairs of shoes, a gold lamé dinner jacket, a diamond-studded tailcoat worth $10,000 and a bugle-beaded tailcoat. In the course of his evidence he referred to his 'English suit', but this turned out, to the horror of Savile Row, to be a 'silk tweed suit with a gold thread'. The attempt by his counsel to compare these sartorial excesses to Beefeaters at the Tower and Masters of Foxhounds at Hunt Balls was hardly likely to convince anyone.

Liberace was aware of the absurdity of this gimmickry, but with some good humour he once told an interviewer that when he gave it up for a year in 1958 it had cost him $400,000. It also emerged that Liberace's home in America was full of piano-shaped things, including a swimming pool with black and white terraces. One witness described going into a room with two hundred models of a piano, only two of which played, and having to stub out his cigarette on F sharp in the ashtray; 'a visitor would be dumbstruck by the extraordinary appurtenances'.

In the opposite corner was William Connor, 'Cassandra' of the *Daily Mirror*. He was turned down by the navy because of his eyesight and so he joined the *Daily Mirror* in 1935. The name 'Cassandra' was bestowed on him by the editor. One of the few errors made by Beyfus in the trial was to suggest that Cassandra was the prophetess of evil. She was, as Gardiner pointed out, a prophetess whose curse it was always to be right but never to be believed.

In the course of the trial Connor was cross-examined about what he had written about doctors, French poodles and Richard Dimbleby. He was a man of extremely forceful views. Gardiner suggested to the jury that he was a man usually standing up for the poor and down-trodden, sometimes blaming, sometimes praising. Beyfus could scarcely contain himself when describing Connor. At the outset of the case he asserted, but never proved that Connor was 'a literary assassin, who dips his pen in vitriol, hired by this sensational newspaper to murder reputations and hand out the sensational articles on which its circulation is built'. Beyfus's ruthless cross-examination committed Connor to a number of propositions as to his style of writing from which he had to withdraw in some disarray. Certainly the case did no harm to Connor and he was knighted in 1966. One witness was to suggest that he and his newspaper deliberately fought the case for its entertainment and circulation value. However, the case did show that he was better employed in the pages of the *Daily Mirror* than in the witness box of the Royal Courts of Justice.

On 8 June 1959 the case was opened by Gilbert Beyfus QC to Mr Justice Salmon and the jury; he said that the first article was 'as savage a diatribe as might be imagined. It meant and was intended to mean that Liberace was a homosexual. Otherwise the words had no meaning.' He described the articles as a serious attack on Liberace's morals and stressed that Liberace's piano-playing was not sexy, but wholesome, homely and in part sentimental. For the defendants, Gerald Gardiner QC denied that the article alleged homosexuality. He argued that the article was fair comment and criticism. He sought to prove that Liberace's performances were sexy, tasteless, riddled with insincerity and beset with gimmicks. The result was a trial that had its

uproarious moments, where feelings ran high and the
evidence ranged far and wide. Liberace's and the *Daily
Mirror*'s views on Princess Margaret were scrutinized, as
were such diverse matters as Liberace's buying perfume at Le
Bourget airport, a strip cartoon reproduced in the *Sunday
Pictorial* entitled 'Bringing up Bonnie Prince Charlie' and
the meaning to be attached to the words 'fruit-flavoured'.

Beyfus sought to prove that the article was suggesting that
Liberace was a homosexual. Gardiner intervened when
Beyfus asked Liberace if he was a homosexual to say that
'there is no such suggestion and never has been of the kind'.
It did appear that Liberace had some grounds for complaint.
Outside the Royal Festival Hall in London there had been a
group of hostile placards. Things got worse as he went north,
as there was a hostile group of young men in Manchester and
when he crossed the Pennines his audience in Sheffield
shouted 'Queer', 'Fairy' and 'Go home, queer'. Liberace told
the jury that this upset him but he had worked hard and won
the audience over.

Despite these denials and disclaimers, the issue of
homosexuality never really left the trial. Various witnesses
were questioned about a music-hall skit on Liberace sung on
television in early 1956 by James Thompson which included
the lines

> I get more and more
> They propose by the score
> And at least one or two are from girls ...
> My fans all agree that I'm really mostly me
> When I play the sugar plum fairy.

The purpose of introducing this seemingly irrelevant
evidence was to seek to probe Liberace's insincerity and
obsession with publicity, for he had, despite these offensive
words, posed for a photograph with Thompson. Liberace
explained that he had not been aware of this skit at the time.
He later sued Thompson, who had to apologize and pay
damages. The defence could not introduce the words to
show that the *Daily Mirror* was saying what others had said,

as that is not a defence to a charge of libel. Reference to the words of the skit did however produce the rather anguished comment that the defendants were seeking 'to justify by the back door'.

Not only did Liberace firmly deny that he had ever indulged in homosexual practices in his life, but he explained that he was against the practice 'because it offends convention and offends society'. Gardiner's cross-examination of Liberace did little to lessen the burden the words had placed upon him:

> 'Are you seriously suggesting that these ordinary English words mean that you are a homosexualist?'
> 'That was the interpretation that was given and understood by everyone I have come in company with.'
> 'I suggest that is quite fantastic. People must have singularly filthy minds if they think the words imply you are a homosexual.'

Liberace explained that the expression 'fruit-flavoured' was one commonly used of homosexuals. Gardiner retorted that it is just a reference to his sugary manner. Liberace replied: 'The reason I am in court is that the article has attacked me below the belt on a moral issue.'

When Connor came to give his evidence, he somewhat unconvincingly denied that he knew the word 'fruit' was slang in the United States for homosexual and said it came as a bit of a surprise to him. He explained that he used the adjective 'fruit-flavoured' in a purely confectionary sense.

Beyfus, in opening the case, had stressed the wholesome nature of Liberace's performance. There was, Liberace asserted, nothing sexy about his performances which were aimed at family audiences. He was not a sex-appeal artist. He considered that sex appeal was something possessed by Brigitte Bardot or Marilyn Monroe. It was scarcely his fault if a female had written for tickets in these words 'we want to be so close that we can feel the breeze from your eyelashes when they flutter' or that a policeman had described the women at the Hollywood Bowl as acting like 'wild animals'.

'I do not consider a person's eyelashes could be considered sexy' and 'the women wanted autographs and I found them well-behaved', Liberace parried. When he denied that women kissing their television screens had anything to do with sex appeal, a somewhat exasperated Gardiner retorted:

'Would you like the truth of your answers to be judged by that one?'

He received a suitably bland if sugary answer.

'I would like the truth of all my answers to be judged by the jury. I am under oath.'

The question was later to be adopted with rather more effect by Beyfus.

There were few areas of Liberace's life that were not considered fair game. Liberace told the jury he had never told any so-called dirty stories, although he did admit to telling one which had a double-meaning about one of his sponsors who made toilet tissue.

Liberace agreed he had sung a song about 'Gloria of the Waldorf Astoria' who had been 'thrilling and willing'. 'Willing to do what?' Gardiner asked with feigned curiosity. 'I did not know. I never knew either.'

One of the reasons why Liberace brought the libel action was the effect the first article had on his mother, who had accompanied him on the trip. He told the court that his only thought at the time was that the September article would certainly have to be kept from his mother. 'I felt this so strongly because my mother has a hypertensive heart condition and further I know that she is extremely proud of her children, perhaps a little more proud of me.' He was asked by his counsel whether he tried to keep the article from her. 'I was unsuccessful; it was brought to her attention by someone.' What effect did it have on her, he was asked: 'She immediately became very ill and was attended by a physician. It was decided by everyone concerned with her welfare that she leave the country.' However, it later emerged in his evidence that she had in fact stayed in England despite medical advice 'because if she went home people would think the article was true'.

In cross-examination, however, Liberace admitted that he had accepted the *Daily Mirror*'s hospitality to go on a pub crawl, after they had written an article which he felt accused him of being a homosexual. He explained that the reason all the drinks were paid for by the *Daily Mirror* was that he did not handle English money. He was then asked by Mr Justice Salmon:

'You must have been in a very forgiving mood when, after your mother had been taken ill, you accepted the hospitality of the paper?'
'I went on the pub crawl with the *Daily Mirror* because I had found that, when people meet me personally, they change their opinions.'

In response to Gardiner's questions he denied that he had ever used the expressions 'mother complex' or 'momism' when referring to his love and devotion for his mother. He did however concede that he had not accepted any of the marriage proposals (of which he received about twelve a month, one even being accompanied by an offer of $200,000 down) because he was looking for a girl like mom. He never did find one.

Liberace's style of piano playing was carefully dissected. His justification of his approach was that it produced a digest of the great music for those who otherwise would never hear it. It encouraged piano lessons and piano purchases. His Beethoven's Moonlight Sonata took a mere four minutes as opposed to the usual seventeen 'lest', one critic suggested, 'American womanhood yawn'. He reduced Tchaikovsky's First Piano Concerto from one hundred and fifty-five pages of music to twenty-three, adding for good measure four bars of his own. It was put by Beyfus to Charles Reid, the music critic of the *News Chronicle*, who was called for the defence, that Liberace's performances had produced an enormous increase in piano sales in the United States and in those wanting to learn the piano. 'I trust they do not maltreat the classics as Mr Liberace does', he commented.

The defence were perhaps on stronger ground when they sought to establish the tastelessness of Liberace's performances. He denied that in one show he went straight from playing *Ave Maria* into the Beer Barrel Polka. He did admit that on a television programme he played *Ave Maria* as curtains were drawn back to disclose a stained glass window and a woman praying to a statue of the Virgin Mary, while a choir boy put yet another candelabrum on his piano. That number was done he explained 'because it is one of the most highly requested in any television programme ... I try to present it with proper respect. In my opinion a young woman dressed as a nun praying to the Virgin Mary is showing proper respect ... It met with the approval of every church dignitary I had ever met.' Not surprisingly Connor saw things a little differently; he commented 'The woman dressed as a nun began to writhe in front of the madonna. I felt a sacred occasion was being misused by Liberace.'

Liberace was asked about the various books publicizing him which he had endorsed. In a foreword he had written of 'my friend Anton Birney, every word in this story about me is true' and somewhat improbably, 'I really wanted *TV Mirror* to publish my story'. It was pointed out to him by Gardiner that Birney had written about him in scarcely the friendliest of terms. Liberace explained that he had never met Birney, but he thought anyone who would take the trouble to write the Liberace life story must be his friend. 'But after reading the story I would not say he was a friend of mine. I did not know his story was going to be untrue in any detail.' Hundreds of books had been written about him. However, he was even more specific in a magazine article serializing his life, in the foreword to which he wrote: 'I find I have been moved by every sentence, at times so much so that tears have sprung to my eyes'. This it turned out was a slight exaggeration, as he had neither read the article nor had he even written the foreword.

At that time there was a view that it assisted your libel action, if your opponent could be shown to have been disrespectful to the Royal Family. Certainly Evelyn Waugh felt in his action against the *Sunday Express* that the jury were in part motivated by a desire to punish the paper for being rude about the Queen. Liberace was therefore reminded of what he said on the Ed Morrow television show in the United States in January 1956. 'I was reading about lovely young Princess Margaret. She's looking for her dream man too.' In court he used the expression, 'looking for a mate', 'I hope she finds him someday'. In the interview he appeared to be volunteering himself; 'we have the same tastes in theatre and music and besides she is pretty and single'. However, at the trial it became clear that a new entry in Debrett would not be necessary. He explained it was a jocular remark. There was no connection between his views on marriage and Princess Margaret. 'Since it appeared to be a foregone conclusion that I appealed to matronly women, it would have been very lovely and wonderful to be accepted in my performance by the lovely young Princess.'

The *Daily Mirror* itself did not come unscathed out of this contest. Beyfus suggested both to Connor and Hugh Cudlipp, his editorial director, that the *Daily Mirror* poll of its readers as to whether Princess Margaret should marry Group Captain Peter Townsend was most distasteful. Furthermore, it was pointed out with some force that the decision of the *Daily Mirror*'s sister paper the *Sunday Pictorial* to reproduce an American strip cartoon entitled 'Bringing up Bonnie Prince Charlie', albeit under the headline 'Thousands may laugh at this, but we call it a stupid insult' had the result that millions of readers had seen the cartoon.

The connection between this and Liberace's piano playing was not immediately obvious, but the defendants had raised the Liberace-Morrow interview in their defence. It seemed that the jury was persuaded that an American entertainment artist could be flippant about Princess Margaret, but an English national newspaper could not be disrespectful about the Royal Family.

Beyfus then called Arthur Coppersmith, the musical director of the Café de Paris night club and George

Melanchrino, a musical director and composer, who gave evidence of Liberace's qualities. Then came Miss Betty Ambler, a thriller writer, whose evidence turned out to be most damaging to Connor. Not very long before the trial, she visited the Connor household to interview and photograph 'Cassandra' and his cat. During their conversation they had talked about the Liberace action, and Connor had allegedly said, 'It is going to be a lot of fun and Liberace will get a lot of money from the *Daily Mirror*, but it will be worth it for a week's publicity. I don't know who will look the bigger buffoon in the witness box. They can object to the jury, because men do not like Liberace and they will make sure there are only women on the jury.' Connor denied the accuracy of this account of their conversation, although he did admit to a jocular remark about who would look the bigger buffoon.

In fact the disputed part of the conversation turned out to be a reasonably accurate assessment of the case.

The effect of Betty Ambler's evidence was slightly lessened by her cross-examination. She was asked whether she had written a book called *The Elusive Husband*. That might have been one of her paperbacks, she conceded; they went back a long time. She could not recollect a bookseller being fined for selling it on the grounds it was obscene but, on the question being repeated, she somewhat vaguely recalled that it was just before she went to do 'the Errol Flynn dialogue'. That, Gardiner was to suggest, made her evidence unreliable, but her evidence seemed to carry weight with the jury.

Cecily Courtneidge passed through the witness box to tell the jury she had seen nothing dirty or suggestive at performances given by Liberace. Bob Monkhouse likewise found nothing suggestive or improper in Liberace's performances and nothing sexy to stimulate the sexual appetite. Despite the judge's acid comment that the trial was taking place in Court Four of the Queen's Bench, he was permitted at the request of Mr Faulks to perform the opening words of his burlesque about Liberace. His request for a grand piano was turned down and he had to strum on the edge of the witness box instead. With this and equally complimentary evidence from Liberace's Hollywood lawyer, John Jacobs, and from Helen Cordet, the owner of the Maison de France club, Liberace's case ended.

The jury then heard Gardiner open the case for Connor. Connor had hitherto enjoyed a good libel track record. Sir Oswald Mosley had been paid £50 damages, a 'Soho gentleman' had sued but then thought better of it, as had a property dealer. Counsel referred to but did not give details of an award of £250. These damages were in fact awarded in 1955 to an 'infant' plaintiff called Lester Piggott, who was falsely accused of rather too adult behaviour in the King Edward VII Stakes at Ascot. Gardiner explained that Connor felt that Liberace was playing on the finest of human emotions to an illegitimate extent. The suggestion that Liberace was a homosexual was fantastic.

Connor entered the witness box and told the jury that what he wrote represented his honest opinions. He had seen on television one and a half of Liberace's performances. The half represented as much as he could stomach after his initial astonishment had turned to nausea. He had found it slickly oversentimental with a note of calculated commercialism behind it. He said that part of Liberace's technique was to exploit religion, love, affection and friendship for what he can get out of them. That he explained was the opinion he held then and the opinion he held now.

The case turned on Beyfus's cross-examination of Connor. Liberace had successfully parried Gardiner's questions, although some of his answers had been revealing. Beyfus's cross-examination was ferocious. Connor was not misled by Beyfus's 'how's your father' wink, which was no more than his involuntary twitch. He sought to establish that Connor was a violent and vitriolic writer, which Connor denied. Connor did admit he was wrong to attack the medical profession in the way he had ('their smooth, lying inefficiency and their blunt assumption that the disease-laden clients have the mentality of sick cattle'). Ultimately he did admit that these were shocking and vitriolic words. He was reminded of his description of Richard Dimbleby ('quietly sizzling and gently bubbling like an over-rich Welsh rarebit'); it might hurt Richard Dimbleby and his family, he eventually conceded.

Connor was even asked about what he had written about poodles ('mincing and prancing in attendance on the fancier tarts of the town'). Somewhat superfluously he explained that did not mean that every female poodle owner was a tart. It was a point directed to the jury's sympathies and even the judge, apparently a dachshund fancier, was to make a passing reference in his summing up to poodles as 'what many people thought a very brave and rather sporting race of dogs'.

Connor's alleged unkindness about dogs was followed by the questioning about what the *Daily Mirror* had written about the Royal Family. His attempt at repartee with Beyfus was not a success. It was suggested to him that he was trying to hack out a good living by making himself useful to newspapers.

'In the same way as distinguished advocates of the Bar do the same thing.'
'I was going to refer to your rudeness, but you have given a good illustration of it,'

Beyfus retorted, underlining the strength of the position of the cross-examining advocate.

Slowly the strings were drawn tight by Beyfus. He asked if the article in question was to express his detestation of Liberace.

'Dislike, I did not detest Liberace.'
'Was it not intended to hold him up to hatred, ridicule and contempt?' Beyfus asked.
'I don't know whether it was. I wrote what I thought about it. I cannot accept any legal interpretation of it. I do not think a person reading the article would think Liberace was a hateful person.'
'Would he not be a contemptible figure?'

'I don't know about that. I think he would become an unworthy figure. I thought the article would reduce him to his correct proportion as a preposterous clown.'

He was reminded about his reference to Liberace as vomit and the judge was later to suggest to him that, if people accepted the opinions in the article, it would be scarcely likely to endear Mr Liberace to them. Connor agreed.

Connor was questioned about Miss Ambler's evidence. 'Who do you now think is the biggest buffoon in the witness box?' he was asked. 'That is a most embarrassing question', he replied.

Finally, Connor told the jury that he had freedom to write what he chose at the *Daily Mirror*. 'I have no fan club and I don't care what my readers think.'

A succession of journalists was called by the defence. Stanley Bonnett, a *Daily Mirror* reporter, admitted in cross-examination that he was wrong to describe Liberace as wearing a ring showing a miniature piano carved in ivory – the piano was in fact represented in small diamonds. Peter Stephens, chief of the *Daily Mirror* Paris bureau, was asked why he formed the view he did of Liberace buying perfume at Le Bourget airport. Donald Zec, the *Daily Mirror* show columnist, said he was astonished to be thanked so warmly by Liberace about a very sarcastic article he had written about him. He had written about Liberace as being 'fragrantly perfumed with toilet water'. Hugh Cudlipp, editorial director of the *Daily Mirror* and *Sunday Pictorial*, gave evidence to explain Connor's position of independence at the *Daily Mirror*, only to be accused by Beyfus of turning that 'gentlemanly and decorous newspaper into a sensational one'.

With some justice Gardiner observed in his closing speech to the jury that the evidence had travelled far and wide and that they had heard a certain amount of irrelevances. He referred to what had been written about Connor. 'It had never been a question of what makes Connor tick but what makes Connor clang.' These words might well be put on his tombstone, Gardiner suggested.

Beyfus took up Gardiner's suggestion that he would match Connor's style of language and suggested that the newspaper was violent, vicious, venomous and vindictive, salacious and sensational, ruthless and remorseless. He spoke of the butchering of reputations and suggested the jury award a sufficient sum to persuade the directors of the paper to behave in a somewhat more gentlemanly and decorous fashion.

In his summing up of the case the judge directed the jury that 'we are all free to state fearlessly to anyone our real opinion honestly held on any matter of public interest – in any way we like, diffidently, deviously, politely and discreetly, or pungently, rudely or even brutally. Violence of language does not necessarily mean the views were not honest views or views which could not be held by fair-minded men.' He suggested that they should not attach much importance to the use of the words 'fruit' or 'fruit-flavoured'. He said that, whatever they thought about Miss Ambler's motives in going to the Connor household, her evidence, if they accepted it, was of considerable importance. He could not direct the jury how much to award if they found in Liberace's favour, but they should be neither niggardly nor extravagant. They could not give Mr Liberace any money because his mother was not well.

The jury retired to consider their verdict for three and a half hours. They returned to announce they had decided that the words in the first article did allege that Liberace was a homosexual and that they were neither true nor fair comment. They awarded £8,000 damages of which they attributed £2,000 to the false allegation of homosexuality. They felt the case was not proved in respect of the second article and therefore awarded no further damages in respect of it.

Before giving Liberace his judgment for £8,000 with costs, the judge said that he had come to the conclusion that the words were just capable of the meaning which the jury had found, although he was by no means certain he would have come to the same conclusion.

There was one wink left in the case in that a widow on the jury winked at Liberace before the verdict was given and mouthed the words 'It's all right'. When Liberace arrived at the Savoy Hotel, she was there to greet him and to get his autograph. 'I wanted to go up to his rooms to wish him the best of luck with all my heart', she was reported as saying.

During the trial, the sub judice rules had been scrupulously observed. 'Cassandra' had not written his column and Liberace did not mention Mom or his poodle or even wink during his appearances on stage.

It is difficult to draw any very serious conclusions from the trial. There was nothing accidental about what was written. 'Cassandra' approached the trial with some relish and Liberace had an entourage of nine accompanying him. The article could have been written in a non-libellous fashion, without losing much of its invective. Critics are permitted to express their honestly held views in an exaggerated or prejudiced fashion. Where 'Cassandra' erred, as the jury found, was in making false allegations of fact against Liberace and in criticizing his private life rather than his public performances.

It was, however, refreshing to see that when Liberace came to England in 1981, the *Daily Mirror* was not inhibited in its comments, referring to Liberace in his pink outfit as a 'well-shod flamingo'. In another show he was so well wrapped up in furs that his act was interrupted by animal rights protesters.

This was not the last litigation in Liberace's life. In 1957 he had sued *Scandal* magazine in the United States for $25 million damages. In 1974 he was sued by a young lady called Joanne Rio Barr for $1½ million damages. She claimed Liberace had ridiculed their romance, although she had herself published an article in a magazine entitled 'I kiss Liberace in the dark'.

In 1982 it was a young man who sued Liberace. His name was Scott Thoron, variously described as Californian, blond, with a face like an angel, six foot two and 'Boober'. He had been Liberace's chauffeur for six years before being dismissed. He felt that his conditions of service entitled him to some $65 million damages for what is described in the United States as 'palimony'.

Like so many other things connected with Liberace, the

case was suitably bizarre. Judge Irving Shimer ruled that the writ had not been validly served when the process server told him that he had served it personally on Liberace, whom he identified as having been dressed in a brown suit. 'Liberace wouldn't be caught dead in a brown suit', snarled the judge and sent the process server packing.

When the proceedings got under way, evidence was filed that, upon the termination of Thoron's employment, an agreed settlement had already been reached whereby he had received the not ungenerous sum of $75,000, an interest in a Las Vegas house and some of its furniture, a Rolls Royce, another luxury car and two dogs.

Liberace bitterly complained that Scott Thoron's action was an attempt at character assassination, that there was not one word of truth in the allegations, which he claimed stemmed from the *Daily Mirror* libel action and that he had merely attempted to help Scott by employing him.

Ultimately the claim was dramatically reduced to one for breach of contract in the more modest sum of $200,000. Nevertheless the case still had one more bizarre twist. In May 1983 Scott Thoron issued a libel writ in America claiming $4 million from the unfortunate Liberace who he claimed had paid Scott's half brother to write an untrue magazine article calling Scott a male prostitute. However, Liberace's estimable track record in his litigation makes it unlikely that he will succeed.

Twelve

The Destruction of
The Destruction of Convoy PQ17

In August 1968 David Irving's book *The Destruction of Convoy PQ17* was published by Cassell. For the previous eighteen months there had been some question as to whether it would be published because of the risk of libel actions for, from the moment he had seen the typescript on 6 November 1966, Captain John Broome, who had been the commander of the convoy's destroyer escort, had threatened to sue. He issued the first writ when the proof copies were distributed, the second for the hardback and the third for the paperback editions. The author and the publisher did not back down and the case went to a trial which lasted seventeen days.

The Destruction of Convoy PQ17 was an account of the disaster that befell that convoy of merchant ships taking supplies to Russia in July 1942. Commander (later Captain) Broome was in charge of the escort of six destroyers, four corvettes and fourteen other vessels. On 4 July 1942 he was ordered by the Admiralty to scatter the convoy. The merchant ships were left defenceless in the middle of the Barents Sea against German planes and submarines and were decimated.

Only eleven out of the thirtyfive ships reached Russian ports. Twentytwo ships were lost in the period 4–9 July, 153 merchant seamen perished; 3,350 out of 4,426 vehicles, 430 out of 594 tanks, 210 out of 297 aircraft and 100,000 out of 156,000 tons of general equipment were lost. Three more ships were sunk on the return journey.

David Irving's view was that the merchant seamen were the real heroes as 'sitting ducks in mostly unarmed

steamships with cargoes of petroleum and explosives for a
country already overflowing with both commodities'. The
questions he set out to answer in his book were who at the
Admiralty was responsible for the order to scatter, and
which of the officers were to blame for the loss of the ships.

At the Admiralty, Irving considered Roger Winn (later
Lord Justice Winn) was at fault. He says he was tipped off by
Vice-Admiral Sir Norman Denning (at the time a Commander and the Director of Naval Intelligence) that Winn,
as the commander of the Admiralty's submarine tracking
room, had been responsible for the faulty assessment of
naval intelligence which led the naval staff to conclude that
the *Tirpitz* had eluded the British submarines and was about
to pounce on PQ17.

Captain Broome had received from the Admiralty an
order emanating from the First Sea Lord in unequivocal
terms, prefixed 'Most immediate ... convoy is to scatter'.
Irving wrote of Captain Broome in terms that were found to
be highly defamatory and unjustified: 'The Royal Naval
vessels had thus very efficiently escorted themselves to arrive
thus far unscathed ... when the order to scatter came,
Broome needed no second bidding ...' Broome 'was a
broken man for the rest of the fast passage back to
Londonderry ... The point of error was Broome's
withdrawal of his escort destroyers.'

Inevitably there were perils in writing such a book while
the chief actors were still alive and in criticizing the Royal
Navy and the Admiralty in these terms. One member of
Cassell's staff commented that they were fighting Captain
Broome and Nelson. However, it was the tone in which the
book was written that was its undoing. Irving's turn of
phrase was a turn of the knife. To British readers it was
uncomfortable to find themselves looking at PQ17 through
the periscope of a U-boat.

The book was read as suggesting that Captain Broome
had disobeyed orders regarding the routing of the convoy,
that he was responsible for withdrawing the protection of the
convoy, that he had taken the convoy closer to German
airfields than he had been ordered to and that he was

indifferent to the fate of the merchant ships and their crews.

The jury never heard Irving's account. Since the trial he has said that such criticism as he was making was confined to the positioning of the convoy within the range of the Banak airstrip in Northern Norway and to the withdrawal of all the destroyers and corvettes after the order to scatter. His view was that only the two destroyers fitted with torpedo tubes would have been of any use in a confrontation with the German heavy battleships and that the other ships in the escort should have stayed with the convoy. He also stated that such phrases as 'needed no second bidding' were given a wholly unintended meaning. He was merely indicating that, whereas on a previous occasion, a particular signal had had to be repeated by Rear-Admiral Hamilton, that was not necessary in this case. In any event, these contentions were not to be tested as Irving chose not to give evidence.

These criticisms were contrary to conventional wisdom. Captain Broome had submitted his ten-page Report of Proceedings four days after the order to scatter. The conclusion of Admiral Sir John Tovey, Commander-in-Chief of the Home Fleet, in his report to the Admiralty on Convoy PQ17 was that he did not consider Captain Broome in any way to blame for the heavy losses. Broome was held to be correct in his decision to concentrate his destroyers and join the Squadron Force. He was not aware at the time that the cruiser force had been ordered to withdraw from the area.

Contrary to normal practice Irving was permitted by the Admiralty to see this report on 6 February 1967. His view was that it reinforced his position and made his defence against any claim Captain Broome might bring more secure.

Captain Stephen Roskill, the official naval historian, in *The War at Sea, 1939 to 1945,* volume 2, did not seek to blame Captain Broome for the disaster that befell Convoy PQ17. Indeed, when Irving's book was published, he was one of the former naval officers who offered Captain Broome financial assistance in his libel action. He was asked by William Kimber, to whom Irving first submitted his manuscript, to report on the book. His opinion, which was

to earn high praise from the trial judge for its prophetic
qualities – only to be surpassed by William Kimber himself –
was:

> This book reeks of defamation and any publisher should
> be very cautious before issuing it. I am no legal expert, but
> I would be very surprised if the publisher of this book, as it
> is written, did not end up in the law courts.

On 27 June 1942 Convoy PQ17 had set sail. Its predecessor
PQ16 had in the terms of such convoys been relatively
successful, having only lost seven out of thirtyfive merchant
ships. The Germans had decided that they would make a
concerted attack on the next Russian convoy and had
accordingly moved their heavy battleships, including the
Tirpitz, to Trondheim and Narvik in Northern Norway.
They had also assembled a fleet of 264 operational aircraft
round the North Cape. The convoy was therefore exposed to
the perils of simultaneous attack by heavy ships, light
surface forces, aircraft and U-boats. It was protected by
Captain Broome's destroyer escort and by Rear-Admiral
Hamilton's cruiser squadron of four cruisers and thirteen
destroyers which was instructed not to proceed east of Bear
Island off the northern tip of Norway. The squadron was
kept out of sight of the convoy; it was only to be brought up
in the event of a surface attack.

The early attacks on the convoy were fought off and,
although three ships were lost on 4 July, Captain Broome
felt that, 'provided the ammunition lasted, PQ17 could get
anywhere'. The Admiralty view was that a heavy German
surface attack was imminent. On 3 July a number of German
ships including the *Tirpitz* and *Scheer* had moved up to
Altenfjord. There was a considerable increase in German
radio traffic, including a buildup of orders for the *Tirpitz* to
sail. It was felt by the Admiralty that, if these ships evaded
the British submarines, the convoy would be overwhelmed.

The *Tirpitz* had been ordered to sail on 5 July to cut off the
convoy. There is now some question as to the extent that the
Germans in fact intended to commit the *Tirpitz* to any naval

engagement. However, the Admiralty felt that the *Tirpitz* had by then eluded the British submarines. The task of evaluating intelligence information was not assisted by an accident to one of the long-range air reconnaissance aircraft which left a crucial gap in intelligence cover from 11 am to 5 pm on 4 July.

In the event Admiral Pound, the First Sea Lord, overrode the advice of his intelligence analysts, particularly Commander Norman Denning. A series of messages was sent with what was later described as a rising crescendo of urgency.

The first went to Rear-Admiral Hamilton shortly after 9 pm:

Most immediate. Cruiser Force withdraw to westward at high speed.

At 9.23 pm a message prefixed 'Immediate' was sent to Broome:

Owing to threat from surface ships, convoy is to disperse and to proceed to Russian ports.

This was followed by a further signal to Broome at 9.36 this time prefixed 'Most Immediate':

My 9.23 of the 4th, convoy is to scatter.

The third message countermanded the second. The second was probably the result of an error in transmission. Dispersing and scattering were different means to the same end. Dispersing meant breaking the convoy into smaller groups each with its own escort. Scattering was altogether more perilous, as not only was the convoy broken up, but each ship started off in different directions. The purpose was to break up the target for the enemy. If the convoy was merely dispersed, it still remained a worthwhile target. In the event the order left a number of unprotected targets which the Germans were able to pick off for the minimal loss of five aircraft.

The exact reasons for the order to scatter still remain secret. Only on two other occasions, once in the first world war and once in the second had the order to scatter been given. Then the decision had been taken by the officer in command and not by someone at the Admiralty. The other instance in the second world war had involved the proper use of the tactics of scattering, when Captain Fegan on the armed merchantman *Jervis Bay* ordered his convoy to scatter while he took on a German pocket battleship. Fegan was later awarded the Victoria Cross.

Captain Broome and his fellow naval officers assumed that there must be some additional intelligence information known to the Admiralty. There was not and the German fleet had not sailed. Admiral Pound's judgment was at fault. He resigned on 4 October 1943 and died of a brain tumour seventeen days later.

The order to scatter had come in compelling terms from the Admiralty. The officers expected to see the *Tirpitz* come over the horizon at any moment. When there was no attack their feelings turned to shock and shame at abandoning the convoy to its fate. Some twelve hours later the *Tirpitz* did make a brief sortie, but the attacks on the convoy were made by aircraft and U-boats.

At the trial Captain Broome explained that his first responsibility was to see that the order of the Admiralty was carried out and his second was to face the threat that was imminent. The order had come like 'a sudden powerful electric shock'. It was the most unpleasant decision he had ever had to take in his life. Once the convoy had scattered, it could not be regrouped and disaster was inevitable if there were enemy aircraft or U-boats in the area.

The escort steamed at high speed south to place itself between the scattering convoy and the direction from which the attack was expected. The destroyers were placed at action stations in anticipation of meeting a far superior force of enemy battleships.

The strength of feeling of Captain Broome and his fellow officers was evident from his agreement at the trial that 'the order to scatter could be described as murder in a single word and murder perhaps on a hideously large scale'. The feeling of the merchant seamen as they saw the Royal Navy steaming away was even more bitter. The suggestion, which David Irving was held to have made some twentyfive years later, that Captain Broome was in large part to blame for the disaster was bound to be met with hostility and a sense of outrage.

David Irving's book was the result of five years' research from 1961 to 1966. Originally he had worked in collaboration with a German called Karweina on a project entitled *Knight's Move*, the codename for the operation to destroy the convoy. He fell out with Karweina over translation rights.

Irving was a small boy at the time of PQ17, but his father, a naval commander, had served on such convoys and was badly injured when the *Edinburgh* was torpedoed while on escort duties. He had already established a reputation as a propounder of controversial historical theories about the second world war, foremost among which were his accounts of the death of General Sikorski and of the destruction of Dresden.

The research involved interviewing 150 survivors and three trips to Washington to examine American and British naval archives. It was accompanied by a methodical recording of interviews and telephone conversations, which were set down in diaries and logs and photographed on microfilm. When these records were disclosed to Captain Broome's solicitors, they were to form the basis of his claim that Broome should be awarded not only compensatory but also punitive damages. Cassell were aware of the existence of these logs and diaries, but not of their contents.

In two unpublished articles Irving wrote about the trial he was to complain about selective quotation and his inability to place his comments in context. He was deprived of the opportunity to do so when he was advised by his counsel that it would not be in his interest to enter the witness box and that he should base his defence on the documents disclosed in the case. The result was that some seemingly unwholesome comments of Irving remained unexplained.

Irving wrote on 6 January 1965 to Karweina: 'Attack someone like Captain Broome, you will have press counter-attack and more publicity.' Irving later explained that this related to some advice he was giving Karweina. On 13 October 1965 he wrote in his daybook: 'I said *Knight's Move* was a book with a difference, as all were shown to be cowards.' Had Irving given evidence he would have pointed out that he would have added 'from whom the real heroes then emerged', as he did in the introduction to his book. The effect would have been very different. On 5 February 1968 Irving noted in his telephone log: 'I do not see what locus he [Broome] has to take action. I have always said that one can say some pretty near the knuckle things about these people. If we say it in a clever enough way, they cannot take action.' Irving later said that this merely referred to his belief that, provided he based himself on what was said in the Admiralty reports, Broome could not sue him.

Irving signed a contract for his book with William Kimber. In October 1966 he completed the work and submitted the manuscript to the publisher. On 6 November 1966 he took a copy round to Captain Broome who telephoned him the next day saying that it was 'a highly fictional account, full of inaccuracies'. Irving then proceeded to what he termed his 'next gambit' which was to suggest to Broome that he should identify the inaccuracies and make corrections. Captain Broome replied that he was under no duty to help him and that no doubt Irving would make a great deal of money out of this, but God help him if he published the manuscript in its present form. For good measure, Captain Broome wrote to Kimber on 9 November 1966 that the book was unquestionably libellous in its present form.

The manuscript was also submitted to Captain Litchfield, who had been second in command of the *Norfolk* and was later Conservative MP for Chelsea. He replied, 'Your criticisms of Broome, are not supported by either the facts or indeed your own evidence'. A similar but rather more sympathetic comment came from Donald McLachlan, who had been in Naval Intelligence and latterly editor of the *Sunday Telegraph*.

Kimber's enthusiasm for the book had waned further after receiving Roskill's report and William Kimber wrote on 21 November 1966 to Irving referring to his book as 'a continuous witchhunt of Captain Broome, filled with exaggerated criticisms of what he did or did not do'. With something approaching second sight, he commented, 'You might well be faced with a claim for punitive damages, if you do not justify every word you have said, because Captain Broome has issued warnings'.

Irving's account is somewhat different, but disputed by Kimber, in that he says they were thereafter satisfied by his revisions to the text. The difficulty was not the manuscript but a copyright problem. In any event he had on 9 November 1966 decided to take the book to Cassell and on 8 March 1967 he signed a contract for the book with them.

Captain Broome learnt of Cassell's involvement when he saw an announcement in *The Times* Saturday Review that they were to publish the book. He wrote to them on 27 December 1967 reiterating his view that it was unquestionably libellous in its present form. Cassell replied that 'you will be glad to know that, in light of your comments, David Irving has made drastic revisions to the text'. Broome's previous involvement with Cassell had been when he acted as naval advisor for the filming of a book by Nicholas Monsarrat, a Cassell author.

At the trial much was made of a Cassell internal memorandum saying that any threatened libel action was first-class publicity. In retrospect that may appear an unguarded remark. It is true that a little controversy may assist the promotion of a book, but the conclusion drawn by the court that the publisher was prepared to gamble on the libel damages being outweighed by increased sales was unfair. Calculations are often made by publishers as to whether a person will sue, but not as to whether sales will exceed libel damages and costs. No publisher would contemplate making such a calculation. It would be a cynical assessment based on nothing more than pure guesswork. In any event Cassell only proceeded with the book after they had taken advice on such information as they then had.

In early February 1968 sixty proof copies were distributed

and one of them was supplied to Captain Broome seemingly by way of the journalist Godfrey Winn. On 15 February 1968 he wrote to Cassell saying that such drastic revisions as had been made certainly did not apply to him. Cassell immediately put an embargo on the book. Broome issued a writ on 5 March in respect of the proof copies; the publication date (originally 8 April) was postponed.

On 14 June 1968 Cassell submitted a defence of justification to Broome's claim that he had been libelled. On 7 August the embargo was lifted and the hardback edition of the book was published in virtually the same form as the proof copies. On 23 August the second writ was issued in respect of that edition.

The third writ was issued when the Corgi paperback edition was published on Friday, 23 January 1970 just before the libel action was due to be heard on the following Monday. That somewhat overconfident step was to be the subject of considerable criticism of Cassell.

Broome and Irving approached the trial with markedly different feelings. Captain Broome felt that it was his duty to stand up for the Navy. It was a view shared by a number of fellow naval officers and comrades. Three of them, Captain Litchfield, Captain Stephen Roskill, and the former war correspondent Godfrey Winn, felt strongly enough about the matter to agree to guarantee Captain Broome's legal costs in the total sum of £5,000. That amount was to be a mere fraction of what the action cost. By the time of the trial it appeared that more substantial help had been forthcoming.

David Irving approached the trial with increasing confidence. This continued until the second day of the trial judge's summing up. He rejected the idea discussed before the trial that he should pay £550 into court. He even approached brokers for a quotation to insure Captain Broome's life in case he should die before the verdict and before the costs of the action could be recovered from him, but was concerned at the financial burden proceedings would impose upon Captain Broome. As it turned out his anxiety was premature.

The dealings between Broome and Irving provide an interesting background to the case. At the outset Broome was willing to assist and he wrote in reply to Irving on 2 December 1962, 'PQ17's only claim to fame was that our own First Sea Lord practically annihilated it'. The correspondence continued in a reasonably friendly vein until January 1965, although Broome began to find it wearisome. Irving took exception to some of Broome's replies such as 'really you amateur tacticians and historians frighten me' and 'didn't your father ever tell you captains' conferences at sea went out with sailing ships?'

In 1965 Irving decided to make a personal approach to Broome. He wished to reproduce one of Broome's cartoons in his book and this provided the means of effecting such a meeting. Broome was a cartoonist of some distinction. One, of an admiral sharing a bath with a Wren to whom he was explaining 'This is how the torpedo goes, Miss Snodgrass', enjoyed a wide circulation. It featured briefly in the libel action, because it was incorrectly stated in the book that both the admiral and the Wren were identifiable. In any event it was of sufficient quality for the original to be lodged in the National Maritime Museum.

Irving arrived uninvited at what he described as Broome's 'expensive Chelsea cottage', when Broome and his wife were preparing to go out to the theatre. Broome was naturally somewhat taken aback to be asked whether it was true that he had shot some German airmen he had picked up from the sea. It was an allegation that shocked the jury. They did not hear Irving's account which was that this was a fault of Captain Broome's memory and that he was confusing Irving's questions about two rescued airmen with a passage in the book when his destroyers opened fire on a crippled German aircraft which had ditched in the sea after being shot down.

In any event Captain Broome felt released from any obligation to cooperate and Irving's views about Broome became more entrenched. 'I am glad the planned confrontation is approaching.' He wrote on 13 December 1966 of Broome as a 'fly and slippery character who has not put a foot wrong'. He was surprised at Broome's reaction to the book, although 'the manuscript was admittedly very frank about him in places at times'. He was later to allege that Broome gave evidence with all the warmth and conviction of an airline stewardess relating her lines about the safety equipment to the passengers.

In fact the trial was a one-sided affair. The issues were whether Broome was responsible for the disaster, whether or not he was 'a broken man' after the signal to scatter, and whether with the melting polar ice he should have been further north to lessen the danger of air attacks from the Banak airstrip. Every witness who gave evidence during the seventeen-day trial supported Captain Broome.

Vice-Admiral Sir John Hayes, then a staff officer in Rear-Admiral Hamilton's flagship, testified as to the 'absolutely shattering' signal – they wondered why the signal had been given when they were doing so well. There had been some question as to whether Broome should have been further north but it had not given rise to particular concern. (The evidence was interrupted by a phalanx of twentytwo Welsh demonstrators who invaded the court to protest against the imprisonment for non-payment of a fine of a member of the Welsh Language Society. It was a heroically unnecessary gesture as fourteen of them found themselves imprisoned for three months for contempt of court and eight were fined £50, whereas the original offender, who had wanted to be imprisoned, was released when local magistrates banded together to pay the fine.)

The officers called on behalf of Captain Broome had by then risen to positions of eminence. Admiral Sir John Frewen had been lieutenant commander in the *London* in Hamilton's cruiser force and had now become Commander-in-Chief of the Home Fleet. He explained the dilemma of Broome, heightened by the fact that the Admiralty never gave reasons for its signals.

Vice-Admiral Sir William O'Brien, then first lieutenant in the *Uffa* in Broome's escort, told the court that the order to scatter came like a bombshell. 'You had the dreadful feeling as you steamed away that this was the sort of thing the Navy did not do.' There was a feeling of shame and hurt when the *Tirpitz* did not appear. So far as Rear-Admiral Hamilton's order on 2 July to reroute the convoy was concerned, it was not mandatory to obey, if there were other considerations. A distinction was drawn at the trial between orders and instructions. The evidence was that, although both tended to be called orders, the man on the bridge had little difficulty in deciding which was which.

Vice-Admiral Sir John Eaton, then Captain of the destroyer *Somali*, said that he thought Broome was on very good form. The most telling evidence that Broome was far from being 'a broken man' came from a film taken by Captain John Litchfield in the *Norfolk* which was retrieved from the Imperial War Museum and shown to the jury in the basement of the Royal Courts of Justice. Captain Broome was shown smiling, raising his mug and waving, having just lobbed an egg over from the *Keppel* onto the bridge of the *Norfolk*. Captain Litchfield spoke of Broome having rendered a most valuable service as a staff officer by keeping everyone cheerful at a time that was not humorous. When a submarine commander, Lieutenant Beckley, had signalled to Broome, 'I intend to remain on the surface', he received the laconic reply from Broome, 'So do I'.

Captain Roskill gave evidence for Broome and, unusually in a libel action, he was able to give his opinion of whether the book was libellous – the question the jury had to decide. The reason for this was that he could give evidence that Irving had been warned the book was libellous. He felt that Irving had set himself up as a hanging judge and the original draft was libellous and full of prejudice. His evidence was that the book as published was to all intents and purposes the same as the draft. This is something Irving disputes, saying it was materially different and 150 pages had been retyped.

Not all Broome's witnesses were so exalted. His Leading Signalman, Basil Elliott, then a police constable at Scotland Yard, found himself called as a witness, after sending a message wishing Broome luck at the beginning of the trial. Broome was an angry man, but he carried out his duties in the normal way during the emergency, he said. Similar evidence was given by Broome's Chief Yeoman of Signals, Mr Blood.

Shortly before the defence case was opened on 10 February 1970, to his dismay Irving was advised that he should not give evidence. He was referred by his counsel, Colin Duncan QC, to the flagged copies of virtually every book he had written which were laid out for use in cross-examination by David Hirst QC, Captain Broome's counsel. Irving was advised that calling evidence could prolong the case by ten days and that he would be cross-examined for three days. 'The mud that Hirst will sling today is nothing compared with the slaughter Hirst will do to you in two days' cross-examination', Duncan told him.

The decision not to call evidence was made in the belief that the judge would withdraw the issue of punitive damages from the jury. In fact he refused to do so. By this time the election had already been made, although the decision about not calling Irving would probably have been the same, even if the judge's ruling had then been known. The other reason for not calling Irving was that he could not give any direct evidence of what happened to the convoy and that he had already produced all his documents in support of his case. That reason was less compelling if the judge let the issue of exemplary damages go to the jury, which would make evidence as to Irving's state of mind highly material.

The decision not to give evidence gave Irving the advantage of his counsel addressing the jury last and of not being cross-examined. The advantage of the last word to the jury is overrated, as it is in any event the trial judge who has the last word.

With a defence of justification, the jury was likely to take a dim view of Irving's failure to go into the witness box, notwithstanding his documents. A silent defendant in such a libel action normally loses. The real disadvantage to Irving was that he was deprived of an opportunity of seeking to rebut Captain Broome's evidence or of explaining what he had written in his logs and diaries.

Mr Justice Lawton, the trial judge, summed up in a

characteristically forthright manner. 'If the words mean what Captain Broome thinks they mean, can you think of anything more hurtful to a man at the end of his distinguished career?' He invited them to consider whether or not this was the picture of an arrogant-minded young man who would not listen to other people because he felt that his version of what happened was the truth. The judge observed that Irving had called Broome a 'fly and slippery character' and suggested that, if anyone was fly and slippery, it was Irving trying to get this naval officer into a position where he could not complain.

The judge did deal rather more sympathetically with the evidence called on Broome's behalf: Elliott, 'a typical professional lower deck sailor', Stephen Roskill, 'an eminent naval historian' and Litchfield, 'a distinguished retired naval officer'. However, these were no more than comments on the evidence and the jury had little difficulty in forming their own view of the matter.

The real problem with the summing up turned out to be not any imagined partiality but the introduction of punitive damages. The normal approach was for a jury to award a sum which reflected the gravity of the libel and it was a system which worked perfectly well. However, a claim was made for punitive damages. The effect of this was that, if the jury thought Irving or Cassell had 'recklessly, knowingly and wilfully peddled untruths for profit', the jury could award punitive damages above the amount they felt was appropriate to compensate Captain Broome for the injury to his reputation. They could, in other words, fine Irving and Cassell for their conduct in publishing the book.

Captain Broome was awarded £14,000 compensatory damages for the hardback edition plus £1,000 for the proof copies. To this £15,000, the jury added the sum of £25,000 punitive or exemplary damages. In other words, the jury fined the author and publisher £25,000 over and above the sum they felt reflected the damage to Captain Broome's reputation. The claim in respect of the paperback edition was settled out of court for £2,500 in a separate action.

£40,000 was an enormous award of damages. However,

the fact that the sum was divided into compensatory and punitive damages led to considerable legal difficulties. The punitive damages were no doubt awarded by the jury to indicate what view they had formed of the defendants, Cassell and David Irving. It was, however, an unsatisfactory way of dealing with the matter. There is no very clear logical distinction between compensatory and punitive awards of libel damages. The £15,000 compensatory damages were, after all, only what the jury considered a suitable sum to mark the gravity of the libel and the damages to Captain Broome's reputation. It was a figure plucked from the air and it did not represent what he had actually lost as a result of the book being published. If the jury wanted to award Broome £40,000, it would have been a great deal simpler if they had made one rather than two awards.

The Court of Appeal, to whom Irving and Cassell first appealed, had no doubt that the jury was right to find for Broome. Lord Denning felt that Irving was after a *succès de scandale*. He observed that neither the official naval historian Captain Roskill nor Winston Churchill had condemned Captain Broome, adding – perhaps a little unfairly – that the condemnation was made twenty years later by an author who knew nothing about the war because he was a small boy at the time. Lord Justice Phillimore was even more unambiguous. 'Irving's diary shows him to be a grasping, conceited and foolish young man – the book was anti-British and a deliberate attack on the Royal Navy, facts which I find unattractive but which are not directly in point.'

With such unequivocal statements the Court of Appeal rejected the appeal. That it took nine days was largely due to the fact that Lord Denning disagreed with the ruling given by the House of Lords in the case of *Rookes v Barnard* some seven years earlier. (That was a case concerning Douglas Rookes, a BOAC draughtsman who was forced out of his job when he failed to join the closed shop operated by the Association of Engineering and Shipbuilding Draughtsmen. In those days the courts had little difficulty in castigating the closed shop as a conspiracy and intimidation. Rookes was awarded £7,500 damages, but the lasting importance of the case was that it laid down the criteria for when exemplary damages could be awarded. In a sense Rookes was even more unfortunate than Captain Broome in that his award of £7,500 was set aside on the grounds of a misdirection in law and there had to be a retrial on the issue of damages.) Thus exemplary damages could be awarded if the jury felt that the defendants had calculated that the profit they would make might well exceed the damages which they might have to pay the plaintiff. There followed a thirteen-day hearing in the House of Lords. Captain Broome was to complain with some understatement after the hearing that it seemed hard luck that the litigants should pay for tidying up the law when the judges disagreed.

By the time the case reached the House of Lords it had been agreed that Captain Broome should have his £15,000 compensatory damages. Irving's resources had been depleted, so he took no further part in the proceedings. The sole issue was the award of punitive damages. Was the summing up adequate and if so, were the damages excessive?

Captain Broome won by the narrowest of margins in a fashion more reminiscent of the better cup finals than of a declaration of the law by the highest court in the land. He built up an early 3-0 lead with judgments in his favour by the three senior judges, Lord Hailsham, the Lord Chancellor, Lord Reid and Lord Morris of Borth-y-Gest. Viscount Dilhorne, Lord Wilberforce and Lord Diplock levelled the score at 3-3 and it was only when Lord Kilbrandon had read his judgment that the parties knew Captain Broome had been successful.

The problem was that the trial judge had correctly set out the basis on which punitive damages could be awarded, but he had not made it clear that the jury could award punitive damages *if and only if* they were satisfied that compensatory damages were inadequate. The dissenting judges felt this was a serious omission in the summing up and that the damages were excessive. They would have ordered a retrial. Lord Hailsham was not altogether happy with the summing up which he felt was only barely sufficient; he was even less happy with the approach of the Court of Appeal. However, he was satisfied that the jury, as the legal and constitutional tribunal for deciding libel actions, was entitled on the evidence and the summing up to reach the decision which they did. Common sense prevailed by a whisker.

That was not quite the end of the matter as a second short hearing in the House of Lords was necessary to determine the question of legal costs. The argument about the correctness of *Rookes v Barnard* deprived the unfortunate Captain Broome of half his legal costs in the Court of Appeal and the House of Lords. So he received £13,324.68 of the total £42,500 damages he had been awarded.

Irving denies that he was motivated by a cynical scheme to profit at the cost of Broome's reputation, pointing to the modest £1,000 advance he was given on the book. If he had been, there was one ironic consequence. While he made no money in England, he did receive 5,000 roubles for a pirated edition of the book that appeared in Russia once a few unflattering references to the Red Navy had been excised. The first Irving officially knew of the publication of his book in Russia was the arrival of the Russian naval attaché on his doorstep, informing him that he could come to Russia and spend the rouble royalties, which he did.

In 1972 Irving was sued by Cassell under the indemnity clause in his contract whereby he had to reimburse his publisher in respect of any libel damages and costs they had to pay on his book. They claimed £100,000. On the advice of the Society of Authors, Irving had inserted a provision in his contract that restricted his liability to breaches of his warranty that the book was free of libel unknown to the publisher. His argument was that the Court of Appeal and the House of Lords had decided that Cassell knew of the facts. In the end Cassell's claim against Irving was not proceeded with.

Captain Broome was not the only person who sued Irving for libel in *The Destruction of Convoy PQ17*. Godfrey Winn had been on the convoy as war correspondent for Beaverbrook Newspapers and had reached Russia on the *Pozarica*. He had written a book about PQ17 which sold over a quarter of a million copies. He issued a writ against

Irving but never served it. He objected to a passage which Irving had quoted from a lieutenant's diary where Winn was reported as saying: 'Captains are heavenly, but Admirals make me shy'.

Irving's attitude to Godfrey Winn and his brother Roger, a Lord Justice of Appeal, bears some comparison with the stance he adopted to Captain Broome. He felt that the Winns were out to destroy him and that Lord Justice Winn had used his position as Chairman of the Security Commission to have his telephone tapped. Where Irving is on stronger ground is that Godfrey Winn did summon two directors of Cassell to his flat on 14 February 1968 and berated them for two hours about their plans to publish the book. His initial concern was with two minor errors about himself, whether he had been organizing party games and whether a particular incident occurred to port or starboard. He said he would issue a writ for libel against the book even if he spent £50,000 doing it and could call Lord Mountbatten, Rebecca West and his brother as witnesses. He stated in unequivocal terms that it would be the worse for Cassell and their directors if they proceeded with the book. The interview ended with Winn pointing to various pictures on his walls which he said had been given to him by the likes of Beaverbrook in settlement of his libel claims.

Irving's dealings with Roger Winn were also acrimonious. He received a letter of 9 April 1963, written in rather stronger terms than those normally used by a High Court judge, complaining that Irving had barged into his home uninvited and that his behaviour was that of a cad. Irving wrote back to the judge alleging he had been 'damnably rude' to him on the telephone and was guilty of 'surprisingly uncivilized conduct'. The upshot was that, although Roger Winn did have the good grace to correct certain matters in the draft, he wrote to Irving, 'I think that is a dangerous, maliciously anti-British book and FORBID the inclusion of my name in the list of collaborators'.

Irving was also sued by Captain Lawford for libel. This case was settled out of court with a sum being paid to charity and Captain Lawford's legal costs being met by Irving.

£1,384 was deducted from his royalties in consequence of that action.

The Destruction of Convoy PQ17 was eventually published by William Kimber in 1980 in a version which was based on the Norwegian edition of the original book. This had the advantage that it had been vetted by Captain Broome's lawyers who required only relatively minor amendments from the version that led to the libel action, for example Broome 'needed no second bidding' became 'Broome at once complied'.

From a legal point of view, the action was unsatisfactory in that Broome found himself subsidizing a legal argument which was not of his making and which was only marginally relevant to the merits of the case. So far as the facts were concerned, it was a dangerous matter for Irving to write so critically on such a sensitive issue. In the light of the order that Captain Broome had received on 4 July 1942 and the evidence the jury had heard from Captain Broome and his witnesses and of the way that Irving had approached writing the book, it was scarcely surprising that they reached the conclusion that they did. Furthermore, the book made statements about Broome's state of mind which could not be proved. It may have been difficult for the jury to form their own view on Irving's account of Convoy PQ17, but there were some incidents on which they could do so, and they probably were able to reject his account of Broome being 'a broken man'.

It is a cautionary tale with many morals, not least of which is that if you are seeking to argue that your book does no more than set out a few well-reasoned criticisms and explanations of a naval reverse, you do not allow your publisher to print these words on its dust-jacket:

Many people were convinced that the merchantmen had been shamefully deserted by a Navy which lost only a fleet oiler in the convoy's passage ... The massacre of PQ17 was due to blunders, miscalculations and misunderstandings which they wanted to remain hidden like so much dirty linen ... Elaborate deceptions had been practised to ensure this.

For Cassell, a publishing house of the highest repute, it was a most unhappy saga. They were subject to severe and often unfair criticism, although they had acted in good faith throughout. Shortly after the verdict was announced they were taken over by an American publishing house, Crowell Collier Macmillan. Cassell's imprint was kept for their dictionaries, but gradually they contracted and ceased to have a separate identity

David Irving emerged relatively unscathed. The book sold well in the United States, where it was not the subject of any legal action; there was no shortage of publishers prepared to publish his subsequent works on the second world war and on the question of whether Hitler knew about the wholesale murder of the Jews by the Nazis. He remained a controversial historian and, perhaps not surprisingly, entered the recent fray about the discovery of Hitler's war diaries. Originally, he condemned them 'as phoney as a three-dollar bill'. This he did on the basis that he had evidence that the diaries had come from a source which he knew to be tainted. Irving was subsequently assured that the diaries came from some other source. In those circumstances he was prepared to endorse the diaries as being genuine, provided they passed the appropriate ink and paper tests. He was impressed that the handwriting was consistent with that of a person suffering from Parkinson's disease, as Hitler was.

The diaries turned out to be fakes and were the subject of some hiliarity – except to those involved. Particularly intriguing were the diametrically opposed views held by David Irving and Professor Hugh Trevor-Roper (Lord Dacre of Glenton). At the outset, the Professor had enthusiastically, but incautiously endorsed the diaries in the *Sunday Times* while Irving was denouncing them in the *Observer*. When doubts crept into Trevor-Roper's mind, Irving was prepared to advance the theory that the diaries were genuine.

Thirteen

Should Editors Go to Prison?

The origins of the law of criminal libel are obscure. Some trace them back to a decree of King Alfred, whereby a convicted slanderer had the bizarre choice between losing his tongue or his head. The more generally accepted view is that the origins are to be found in 1275 in the offence of *Scandalum Magnatum* (Slander of Magnates). This description of criminal libel seemed particularly appropriate in the Goldsmith case some seven hundred years later. The law was administered by the Court of Star Chamber. In the sixteenth century the going rate for libel was loss of the right hand and for slander, rather less logically, loss of the ears.

Criminal libel survived the demise of Star Chamber in the seventeenth century, as it was thought useful as a means of discouraging duelling. There were many cases, however, where there was no danger of any breach of the peace. In 1838 the Rev Augustus Gathercole was prosecuted for libelling a group of nuns. He referred to them as 'living in a brothel of prostitution'. There was no evidence that any of them intended to do him any violence.

Criminal libel also served as a useful means of suppressing unwelcome publications and of keeping newspaper editors in order. Even the editor of *The Times*, John Walter, spent sixteen months in jail for libelling the Prince of Wales and the Duke of York for the insincerity of their joy, when George III recovered from his illness in 1789. He was however relieved from the other part of his sentence which was to stand for one hour in the pillory at Charing Cross.

In 1802 Jean Peltier had the misfortune to be prosecuted at a time when friendly relations between England and France briefly existed after the Treaty of Amiens. He had suggested that Napoleon was 'a tyrant worthy to be deposed'. However, war broke out before he was sentenced and the case was quietly dropped.

The nineteenth century had seen a number of editors imprisoned for what they had written. In 1879 Adolphus Rosenberg, the editor of *Town Talk*, received eighteen months for daring to suggest that the Prince of Wales was having an affair with Lillie Langtry. In 1884 Henry Labouchere, the editor of *Truth*, had been prosecuted, but acquitted on a technicality, for alleging that the fortune of the Duke of Vallombrosa was founded on sending the corpses of dead French soldiers back to the French army as edible meat. In 1890 the editor of the *North London Press* was sentenced to twelve months for blowing the whistle on a homosexual brothel in Cleveland Street frequented by a number of aristocratic members. He unwisely named an earl as a patron. At the subsequent trial it emerged that the earl had merely visited the place on his way home from his club to see the 'poses plastiques' it advertised. He said he had had no idea that the 'poses plastiques' would involve telegraph boys.

Edward Mylius, editor of *The Liberator*, was unwise enough to accuse George V of committing bigamy in 1893. He was imprisoned for two years in 1913.

In 1923 Lord Alfred Douglas, editor of *Plain English* and Oscar Wilde's friend, was jailed for six months for accusing Winston Churchill of using his position as First Lord of the Admiralty to manipulate the news from the Battle of Jutland to depress the value of the English stocks on the American Stock Exchange. This, he said, enabled the financier Sir Ernest Cassel to make a profit of £18 million and to provide Churchill with the scarcely generous payoff of furniture worth several thousand pounds. The authorities would have treated this as pernicious rubbish, if Douglas had not then taunted Churchill in the *Border Standard* for not having taken action: 'if Churchill were editing a newspaper and printed one fifth of what I printed about him, I would have him round at Bow Street with his nose hanging over the edge of the dock to answer a charge of criminal libel, within twentyfour hours'.

Many of the people who had been prosecuted for criminal libel had gone out of their way to provoke such action. In 1896 Lady Scott was sentenced to eight months' imprisonment for circularizing every Law Lord and Lord Justice of Appeal in the hope of helping her daughter obtain her divorce, with the information that her son-in-law, Earl Russell, had been engaging in sodomy.

For fiftythree years after the prosecution of Lord Alfred Douglas, editors had faced nothing worse than the payment of damages for libel which, though large, were paid by the newspaper proprietors. Editors were at greater personal risk when it came to contempt of court. In 1949 the unfortunate editor of the *Daily Mirror* was jailed for three months for the highly prejudicial headline following Haigh's arrest for murder, 'Vampire will never strike again'.

Before the second world war there were about thirteen cases a year. By the early 1970s the figure was down to one or two. Criminal libel was used only to deal with a motley bunch of miscreants for whom no other proceedings were appropriate. A typical example was the man in 1971 who hoped to improve his chances of acquittal by hiring five men to distribute five thousand handbills accusing the police officer in the case of drunkenness. He was sent to prison for six months.

In recent times it was generally thought that the offence of criminal libel was virtually extinct. At the end of 1975, a series of articles in *Private Eye* sought to link James Goldsmith with an alleged conspiracy to pervert the course of justice in relation to the murder of Lord Lucan's children's nanny. They also attacked his fitness to be chairman of Slater Walker Securities, then receiving the kiss of life from the Bank of England. It soon became apparent that the law of criminal libel was anything but dead. (It could still carry a sentence of two years' imprisonment.) The next eighteen months saw a bewildering number of writs issued, injunctions sought, attempts to commit persons to prison for contempt and assorted legal manoeuvring until, some £250,000 in lawyer's fees later, the terms of this drawn contest were announced at the Old Bailey.

On 7 November 1974 Lady Lucan burst into the Plumbers'
Arms in Lower Belgrave Street, bleeding from the head and
shouting, 'Help me, help me! I have just escaped from a
murderer'. Enquiries revealed that Sandra Rivett, her
children's nanny, had been murdered at her house. In June
1975 the jury at the inquest decided, in a verdict reminiscent
of *Cluedo*, that the nanny was murdered by Lord Lucan with
the lead piping in the basement. He had disappeared after
the killing, leaving a series of bizarre notes, some suggesting
he would commit suicide, others that he would 'lie doggo'. In
any event he was never seen again, having either committed
suicide or gone abroad, a place he was said to detest
cordially.

On 8 June 1975 the *Sunday Times* had published a less
than flattering article by James Fox on Lord Lucan and his
Clermont Club cronies, entitled 'The Luck of the Lucans'.
They were less than overjoyed by their portrayal. Dominic
Elwes was suspected of having provided the credentials for
the Old Etonian James Fox to enter this circle. He was
suspected of having provided photographs of his painting of
a group at the Clermont Club, which included Goldsmith,
and of Lucan on holiday with Goldsmith and others in
Acapulco. These photographs could have been obtained
from Lady Lucan. For these misdemeanours Elwes was sent
to Coventry, which in this milieu consisted of being banned
from the Clermont, Annabel's and the nearby watering-hole
called Mark's. This and other pressures led him to take his
own life, leaving notes cursing his former friends from the
grave. At Elwes's requiem mass John Aspinall gave the
address. This moved Elwes's cousin, Tremayne Rodd, to
punch him on the jaw outside the church with the words
'That's what I think of your bloody speech, Aspinall'.

This event was chronicled and photographed by Fleet
Street. It aroused Richard Ingrams's curiosity. (He has
described the investigations he carried out and his reasons
for doing so in his book *Goldenballs*.) The result was an
article in *Private Eye* on 12 December 1975 written by
Patrick Marnham entitled 'All's well that ends Elwes'. It
carried a prominent photograph of Goldsmith.

The article suggested that there was a conspiracy to obstruct the police investigations into the Lucan affair and that the principal member of this 'conspiracy' was 'its richest and most powerful figure', James Goldsmith. The article described a lunch given by Aspinall at his house in Lyall Street on the day after the murder. Those present were John Aspinall, Dominic Elwes, William Shand-Kydd (Lucan's brother-in-law), Daniel Meinertzhagen, Charles Benson and Stephen Raphael. *Private Eye* suggested Goldsmith was chairing this lunch and had despatched Dominic Elwes to see Lady Lucan in hospital to discover what she had told the police. In fact, Goldsmith was doing nothing more sinister at the time than addressing the Institute of Chartered Accountants in Ireland (a fact which had been published elsewhere). Although such a lunch did take place, there was no evidence of any conspiracy.

The article also suggested that Goldsmith was responsible for the failure of Greville Howard, who had given a statement to the police, to attend the nanny's inquest. Howard, *Private Eye* suggested, was 'pillowing his head upon a sackful of certificates from fashionable doctors. When he feels stronger, Greville Howard works for Goldsmith at Slater Walker.' This was also inaccurate. Howard had worked for Goldsmith at Cavenham and subsequently did work at Slater Walker, but at the time of the nanny's inquest he was not working for Goldsmith, who had not yet taken over at Slater Walker.

When the 12 December article was published, Goldsmith was in Singapore, engaged in negotiations between Slater Walker and Haw Par International. While he pondered how he should react to the 12 December article, he was further attacked in the 26 December issue in an article in *Private Eye*'s Slicker City column by Michael Gillard. This suggested he was unsuitable to be Chairman of Slater Walker.

On 9 January 1976 *Private Eye* wrote an article about what it termed an 'intriguing link' with T Dan Smith, then serving a jail sentence for corruption in the Northeast. For good measure they threw in a few allegations about

Goldsmith's behaviour at a nightclub in Gstaad. where he had spent his Christmas holiday. This link turned out to be no more than the fact that the solicitor whom Goldsmith had been using for the affairs of Slater Walker, Eric Levine, had also acted for T Dan Smith and had been on the board of a number of Smith's companies. In fact, Goldsmith had never met T Dan Smith or had business dealings with him and his activities at the Gstaad nightclub amounted to no more than meeting his son.

In legal terms it was an unwise article to write. It was long on innuendo, but short on substance. It had no point unless it was calling into question the integrity of Eric Levine or of Goldsmith for using his services. If the purpose of the 9 January article was to drive a wedge between Goldsmith and Levine, it backfired spectacularly. Goldsmith was to adopt a very protective attitude to his solicitor. He was not going 'to let *Private Eye* crucify him'. Levine never sued *Private Eye*, although he did act throughout on Goldsmith's behalf. In an unusual reversal of roles, Goldsmith sought an injunction to protect his solicitor. It is more normal for solicitors to seek injunctions to protect their clients.

The 9 January article was the last straw as far as Goldsmith was concerned. An avalanche of writs decended upon Greek Street. Not only were the editor, the publisher, and principal distributor of *Private Eye* sued, but seventy-four writs were issued against a further thirtyseven wholesale and retail distributors of *Private Eye*.

There followed a spectacular but indecisive legal battle which lasted for eighteen months until, on 18 May 1977, Richard Ingrams, Patrick Marnham, the publisher (Press-dram Ltd) and the principal distribution company (Moore-Harness Ltd) of *Private Eye* were acquitted of criminal libel at the Central Criminal Court and the civil actions were settled. All told, some ninety writs were issued. When Goldsmith was asked at the criminal libel proceedings by James Comyn QC, who was appearing for *Private Eye*, about the large number of writs, he replied that he had only issued one writ against a newspaper before. 'You are making up for it now', Comyn wryly commented.

There were ten separate court hearings. There were
injunction proceedings to prevent *Private Eye* mentioning
Goldsmith or Levine. There were two separate attempts to
have Richard Ingrams imprisoned for contempt of court and
the assets of *Private Eye* sequestrated. There was a
protracted battle to get Goldsmith's actions against the
distributors struck out on the basis that they were aimed at
putting *Private Eye* out of business and, as such, were an
abuse of the process of the court. The result was an expensive
draw which cost James Goldsmith £250,000, and *Private
Eye* not less than £85,000.

Private Eye's principal allegation that Goldsmith was the
leading member of a conspiracy to obstruct the course of
justice was unquestionably libellous. On 5 April 1975
Private Eye's solicitors admitted that it was untrue. It was a
case where Goldsmith could in the normal course of events
have expected to receive a substantial five, if not six-figure
sum in a civil claim for libel.

Although he did issue a large number of libel writs,
Goldsmith chose to bring a criminal prosecution and to
leave the civil actions in abeyance. The prospect of obtaining
very substantial damages did not seem greatly to interest
Goldsmith. His view was that the damages he might recover
were insignificant in the terms of the profit and loss account
of the company he headed. He was personally an extremely
wealthy man to whom the prospect of a large tax-free sum of
libel damages did not have its usual glitter. He felt that civil
libel actions were cheap advertising for *Private Eye*.
Fighting a civil libel case against them was therefore a gift or
a subsidy. He considered that, until juries awarded libel
damages that bore some relation to the cost of advertising, a
libel action against *Private Eye* was more of an advantage
than a disadvantage to them. In fact, *Private Eye* was to
obtain far greater publicity from the criminal proceedings
than from any civil libel action.

To a limited extent libel actions have assisted *Private Eye*
in its spectacular increase in circulation. The current
provision for libel actions in their accounts of some £85,000
to £100,000 is extremely high in relation to their turnover.

Private Eye had turned certain libel actions to their advantage by appeals to readers for funds and has emerged from them stronger rather than weaker. The value of the victories secured by the late Lord Russell of Liverpool (Lord Liver of Cesspool) and Nora Beloff were each lessened, the one by a gala evening (The Rustle of Spring) at the Phoenix Theatre, the other by the launch of the Ballsoff Fund. These events ensured the survival of *Private Eye*. At the same time, they perpetuated the libel and probably caused more damage to the reputations of Russell and Beloff than the original libels.

Goldsmith's resolve was reinforced by the opinion that he had formed of *Private Eye*. He thought it was an evil publication with a small core of rot, 'maggots and scavengers', and with a lot of trendies involved who did not know what they were doing. There was, he felt, an orchestrated plot among a number of journalists working for different newspapers who were engaged in a campaign of vilification and ridicule against him by contributing anonymous articles to *Private Eye*, often in breach of their contracts of employment. These people were responsible for the seemingly uncoordinated references to him and his family in the financial and gossip columns of major newspapers. Constant repetition built these matters up into news stories.

The object of this group was, he felt, to undermine the financial institutions, including his Bank of England-supported rescue of the ailing Slater Walker companies, and to bring about the nationalization of the City of London. He was the person that *Private Eye* believed they could attack more effectively than the others involved, such as Charles Hambro, Lord Rothschild and Sir Ronald Leach. The Lucan affair was merely a pretext to attack him. Goldsmith was reinforced in these views by his belief that *Private Eye* had deliberately published a story which they knew was untrue. He considered that this case was not so much about freedom of speech as freedom to lie.

When these articles appeared in *Private Eye*, James Goldsmith wanted to discover more about this group which appeared set upon discrediting him. His solicitors engaged a firm of private detectives to analyse the contents of *Private Eye*'s dustbins. The purpose was to examine the drafts of their stories to see who was writing them. These drafts would then be photocopied and put back in the dustbin to avoid any accusation of theft. He had meetings infiltrated where journalists from different newspapers apparently discussed their stories and coordinated their planning. Such meetings were recorded; so too were their restaurant meals including their discussions before and after the meals by placing listening devices in a mackintosh on the coatstand.

Ingrams never resorted to such methods against Goldsmith. There were nevertheless some similarities in the views that the two adversaries had formed of each other. Ingrams considered that Goldsmith was the leader of a tight-knit group. He too had a conspiracy theory of his opponent and an almost obsessive interest in him. He was perhaps more obsessed against than obsessed with. Visitors to his office were confronted by a cardboard cutout of Goldsmith. Goldsmith and Ingrams never met except in court and then they did not exchange words. An arrangement that they should meet for lunch was made when the case was settled, but it was vetoed by Mrs Ingrams.

As *Private Eye* was in law a newspaper, it was protected by the Newspaper Libel Act 1888 and so, on 15 January 1976, Goldsmith had to ask the leave of a High Court judge to bring criminal libel proceedings against *Private Eye* in respect of the issues of 12 and 26 December 1975 and 9 January 1976.

The reasons, as later set out in Goldsmith's affidavit for proceeding with his private prosecution of *Private Eye*, were firstly that he considered the allegations of conspiracy to obstruct the course of justice exceptionally serious; secondly, he occupied a position of public prominence and was entrusted with the safety of funds belonging to the public; and thirdly, *Private Eye* had embarked upon a virulent campaign against him which he could no longer allow to go unchallenged and uncontradicted.

On 13 and 14 April 1976 Mr Justice Wien heard

Goldsmith's application for leave to institute criminal libel proceedings. On 5 April 1976 the solicitors for *Private Eye* had written to Goldsmith's lawyers indicating that *Private Eye* was satisfied that there was no truth in the suggestion that Goldsmith was a party to any attempt to obstruct justice. The letter stated that *Private Eye* had honestly believed, when the article was written, that Goldsmith had been present at the Aspinall lunch. They now offered to make a public withdrawal and apology.

It was a conciliatory gesture, but Goldsmith was not at that stage disposed to settle. The retraction stripped *Private Eye* of any substantive defence to the charge of criminal libel and it was used as a stick to beat them in the hearing before Mr Justice Wien.

While these legal overtures were being made, *Private Eye* published a particularly uncompromising article in the City column about Goldsmith leaving Slater Walker. It referred to him variously as Goldshidt and Goldenballs. It appeared in the 16 April issue, which was on sale on 14 April, before the Wien hearing ended. It is normally a bad sign when a judge comments, as did Mr Justice Wien, that he was not influenced by these terms of abuse. He did nevertheless refer somewhat ominously in his judgment to the fact that the campaign of vilification continued month after month with no let-up – 'not even when it was known this application was being made'.

Mr Justice Wien decided that there was a clear prima facie case of libel and that the libel was so serious that a criminal prosecution could be brought. Goldsmith's next step was to issue a summons for criminal libel, now that he had his leave. Before this happened, negotiations took place. There was talk of £20,000 damages, a five-year ban on *Private Eye* mentioning Goldsmith or Levine and after the five years a fortyeight hour early warning system before Goldsmith or Levine featured in *Private Eye*. Goldsmith was prepared to drop the five-year ban and his claim for damages, but negotiations floundered on 11 May over the vetting procedure. On 12 May the summons for criminal libel was issued.

On 21 May *Private Eye* gave a temporary undertaking in
the High Court to Mr Justice Chapman not to publish
anything about Goldsmith or Levine until the case for an
injunction was fully argued. They did manage inadvertently
to breach this undertaking five times. The undertaking was
not wholly ineffective in that it did prevent *Private Eye* from
commenting on the controversial Wilson resignation
Honours List in which Goldsmith was unexpectedly
knighted. Accordingly, on 5 July 1976 Goldsmith applied
for the undertaking to be made into a permanent injunction.
The hearing lasted seven days before Mr Justice Donaldson
who dismissed the application and ordered Goldsmith to
pay the costs.

The case was unusual because of the injunction sought.
Not only was Goldsmith trying to prevent *Private Eye* from
publishing matters about him which might prejudice
potential jurors, he also wanted to stop *Private Eye*
disparaging his solicitor, Eric Levine, or his firm. The judge
felt this was far too general and very unusual in that it was
not brought by the person who was the main object of the
campaign; Levine had not issued any proceedings on his own
behalf.

The case was also notable for some of the devices used by
Private Eye's Lord Gnome to refer to Goldsmith in his
editorial column without actually naming him, and breaking
the court undertaking. For instance, Richard Ingrams
denied that Lord Gnome had in mind Goldsmith's well-
known domestic arrangements, when he referred to his
second ménage with Miss Rita Chevrolet. Lord Gnome has
things in common with a lot of people, Ingrams ventured
rather unconvincingly. However, Lord Gnome's denunciation of peeping-tommery in journalism bore more than a
passing resemblance to Goldsmith's denunciation of 'peeping-
tomism' on Ludovic Kennedy's television interview on 16
June. The attempt finally fell on its face on 9 July when Lord
Gnome's otherwise obscure Dutch address of Heerengracht
was revealed to be the site of a bank owned by Goldsmith.

In its attempt to defend the cases, *Private Eye* thought it
would be worthwhile investigating his solicitor, Eric Levine.

Michael Gillard, who had been involved in writing the
'Slicker' articles, telephoned John Addey of John Addey and
Associates, a firm of public relations consultants in the City
of London. Gillard thought Addey might have some useful
information about Levine, as both he and Levine acted for
Trusthouse Forte.

The involvement of John Addey gave a curious twist to
the case. Initially he supplied *Private Eye* with material
which appeared to discredit Levine. Shortly afterwards he
recanted and accused Gillard of blackmailing him. This
allegation cost him £5,000 libel damages.

According to Gillard, Addey immediately volunteered to
go and see 'his old mate', Leslie Paisner, a solicitor who had
been a partner of Levine in the firm of Paisner & Co. This he
did and Paisner told him about three incidents which led to
Levine leaving Paisner's practice on less than amicable
terms.

Although Addey's recollection was somewhat different, it
seems that he discussed Levine and the Goldsmith action at a
Private Eye lunch on Wednesday 21 April 1976, referring
obliquely to some alleged scandal involving Levine. Of the
ten people present, Brian Walden MP and three journalists
had a distinct recollection that they heard Addey discussing
Eric Levine, Leslie Paisner and the Goldsmith action. Addey
was adamant he did not mention Eric Levine in this context.
According to Michael Gillard, Addey repeated these
allegations at their dinner at Burke's restaurant that evening.

Following this dinner, Patrick Marnham was despatched
to see Leslie Paisner to check what Addey had said. He saw
Mr Paisner on 5 May and found him unusually willing, for a
senior city solicitor, to discuss the qualities of his former
partner with a journalist. He told Marnham he was prepared
to help because of the criminal libel proceedings against
Private Eye.

On 28 April Goldsmith heard that *Private Eye* was
sniffing around Eric Levine. He was told of this by his
stockbroker, Alexander Gilmour, who had himself been told
by Addey on 23 April of the *Private Eye* investigations into
Levine. Goldsmith personally investigated the matter with

remarkable zeal. He was ready to see Paisner on 13 May,
who repeated his allegations against Levine. He then
interviewed Addey at his offices in Leadenhall Street, who
made similar accusations and others beside. Levine was
summoned by Goldsmith. He vehemently denied the
charges, suggesting that Goldsmith should see the people
who were said to have made these allegations of misconduct
against him. Goldsmith arranged to see one of them in Paris.
On the morning of Sunday 16 May a Mr Refson came with
his lawyer to Goldsmith's house in Paris. He categorically
denied what he was said to have alleged against Levine, and
that there was any truth in such allegations. He agreed to
provide an affidavit in London but in the end did not do so.

Goldsmith then saw David Karr, the Chairman of a
French subsidiary of Trusthouse Forte, who likewise
confirmed that Levine had not behaved improperly in
relation to Trusthouse Forte's affairs. Sir Charles Forte also
swore an affidavit to this effect. A solicitor called Solomon
swore an affidavit also proving a negative: that Levine had
not been guilty of any misconduct in relation to his
professional behaviour at Paisner and Co.

On the evening of 13 May Addey telephoned Roland
Franklin, a business associate of Goldsmith who had been
present at the meeting between Goldsmith and Addey earlier
that day. Now Addey's account changed dramatically. He
admitted he had made a 'terrible mistake, a terrible
confusion'. The following day he lunched with Franklin and
retracted his allegations. After lunch he unburdened himself
by writing two letters, the first to Paisner:

> The whole of that story has been a pack of lies from
> beginning to end. I am deeply ashamed of my conduct.

The second was to Levine and even more abject:

> I admit unequivocally that this story was a whole tissue of
> lies from beginning to end. I am deeply ashamed. I beg
> your forgiveness.

This was followed by an affidavit in similar terms sworn by

John Addey in the presence of a partner of the firm of City solicitors Clifford-Turner as an independent observer.

On Saturday 15 May after Addey had told Paisner that he had withdrawn all his allegations, Mr Paisner telephoned Eric Levine saying he had 'done something terrible' and he wanted to retract. He swore an affidavit at his home on 16 May. It was later described by the Lord Chief Justice, Lord Widgery as 'a grovelling apology'. It contained similar clichés: 'a complete pack of lies from beginning to end . . . I saw him [Addey] as an opportunity to ensure Eric Levine would be ruined'.

Paisner explained that he had acted as he had out of a 'strong desire to destroy Eric Levine'. Addey's reason was rather different. He suggested, although he later changed his story, that he had become involved in these matters as a result of blackmailing pressure from Michael Gillard who had in his possession an anonymous article about his chauffeur and his company. This allegation was vigorously denied by Gillard. Although Addey was to apologize for this charge and pay £5,000 damages, Goldsmith chose to repeat the allegation and was later sued by Gillard for libel and slander.

These two affidavits from Paisner and Addey, their two principal witnesses, hit *Private Eye* like sandbags. Richard Ingrams went to see Addey in his set of chambers in Albany on 19 May. Addey told Ingrams that he had sworn his affidavit because of his fear of being prosecuted for criminal libel, 'I never realized they were so powerful', he said to Ingrams.

Addey never gave his account of this meeting, for a few days before the court hearing he remembered a pressing engagement in Italy, omitting to instruct his office to release his forwarding address or his likely date of return. He was quite entitled to do so, as he had not been subpoenaed. His absence was, as Mr Justice Donaldson observed, 'unfortunate'. The consequences were punishing for Addey. He was sued for libel by Gillard. Initially he agreed to resign from his company. However, he changed his mind and instead six out of nine directors left.

Paisner did not turn up at court to be cross-examined on
the contents of his affidavit either. However, his counsel,
John Wilmers QC, and his doctor did. 'He was extremely
confused and withdrawn and threatening suicide', it was
explained. His doctors diagnosed him to be suffering from
an acute depressive illness and advised him that he was quite
unfit to attend the hearing. Shortly after the hearing he
retired from practice and his health never recovered. He died
on 28 March 1979 aged 70.

On 16 July Mr Justice Donaldson refused to grant
Goldsmith the injunction he sought – to prevent *Private Eye*
from publishing anything about him or his solicitor. It was
Private Eye's first success in the campaign, but the battle
gave some flavour of the fighting to follow. The judge issued
dire warnings that *Private Eye*'s convoluted style did not
fool the court and that it was difficult for an editor to justify
an obsessional interest. He observed that breach of an
undertaking given to the court was a serious matter. Ingrams
was fortunate, he said, that the breaches of the undertaking
given to Mr Justice Chapman on 21 May were not the
subject matter of an application to commit him to prison.

Richard Ingrams did not have long to wait for such an
application to be made. On 6 August 1976 an application
was made to commit Gillard and him to prison for contempt.
They admitted they were in contempt of court and they,
Pressdram Ltd, and Moore-Harness Ltd were fined £250
apiece. The judge, Mr Justice Goff, did not take too serious a
view of the contempt. All but one of the five references were
jocular and nothing had been said about Levine. It had been
possible to make Gillard a party to these proceedings as a
sifting of the contents of *Private Eye*'s dustbins revealed his
writing on the draft of one of the articles.

In the meantime Richard Ingrams, Pressdram and
Moore-Harness had found themselves in court again. On 30
July they were committed for trial on a charge of criminal
libel at the Central Criminal Court. They were later joined in
the dock by Patrick Marnham, the writer of the Elwes
article. Somewhat ominously for *Private Eye*, the Chief
Metropolitan Magistrate rejected the argument that criminal

libel required a likely breach of the peace. Belief in the truth of what was written at the time of publication was relevant only to sentence, he observed.

Having held their fire over the Honours List, *Private Eye* decided they would not remain silent about the hearing before Mr Justice Donaldson. This had been held in chambers, that is to say behind closed doors. The result was an article on 20 August, entitled 'The Erasing of Lazarus', that being the middle name of Leslie Paisner.

A second attempt was made to commit Richard Ingrams to prison for contempt of court. This was heard on 28 October 1976 by the Lord Chief Justice, Lord Widgery, sitting with Mr Justice Eveleigh and Mr Justice Peter Pain. The judges clearly found the turnabout of Addey and Paisner somewhat bewildering. *Private Eye* was stoutly defended by James Comyn QC: 'trial by newspaper is a wonderfully emotive phrase, but it must not be allowed to interfere with freedom of speech or freedom of the press'. Ultimately the court decided that the article complained of did not present a real risk to the fair trial of future legal proceedings.

Appeals by Goldsmith to the Court of Appeal and the House of Lords were unsuccessful. In the House of Lords his counsel, Lewis Hawser QC, argued that the article in question was calculated to put pressure on Sir James Goldsmith not to proceed with his libel action. 'He has shown a great deal of fortitude in resisting this pressure so far', Lord Diplock wryly observed. *Private Eye*'s success in this application showed that the tide had turned in their favour.

While all this had been going on, civil actions had been proceeding against seventeen of the thirtyseven distributors of *Private Eye* who had not settled the libel actions brought against them by Goldsmith. *Private Eye* won the first round before a High Court Master, Master Warren, who held that the action was an abuse of the process of the court as its purpose was to shut off *Private Eye*'s channels of distribution.

Most distributors had been able to settle the claim

brought against them by agreeing not to distribute *Private Eye*. This had led to a 12,000 drop in *Private Eye*'s circulation of 101,000. Sir James Goldsmith stoutly denied that the purpose of this litigation was to smash *Private Eye*. He pointed out that the earlier negotiations would have ensured the survival of the magazine. His appeal to Mr Justice Stocker was successful and a majority of the Court of Appeal, but not Lord Denning, felt that Goldsmith was perfectly entitled to sue all the distributors.

Such wholesale litigation against distributors and retailers was unusual. Distributors can be held liable for circulating libellous material, unless they can establish that they distributed the magazine without any reason to suppose either that the particular issue was libellous or that it was the sort of publication which was likely to contain a libel. Ironically one of the leading cases in this area of the law had come about when W H Smith, the *bête noire* of *Private Eye*, had run foul of Sun Life in Canada in 1934 for material they had distributed.

The view of Goldsmith was that the position of distributors of a poisonous magazine like *Private Eye* was analogous to grocers selling rotten food. They should receive the same treatment.

A somewhat less charitable view of Goldsmith's action was taken by an increasing number of persons who felt that he was indeed attempting to destroy *Private Eye*. The libel was dwarfed by Goldsmith's reaction to it. *Private Eye* established a Goldenballs Fund which had raised £40,000 by the time of the Old Bailey hearing. Contributions came in varying sizes from all over the country with suitable words of encouragement, including a note attached to a donation of £50 from Peter Jay, '*Vivat Oculus. Delendi sunt testes aurei.*' 'Long Live the Eye. Goldenballs must be destroyed.'

The criminal libel proceedings proved something of a liability to Sir James Goldsmith in April 1977 when he was invited by the board of Express Newspapers to intervene in the attempt by Associated Newspapers, the publisher of the *Evening News*, to take over the *Evening Standard*. Goldsmith's intervention took a somewhat dramatic form.

An announcement was due to be made by Vere Harmsworth, the Chairman of Associated Newspapers at the Bonnington Hotel on 28 April. At 9.30 am Goldsmith telephoned from his motorcar with a formal expression of interest which triggered the anti-monopoly provisions of Section 58, Fair Trading Act 1973, in that, while there remained a possibility of the *Evening Standard* surviving as an independent newspaper, Associated Newspapers' bid could not go through. This led Goldsmith, who held thirtyfive per cent of the non-voting shares in Express Newspapers to agree on a joint approach with Tiny Rowland, whose company Lonrho was interested in establishing a foothold in the English newspaper industry to add to its Scottish and African interests. This was scarcely the most promising of partnerships, as Rowland's £5,000 was the largest single contribution to the Goldenballs Fund.

By the end of June Trafalgar House had made a bid and Goldsmith decided not to match it. Consequently it was the *Evening News* that disappeared rather than the *Evening Standard*. These dealings had a direct effect on the criminal libel proceeding in that those people who had persuaded Goldsmith to intervene in the takeover now urged him to settle his case against *Private Eye*.

An armistice was arranged by Simon Jenkins, the editor of the *Evening Standard*. The principal feature of the settlement was an unequivocal apology published in a whole-page advertisement in the *Evening Standard*. It was stressed that this was a genuine apology. *Private Eye* would contribute £30,000 to Sir James's costs, over ten years. They gave an assurance that they would not pursue any vendetta against him in future issues of *Private Eye*.

As part of the settlement, no evidence was offered on 16 May 1977 against the defendants on the charge of criminal libel and they were acquitted. Court No. 1 of the Central Criminal Court then became a civil court and the civil litigation was also settled.

In retrospect Sir James Goldsmith regrets having settled and ascribes it to a moment of weakness. He was advised by everyone at Express Newspapers to settle the action; he was under considerable pressure of work with the bid for the *Evening Standard*, the problems of Slater Walker and the day to day running of Cavenham; he felt too much of his time was being devoted to the action and that, with all the publicity it had received, *Private Eye* might be acquitted or receive a minimal fine. When a bout of influenza added to his problems he was persuaded to settle. Even so he feels that his decision to launch a private prosecution was correct and that, given the same circumstances, he would do the same again.

Who had the better of this contest? In financial terms it was arguable that Sir James did. It did cost him £250,000, which was considerably more than the £85,000 it seems to have cost *Private Eye*. The actual cost of the action to *Private Eye* remained a matter of contention and the subject of a bizarre and unresolved bet by Goldsmith that the real cost was over £100,000. If they could prove to independent accountants that their costs were, on 'an arms' length basis', below £100,000, he would pay the difference between that sum and the £100,000. He remained unimpressed by their figure of £85,000.

Goldsmith could more readily afford these costs than *Private Eye*, despite the £40,000 from their Goldenballs Fund. In purely financial terms, Goldsmith benefited from this litigation. It depressed the value of the Cavenham shares at a time Goldsmith wanted to buy them in order to transfer control of Cavenham to his privately owned French company, Générale Occidentale. Goldsmith's profit on these transactions ran into many millions. The litigation did not further such political ambitions as he had, although he had already decided to wind down his operations in England. He was nevertheless approached by some Richmond Conservatives to put his name forward as a parliamentary candidate. He was likewise canvassed to stand for membership of the European Parliament. Nothing came of either approach.

The disadvantage of this litigation for Goldsmith was that it brought every sphere of his life into the public arena. When *Now!* magazine was launched in September 1979 it was savagely attacked by *Private Eye* who ridiculed its claimed circulation figure of 125,000. They held a lunch at the Savoy to find the newsagent of the year whose order for *Now!* had declined most spectacularly and the prize went to a Mr Sid Smith of Wigan whose orders had plummeted from 250 to 25. In April 1981 *Now!* closed with losses of the order of £8–10 million. *Now!* might have failed in any event. Undoubtedly *Private Eye* was largely instrumental in its speedy demise.

Goldsmith's libel problems were not at an end. In July 1976 he had attacked Philip Knightley, a *Sunday Times* journalist, for lack of objectivity in his report on the *Private Eye* litigation. He had done so by means of a widely circulated letter to the Press Council. In an out of court settlement Knightley received £6,000 damages and an apology.

Still more extraordinary was the slander action brought by Michael Gillard against Goldsmith. This went back to the allegation that John Addey had been blackmailed by Gillard into helping *Private Eye* with its defence. After Addey's spectacular retraction of his allegations against Levine, Goldsmith had telephoned William Rees-Mogg, then editor of *The Times*, William Deedes of the *Daily Telegraph*, John Junor of the *Sunday Express* and Andrew Knight of *The Economist* informing them that Michael Gillard had blackmailed John Addey. Henry Keswick, proprietor of *The Spectator* received the same message, as did Anthony Blond, a director of Pressdram, the proprietors of *Private Eye*.

On 20 May 1977 Sir James Goldsmith repeated the allegation of blackmail in a letter to William Deedes. Someone took a photocopy of the letter but, like the rummager in *Private Eye*'s dustbin, the informant was scrupulous to avoid any suggestions of theft, so the original letter was carefully replaced in its file. Gillard issued another writ, this time for libel, against Goldsmith in respect of that letter.

Against the odds, Sir James Goldsmith successfully defended this action. After all the allegation was not that Goldsmith was being blackmailed but John Addey. It was suggested that the blackmail arose out of an anonymous article that Gillard had received and kept in his drawer, entitled 'The Rise and Fall of John Addey'. The alleged blackmail was that this article would be published unless he produced evidence for *Private Eye* to use against Goldsmith and it would severely damage Addey's relationships with the companies for whom he acted as public consultant.

Quite apart from the evidence of Gillard and his three witnesses from the *Private Eye* lunch of 21 April 1976, who included Brian McConnell (the journalist who had rescued Princess Anne from the attentions of a deranged gunman), Goldsmith had the problem that John Addey, the alleged blackmail victim, had apologized to Gillard for this very allegation and had paid him £5,000 damages.

Goldsmith fought the case without calling Addey (by then back from Italy) to give evidence. The case was dominated by Goldsmith. He was in the witness box for a day and a half. *Private Eye* was to refer to his giving of evidence as a *tour de force*. His answers in the witness box became longer and longer with his repeated references to journalists searching for grime in his background and to an orchestrated campaign against him. Cross-examination became an uphill task. Even Gillard's solicitor did not escape; he was first referred to as Bindman (*Private Eye*'s solicitor), then with suitably profuse apologies as Birnberg (his real name) and finally as the composite Bindberg.

An unfortunate series of coincidences was skilfully highlighted by Lord Rawlinson QC, Goldsmith's counsel. Gillard had not handed the anonymous letter over to Addey for sixteen months and then only produced a photocopy; he had not got in touch with Addey until he needed his assistance on the day that Mr Justice Wien granted leave for criminal libel proceedings to be brought.

Despite Gillard's evidence that he had been a friend of Addey's for eight years and had attempted to contact him on a number of occasions about the anonymous article, the jury found in favour of Sir James Goldsmith. Notwithstanding testimonials from a number of colleagues, Gillard's appeals to the Court of Appeal and the House of Lords failed. Here

again there is some dispute as to what the case cost Gillard.
Goldsmith puts it at about £70,000, whereas Gillard says the
original bill presented to him was substantially reduced on
the court's taxation of costs and that the action did not cost
him more than £50,000.

Gillard did, however, receive some sympathy from Lord
Justice Templeman in the Court of Appeal. He said that
Gillard had fallen victim to the 'no holds barred' feud
between Sir James Goldsmith and *Private Eye*. It did not
follow, he said, from the jury's verdict that Mr Gillard was a
blackmailer in common parlance or that he had forfeited his
right to practise his profession.

The verdict meant that in the charged atmosphere of 1976
Mr Gillard, inspired by loyalty to *Private Eye*, went too far,
and used the article as a means of encouraging or persuading
or spurring Mr Addey to find information derogatory to Mr
Levine.

'It means Mr Gillard has fallen victim to this dreadful feud
which has caused him as well as many others, so much agony
and expense – so far as I can see for no good purpose to
anyone'.

Although this round of Goldsmith's litigation with
Private Eye had ended on a high note, was it worth it? In a
legal sense, he had won the argument. Surprising as it may
seem, *Private Eye* would probably have been convicted.
Goldsmith had shown that the offence of criminal libel was
alive and, if not actively kicking, still capable of landing a
well-directed kick.

In 1982 the Law Commission considered the law of
criminal libel and concluded that there should be such an
offence to deal with cases of character assassination. There
would be two principal elements of the new crime, the
libeller must have intended to defame and he must have
deliberately lied in the sense that he must have known or
believed that what he wrote was untrue. The Law
Commission recommended that the Director of Public
Prosecutions should conduct the proceedings rather than
private individuals.

Had this been the law, a prosecution of *Private Eye* might

still have taken place but it would have failed on the grounds
that *Private Eye* mistakenly believed Goldsmith to have
been at the Aspinall lunch.

What the Goldsmith case had done was to underline how
archaic and unsatisfactory the law of criminal libel is. Truth
alone is not in itself a defence; it also has to be shown that
publication was in the public interest. Fair comment is not a
defence. The whole law of criminal libel is beset with such
anomalies. Unlike civil libel, criminal libel does not need to
be published to a third party. This meant a Mr Adams could
in 1888 be convicted of criminal libel when he sent a young
lady of virtuous and modest character, a letter 'soliciting her
chastity'.

The law of criminal libel had an undesirable aspect in that
the criminal law can be used for settling private squabbles. In
1934 no less a person than Sir Thomas Beecham had
prosecuted Alexander Gifford, an elderly organist from
Lewisham, who had complained in a letter to Beecham's
solicitor that he had been 'trying to get back the guinea
which I foolishly lent a prince of stunters for a fantastic
project [the creation of the Imperial League of Opera] which
would never mature' (which it did not). The organist was
bound over by the magistrate in the sum of £5 to keep the
peace, despite pointing out that he had successfully kept it
for over fifty years.

As an illustration of the fact that the law of criminal libel is
in need of re-examination, it is difficult to improve upon the
words of Lord Edmund-Davies in the case of *Gleaves v
Deakin* in 1980 where he spoke of 'a startling state of affairs'.
The judge was commenting upon the fact that book
publishers and television companies do not have the benefit
of the meagre protection of the Law of Libel Amendment
Act 1888 in that the leave of a High Court judge was not
necessary to bring a prosecution. In that case Mr R C A
Gleaves (aka the Bishop of Medway), somewhat to the
surprise of Lord Edmund-Davies, was able to ignore any
civil remedies that he might have had and to launch into a
criminal libel prosecution. In the first of a series of private
prosecutions Gleaves brought proceedings for criminal libel

against the authors (Michael Deakin and John Willis) and publisher of the book *Johnny Go Home* which was based upon a widely publicized television programme on Yorkshire Television which had been highly critical of Gleaves.

The allegations against Gleaves were undoubtedly very serious but this was a classic instance of a case where there was a strong argument for the evidence to be scrutinized before a prosecution was committed. Gleaves had a series of convictions for offences of homosexuality and violence which culminated in a four-year prison sentence being imposed upon him at the Old Bailey in 1975. The case brought against the authors and the publisher of the book illustrated the complexities of this area of the law. A ruling at the magistrates' court that, although the defendants could cross-examine Gleaves upon his previous convictions, they could not call witnesses at the preliminary hearing on issues as to Gleaves's character, led to a test case in the House of Lords where it was upheld. The trial itself lasted thirteen days before the defendants were acquitted on all eight counts. The trial judge, Mr Justice Comyn, observed that the law of criminal libel was extremely unsatisfactory and wholly unfitted to modern times. The further prosecutions envisaged by Gleaves were stopped by the Attorney General entering a plea of *nolle prosequi*, that is to say announcing that he would not allow such prosecutions to take place.

In such cases where the leave of a High Court judge to bring a case of criminal libel has been required, the tendency has been for the evidence supporting the prosecution to be more closely analysed to see if it really is in the public interest that criminal proceedings should be brought. No one is denying the right of persons such as Gleaves to bring civil proceedings; the issue is whether it is right to allow prosecutions in such cases.

Thus a Mr Paul Desmond failed in April 1982 to persuade Mr Justice Taylor that the *Sunday People* should be prosecuted for their article entitled 'Bully boasts, I beat up tragic deb'. It was a very disagreeable article about Desmond. When the court was told that he had tried to sell the newspaper the story about his relationship with his dead girlfriend and learnt how he had admitted he had treated her, it felt that this was not a matter for the criminal law.

Although these decisions all followed the ruling of Mr Justice Wien in the Goldsmith case, the judges' lack of enthusiasm for private prosecutions for criminal libel was apparent. The law of criminal libel will doubtless survive to deal with the occasional serious libel of such persons as members of the Royal Family, judges or police officers. It is unlikely there will ever be a case similar to that brought by Goldsmith. The probability is that such prosecutions will be conducted in rather less idiosyncratic style by the Director of Public Prosecutions. The Law Commission in 1985 published a report recommending that the crime of criminal libel should be abolished and should be replaced by a narrowly defined statutory crime of criminal defamation.

Private Eye's success, such as it was, turned out to be shortlived. In August 1981 'Slicker' (Michael Gillard) in his City column tried to forge a link between Sir James Goldsmith and Roberto Calvi, the disgraced Italian banker, who had been found hanged from Blackfriars Bridge.

The article falsely suggested that Calvi had been a business associate of Sir James and sought to establish a link between Calvi and Goldsmith through Antonio Tonello's one-time directorship of a Luxembourg company called Basic Resources International SA. For these libels, *Private Eye* had to pay £85,010 being £35,010 damages and £50,000 legal costs. This is to date the largest out of court settlement, where the full financial terms have been publicly announced.

This followed the substantial awards to Lady Havers, wife of the Attorney General, and to Esther Rantzen and her husband Desmond Wilcox. It placed sufficient strain on *Private Eye*'s resources for their property in the Dordogne, the Villa Disraeli, to be placed on the market' and it far exceeded *Private Eye*'s existing libel reserves.

Fourteen

'All I have done ... was to help the Liberal Party'

'All I have done (and God! how I regret it!) was to help the Liberal Party and various Liberals ...' So wrote Jack Arnold Hayward OBE on 20 April 1983 to the Rt Hon Jeremy Thorpe MP, the former Leader of the Liberal Party. He was complaining bitterly about the fact that his financial help to the Liberal Party in the 1970 and 1974 elections had caused him to be accused by a British Sunday newspaper of involvement in a criminal conspiracy to murder Norman Scott.

Mr Hayward was a highly successful businessman in the Bahamas. He had remained relatively out of the public eye, although his charitable and philanthropic activities had earned him the nickname of 'Union Jack' Hayward. These included bringing back the SS *Great Britain* from the Falklands, the purchase of Lundy Island for the nation and the building of the indoor cricket school at Lord's. In the libel action that followed, Lord Denning was to describe him as 'a man of the highest character and reputation, who was intensely loyal to this country and who had used his money to support many good causes'.

Among those who benefited from Hayward's munificence were Jeremy Thorpe and the Liberal Party. Thorpe had met Hayward when he was serving on a committee to raise money for the National Trust to buy Lundy Island. Subsequently Thorpe persuaded Hayward that the Liberal Party was another worthy British institution which needed assistance. Hayward donated £150,000 in May 1970, £40,000 and £10,000 in May 1974, £9,000 in July 1975 and £10,000 in

November 1975 – to meet the expenses of the 1970 and 1974
General Elections. These sums were given in response to
flamboyant letters from Thorpe, laden with news of the
goings on of such a diverse group as the Queen, King
Constantine, President Nixon, Ian Smith, Dr Henry
Kissinger, Pierre Trudeau and Idi Amin.

Few private letters have in recent times been so widely
read. They contained Thorpe's description of what the
money would be spent on and his instructions as to how it
was to be paid. They formed a central part of a charge of
conspiracy to murder. Although Thorpe was acquitted of
this charge, as well as of incitement to murder, the
accusation was sufficient to destroy his political career. It
was unfortunate for him, therefore, that these letters were
still in existence several years after they were written. The
prosecution attached considerable importance to them.

So far as Hayward was concerned, the money had been
donated for and had been spent on such things as election
expenses, posters and television linkups.

All this had seemed totally unrelated to what became
known as the Norman Scott Affair. This involved the
shooting on Exmoor in October 1975, not of Norman Scott,
a male model and friend of Thorpe in the early 1960s, but of
Rinka, his Great Dane. The gunman, airline pilot Andrew
'Gino' Newton was jailed for two years. He was released in
April 1977. He then announced to the press that he had been
hired for £5,000 to kill Norman Scott.

This was a very different account from the one which, with
limited success, he had given to the jury at his trial. Precisely
who had been involved in these events beyond Newton,
Scott and Rinka was to remain unclear until the beginning of
March 1978. The mystery then started to unravel following a
row at the House of Commons between Jeremy Thorpe and
David Holmes, a merchant banker and best man at his
wedding. Holmes had still been sufficiently angry when he
reached his mother's house in Surrey to rush round to the
nearby cottage of an Independent Television News journalist
whom he scarcely knew. He told the startled reporter that, if
he wished to know where the money had come from, he
should ask Mr Dinshaw in Jersey.

This appeared to be the missing link in the case. There followed intensive investigations by the police and the press. At the beginning of April Hayward's house in Sussex was circled six times by a private plane and four reporters turned up asking where he was. On 9 April 1978 the *Sunday Telegraph* decided it would publish a story about the developments in the case and the article appeared on its front page under the headline

TWO MORE IN SCOTT AFFAIR
by Christopher House, Crime Correspondent

The names of two more people connected with the Norman Scott affair have been given to the police. One is a wealthy benefactor of the Liberal Party and the other is a businessman from the Channel Islands. Both men, police have been told, arranged for a leading Liberal supporter to be 'reimbursed' £5,000, the same amount Mr Andrew Newton alleges he was paid to murder Mr Scott. Mr Scott, a former male model, once claimed he had a homosexual relationship with Mr Jeremy Thorpe, the former Liberal leader. Mr Thorpe has repeatedly denied the claim. The new names were made known to the police only during the past two weeks. Inquiries are being made and it may be some time before they are interviewed.

VISIT TO ISLANDS

Police have been told that some time last year the benefactor flew to the Channel Islands where he had a meeting, arranged several days before, with a business friend living there. During the meeting, he was allegedly handed £5,000. He then returned and later paid the money to a leading Liberal supporter, either directly or through another source ...

Although the various individuals referred to were not at that time named, the reference to 'the wealthy benefactor' was to Jack Hayward, and 'the businessman from the Channel Islands' referred to was Nadir Dinshaw, another wholly unsuspecting party to these transactions.

The article was followed up the following week, 16 April,

by another article by Christopher House. This appeared
under the headline:

NEW NAME IN SCOTT AFFAIR

Mr Jack Hayward, the Bahamas-based millionaire, who
once gave the Liberal Party £150,000 to help pay its
overdraft and to boost its election fighting fund, said last
night that the police want to interview him about the
Norman Scott affair. At his home in Freeport, Bahamas,
Mr Hayward, 54, who was once known as 'Union Jack'
because of his many Back Britain campaigns, told me 'I
have been informed that the police would like to interview
me about the Scott affair, but so far no one has contacted
me officially. Obviously, I will help them if I can. But I
have no knowledge of the Scott affair other than what I
have read in the newspapers ...'
Last week I revealed exclusively in the *Sunday Telegraph*
that the names of two people, a wealthy Liberal party
benefactor and a Channel Island businessman had been
given to the police. Both, it has been alleged to police,
arranged for a leading Liberal supporter to be 'reimbursed'
£5,000, the same amount of money airline pilot Mr
Andrew Newton alleges he was paid to murder Mr Scott.

The first article had not said who the wealthy benefactor
was. The second article removed any doubt as to his identity.
As Hayward stated in his letter to Thorpe of 20 April 1978,
his telephone in the Bahamas had hardly stopped ringing
and reporters from virtually every newspaper had been on
the line. The local Bahamas newspaper had repeated the
allegations made by the *Sunday Telegraph*. An ITN news
crew had turned up on his doorstep unannounced.

The 'exclusive revelation' by the crime correspondent on
the front page of the *Sunday Telegraph* pushed Hayward
into the Norman Scott affair and into the limelight. Mr
Thorpe had not then been arrested and there was
considerable press coverage and speculation about the
police enquiries. The picture drawn by the *Sunday
Telegraph* of Hayward going backwards and forwards to the

Channel Islands with money to pay for the gunman's services, and the paper's use of inverted commas round the word 'reimbursed' suggested Hayward was implicated in a criminal conspiracy. It was a very grave allegation and he issued a writ for libel on 27 April 1978.

At the ensuing libel action, Andrew Bateson QC, counsel for the *Sunday Telegraph*, said that there had been no intention whatsoever on the part of the paper to suggest that anyone identified in those articles could be said to have been considered guilty of a conspiracy to murder Scott or suspected of it. However, the test in libel actions is not what the newspaper intended but what the words meant. The jury appeared to have little doubt; they awarded Hayward £50,000 damages.

In any event the article was inaccurate. Hayward had not gone to the Channel Islands at all in 1977. Still less had he had dealings with Dinshaw or handed him £5,000. At the trial cross-examination of House, the paper's crime correspondent, by Lord Rawlinson QC revealed that the story did not accurately record what House had meant to say. It emerged that someone involved in the sub-editing or production of the story had altered the article.

House had written of Hayward (the wealthy benefactor) visiting the Channel Islands and handing over the money to Dinshaw (the businessman) and flying back to England. What actually appeared in the newspaper was Hayward flying to the Channel Islands to meet Dinshaw, being handed £5,000 by him, then returning to England and paying it to David Holmes (the leading Liberal supporter). Precisely how or why these changes were made was not clear, as the original draft of the article had been lost by the time of the trial.

At the trial there was a dispute as to whether Hayward had said to the reporter 'I have been informed that the police would like to interview me about the Scott affair' or 'I have *not* been informed . . .' Unfortunately, the original notes of the conversation by then had also gone astray.

The libel action could not be heard until November 1979 because of the criminal proceedings brought against Jeremy

Thorpe, David Holmes, John le Mesurier and George
Deakin. The result was that by the time the libel case was
heard, it had a distinct air of *déjà vu*.

That was far from being the case at the committal
proceedings at Minehead against Thorpe and three others.
The small magistrates court was ringed by journalists and
television gantries and presented an astonishing sight.
Hayward's arrival from the Bahamas and his evidence were
awaited with interest. Yet he and his lawyer were able to dine
in a local restaurant unrecognized by the news hounds who
were discussing him at length at the surrounding tables.

In contrast, the West Quantoxhead hotel, where he was
staying, fifteen miles from Minehead, was traced by an
enterprising freelance reporter who telephoned every hotel
within a twenty-mile radius of Minehead. The following
morning on drawing the curtains he saw two television crews
and three carloads of reporters camped outside. He travelled
to court followed by a convoy of journalists past hoardings
with suitably local angles on the case such as 'Rinka's niece's
birthday'.

It was a surprising sight to see Jeremy Thorpe, more
usually seen on television or on state occasions, in the dock.
He was an immaculate, confident figure, once he had
overcome his evident feeling of nausea at Norman Scott's
evidence.

Sir David Napley, Thorpe's solicitor, opened his questioning of Hayward by making it clear that he was blameless in
the matter. This was reported in a number of papers,
including the *Daily Telegraph*. It was not mentioned in the
Sunday Telegraph in their background article on the case.
Instead a somewhat chatty piece, mentioning the 'genial
expatriate millionaire from the Bahamas wearing an MCC
tie', was published.

At the Old Bailey the same thing happened when George
Carman QC, Thorpe's counsel, made a similar statement.
Again the *Sunday Telegraph* did not report it, although they
did find space for the fact that Hayward had recommended
an improbably named Southwark pub, The Boot and
Flogger, to the judge, Mr Justice Cantley.

On 22 June 1979, the last day of Royal Ascot, Thorpe and his co-defendants were unanimously acquitted. A West Country vicar unwisely held a service of thanksgiving. The precise operation of divine providence was never made clear.

On the Sunday following his acquittal, Thorpe issued a statement to the Press Association through his solicitor. This announced, as was the case, that £20,000 had been placed in a joint solicitors' account and that it could be reclaimed by Hayward. It led certain newspapers to conclude that this was *the* £20,000 originally paid by Hayward – that is to say the two payments, each of £10,000, in May, 1974 and November 1975 which had never been properly accounted for and which, the prosecution had alleged, had been used to fund the conspiracy. There were such headlines as: 'I've got the £20,000'. Surrounded by reporters and dogs at Hayward's house in Sussex, his lawyer put out a statement to clarify the position. The money was paid to Hayward and there the matter ended.

It was far from clear why Thorpe sought this additional publicity. The idea of letting sleeping dogs lie seemed singularly appropriate. After the trial at the Old Bailey, but before the libel case, the *Sunday Telegraph* found itself censured by the Press Council in October 1979 for a 'flagrant breach' of the Declaration of Principle in Payments to Witnesses. This arose out of a contract which the newspaper had signed in October 1978 with Peter Bessell, the former Liberal MP. Under the terms of the contract Bessell would have received £50,000 for a book on the Thorpe case, if he were convicted. If he were acquitted, Bessell would only receive £25,000 for six background articles.

The newspaper was unfortunate to be so strongly criticized. The real problem was the credibility of Bessell rather than the contract which was dubbed 'a double-your-money' contract. Much capital was made out of the fact that it was in Bessell's financial interest to see Thorpe convicted. However, prior to the committal proceedings, Bessell had been a man of some reputation despite his financial difficulties. The matters that emerged at his trial were not then known. What the paper had been trying to do was to distinguish between the lucrative book serialization rights it would acquire from Bessell, if Thorpe had been convicted, and the much less valuable payments for six background articles, if Thorpe were acquitted. As it was, Bessell's credibility was so tarnished that the paper did not publish anything. It did pay Bessell his £25,000.

In November 1979 Hayward's libel action was tried before Mr Justice O'Connor and a jury. The paper faced the somewhat forlorn task of establishing that the article was not defamatory. The editor, John Thompson, said in evidence that he never minded apologizing when the *Sunday Telegraph* had made a mistake, but they felt that they had not libelled Hayward, even unintentionally.

It was in fact a little difficult to see why the *Sunday Telegraph* had not apologized. The nearest they had come was a letter from their solicitors dated 4 May 1978. This said that the paper had 'the greatest respect for Mr Haywood as a patriot and public benefactor'. As Sir George Baker pointed out in the Court of Appeal, the effect was somewhat reduced by the mis-spelling of Hayward's name.

The paper's defence was that the article did not mean that Hayward was involved in or that he was reasonably suspected of participating in a criminal conspiracy. They argued that they were merely reporting the progress of a criminal investigation and that in this restricted sense the article was true.

After Hayward had given his account of what had happened, the jury returned a verdict for him for £50,000. Unlike the Broome action, the case was not beset by difficulties about punitive damages. Instead Mr Justice O'Connor had directed the jury to award suitable damages, if they found the article libellous. They should reflect compensation and moderation rather than punishment of the newspaper, he told them.

In the subsequent appeal the amount of damages awarded was not greatly in issue. The award of £50,000 was the highest sum of libel damages upheld on appeal.

The criticism of the newspaper by the Press Council was mild in comparison to what the Court of Appeal meted out in June 1981. The *Sunday Telegraph* took their nineteen grounds of appeal before a court consisting of Lord Denning, Sir George Baker and Sir Stanley Rees, a team totalling two hundred and twenty years of age including seventy years as judges of the High Court and Court of Appeal and, no doubt, a few years as readers of the *Sunday Telegraph*.

After a four-day hearing Lord Denning called the story: 'a vicious and unjustifiable libel'. He felt the jury were fully entitled to condemn it and award £50,000 damages. He went on to say that it seemed to him: 'to be a case where, in the search for a sensational story, the *Sunday Telegraph* published these articles which carried the implication that Mr Jack Hayward, a man of the highest reputation, was implicated in a plot to murder. No such story should have been published.'

The *Sunday Telegraph* fared no better with Sir George Baker. 'The Crime Correspondent put the wealthy bene-factor "in" the Scott Affair and he never got him out. If this was merely suspicion of implication, it was so malignant, so virulent, as to be equivalent to a categorical statement of participation in the plot'. He went on to refer to 'interest having to be titillated and the article appearing to be a kind of crossword puzzle or colloquially a "whodunit" on page one with an invitation to solve the identity from the clue "a wealthy benefactor of the Liberal Party"'. He referred unfavourably to the fact that the crime correspondent: 'had failed even to inquire how or why subediting of his article of the 9 April had produced a complete distortion of what he said he wrote and that he had lost his notebook despite a request for its production'.

Leave to appeal to the House of Lords was refused by the Court of Appeal. An application to the House of Lords for leave also failed.

The appeal highlighted the technicalities of the law of libel, Lord Denning ruled. He said that the test of whether or not an article was defamatory was a matter of the impression an ordinary person gets on first reading and not on later analysis. The meaning of the words in a libel case should not be a matter of construction in the way a lawyer construes a document.

Lord Denning also stated that the Court of Appeal should not upset the verdict of the jury on the grounds of a supposed misdirection by the trial judge on a question of law or fact, unless it was plainly such as to lead to a substantial miscarriage of justice.

The articles had been published only a week apart. The first one referred merely to an unnamed 'wealthy benefactor'. The second named him as Mr Hayward and referred with some pride to the 'exclusive revelation last week'. The trial judge's ruling that the jury could look at the words of the article of 16 April to decide who was referred to in the 9 April article was challenged on appeal. This argument appeared to gain some support from a judgment of Lord Denning given only a few months earlier in January 1981. However, with his usual agility, this case was distinguished on the basis that, as the *Sunday Telegraph* had intended to refer to Mr Hayward, they could not escape liability by not giving his name.

If the *Sunday Telegraph* had succeeded in establishing that there had been a substantial misdirection of law, the Court of Appeal would have been bound to send the case back for a retrial. That would have meant a second trial and a doubling of legal costs. As Lord Denning pointed out: 'counsel for the *Sunday Telegraph* said the best he could hope for was a new trial, and – my word – we do not want that'.

If the Court of Appeal had come to the view that the amount awarded by the jury was excessive and unreasonable, it was powerless to alter the award, unless both parties agreed to give the court such power. Again, there would have had to have been a retrial. This would scarcely be just as the jury are not given guidance as to what figure they should award by way of damages. Instead, they have to do the best they can with words such as 'substantial' or 'appropriate' damages and with what they can remember reading about libel awards in their newspapers.

Precisely what did happen to Hayward's two donations of

£10,000 in May 1974 and November 1975 was never made clear, as Thorpe exercised his right not to give evidence at his trial and to remain silent.

Thorpe's defence would have been that as the £20,000 turned out not to have been required for Liberal Party funds, he had lent it to David Holmes. Discussing the case outside court at Minehead he alleged that his trial had been brought about by the malice of Bessell who, he said, had been paid £50,000 by the *Sunday Telegraph*. Thorpe said that the whole case was a put-up job. Penrose and Courtier (the journalists who had set the enquiries in train) had made £160,000 out of spreading these allegations. In fact as journalists they had earned nearer half that sum perfectly legitimately from their writings. However, their invest-igations were expensive to conduct and had led to their leaving their jobs at the BBC. Bessell received a total of £25,000. It was true, however, that he would have received £50,000, if Thorpe had been convicted.

On 3 June 1978 Thorpe handed the police a signed statement in which he gave a rather similar account:

> By reason of other donations it became unnecessary to have recourse of these sums [the two Hayward payments of £10,000]. I therefore made arrangements for the sum of £20,000 to be deposited with accountants and to be held as an iron reserve against any shortage of funds at any subsequent election.

This version of the facts was contradicted by Nadir Dinshaw, the unsuspecting recipient of the money and subsequently a prosecution witness. He had told the police he had paid the two sums to David Holmes, on Thorpe's instructions, one by cheque and the other in cash instalments.

Thorpe's statement to the police was made before there came to light his letter to Hayward dated 19 September 1975 in relation to the second payment of £10,000. That gave a different account:

On the strength of your generous promise, my Jersey friend has actually advanced that sum to pay off the outstanding election expenses and therefore the payment to the accountants will go direct to him.

That was not true. It did, however, cause Hayward to part with his money. Mr Justice O'Connor commented to the jury in the libel action:

Here was a man who was a very eminent politician and a Privy Councillor and none of the ultimate story which came forth had emerged. There was nothing illegal in what was being done. There was no reason why Mr Hayward was not free to send his money to whoever he willed and if Mr Thorpe wanted it paid in Jersey, so be it.

Investigation of these matters in the preparation of the libel action did reveal the secretive manner in which Thorpe administered Hayward's donations of £40,000 in May 1974 and of £9,000 in July 1975.

It emerged that the Liberal Party Organization in July 1978 was totally unaware of the existence of donations totalling £49,000 and, needless to say, of the two other donations of £10,000. This came about because Thorpe asked for the cheque of £40,000 to be made payable to the Liberal Party General Election Fund at Lloyds Bank, Finsbury Circus. There was no such account at Lloyds Bank, Finsbury Circus. The audited Liberal Party General Election Fund account was at Coutts Bank. Thorpe did, however, operate an unaudited account called the 'Direct Aid Committee' account, at Lloyds Bank, Finsbury Circus.

This was an unaudited account which had been opened in September 1973 upon a mandate signed by Thorpe as party leader and countersigned by the then Chief Whip David Steel. Mr Steel was not involved in any way with the running of the account and was unaware that it continued to be operated after 1974. Indeed, when details emerged in 1978 of the continued use of this account, Steel used his powers under the mandate to enable the operation of the account to be investigated. These enquiries showed that the sums of £40,000 and £9,000 had been spent on the political purposes outlined by Thorpe to Hayward.

Thorpe's Direct Aid Committee account at Lloyds bore a very similar name to the account called the Liberal Party Direct Aid Committee Account at the National Westminster Bank in Victoria Street.

When Thorpe received Hayward's £40,000, he paid it into his Direct Aid Committee account at Lloyds. He forthwith paid £5,400 to the Liberal Party Organization in Whitehall Place. Despite the Direct Aid title of the account it went by the somewhat indirect route of being paid into the Liberal Party Direct Aid Committee Account at the National Westminster in Victoria and then being withdrawn on the same day and paid to the Liberal Party Organization. The Liberal Party would therefore have received their money from the National Westminster account, which was also then under Thorpe's sole control, rather than the Lloyds account, into which the funds had originally been paid.

In 1974 the Liberal Party was advised by Deloittes, their accountants, that they should cease to use unaudited accounts. Arrangements for the Liberal Party Direct Aid Committee's finances were therefore altered with effect from 1 January 1975. The account at the National Westminster in Victoria Street, hitherto operated by Thorpe alone, was to have two signatories, the then Treasurer of the Liberal Party and Cyril Smith MP. Thorpe nevertheless continued to operate the second account, the Direct Aid Committee account at Finsbury Circus. The officers of the Liberal Party did not know of this until the summer of 1978.

In July 1975 Hayward contributed a further £9,000 at the request of Thorpe by a cheque made payable to the Liberal Party Direct Aid Committee. It was nevertheless paid by Thorpe into the Lloyds account rather than the National Westminster.

There can have been few libel actions where the movement of such large sums of money had to be traced and unravelled. It was perhaps inevitable that after hearing the figures, the jury awarded a substantial sum.

There are times where the libel is little more than an imagined insult. However, this was a case where a very serious allegation was made by way of an exclusive revelation and was never withdrawn despite the detailed analysis of the facts before the trial. Hayward's circumstances were such that he could maintain an action to clear his reputation in face of the stubborn defence by the newspaper, which was so decisively rejected by the jury and the Court of Appeal. In a field of the law where there is no legal aid, few would have been able to maintain such an action to defend their reputations.

Fifteen

Random Thoughts on the Law of Libel

It is apparent from a number of cases mentioned in this book that the law of libel can be very uncertain in operation, extremely expensive in practice and unduly technical in application.

A distinguished committee including publishers as well as lawyers sat under the chairmanship of a High Court judge, Mr Justice Faulks. It heard a wealth of evidence from those who had come into contact with the law of libel. The committee reported in March 1975 but nothing had been done to implement any of the recommendations. There are, it seems, few votes to be won from legal reform and as a result successive governments have seemed reluctant to find the parliamentary time for such legislation. It is admittedly a specialized area of the law, but it is of great importance to those in the newspaper, television and publishing world who would greatly benefit from a liberalization and simplification of the law.

Very much the same thing happened in 1974 when a committee under Lord Justice Phillimore produced proposals for the reform of the law relating to contempt of court. For some years nothing was done until the government found to its embarrassment that our law of contempt did not meet the standard required by the European Court of Justice. The result was a fairly hastily produced Act of Parliament, the Contempt of Court Act 1981. The committee under Mr Justice Whitford enquiring into the reform of the law of copyright and designs fared little better. It reported in 1977, but it was not until 1981 that the government produced a Green Paper in the form of a consultative document on the proposals. Apart from one or two minor amendments of the law, nothing had been done to implement the Whitford recommendations.

One of the most striking things about the law of libel is the size of awards of damages. A relatively minor libel can result in larger damages than would be awarded for a serious personal injury, even though there is little doubt which is the more permanent. Damages for such personal injuries are fixed by judges and follow an ascertainable scale, where the aim is to try to compensate for the injury actually suffered. In libel law, a jury without any previous experience of libel cases has to pluck a figure out of the air to compensate the plaintiff for the injury to his reputation. Their task is made more difficult by the fact that no one is able to suggest a suitable figure to the jury. If a libel action were brought by a police officer, it would not be permissible for anyone to suggest to the jury that it was, for example, less serious than the case brought by Detective Sergeant Alan Carpenter (£20,000 in 1983) but more grave than that of Chief Superintendent Ronald Day (£10,500 in 1979) (*see* Appendix). Instead the jury are urged to award 'substantial' or 'modest' damages and have to work out what those adjectives mean in cash terms. The jury's task is made no easier by the fact that they are not assessing what the plaintiff has actually lost but what they think would be an appropriate sum to mark the damaging nature of the injury to the plaintiff's reputation.

The system results in libel damages becoming ever larger. The average man sitting on a jury tends only to recollect the more spectacular awards. He may think that the libel he is having to decide is more serious than the one in which, for example, Telly Savalas was awarded £34,000. He is unlikely to know that the award was appealed against and was settled out of court for a lower sum and he certainly will not know what that settlement was, nor will he know whether the original Savalas award was an appropriate sum. He may however feel it is appropriate to award his plaintiff £40,000 and so it will go on.

In a recent case an award of £45,000 to a former undersecretary at the Department of Energy was upheld by the Court of Appeal. While one would not quarrel with the actual decision, it was unfortunate that the court set its face against any policy of altering awards which it believed to be wrong. The court would only do so where the award was one which no twelve reasonable jurors could have awarded if properly directed. Even then it can only amend the amount of damages if both parties agree to allow the court to do so. If they do not agree, there has to be a retrial on the issue of damages.

A very simple way of keeping libel damages within bounds would be for the trial judge to be able to suggest to the jury a range of damages which would be appropriate according to the view they took of the facts. Thus, if they were to decide that a particular statement suggested that the plaintiff was a sharp and not altogether trustworthy businessman, the judge might suggest that on the particular facts an award in the range of £5,000 to £10,000 might be appropriate; whereas, if they thought the words meant that he was thoroughly dishonest and deserved to be prosecuted, the range might be £15,000 to £20,000. This would provide a greater degree of consistency, while leaving the jury to make the appropriate findings of fact. It would also make it easier to see what the jury decided and, if need be, for the Court of Appeal to adjust the libel damages if the trial judge's original figures were too high or too low. It would also go some way to removing the appalling consequence of most successful libel appeals that the Court of Appeal is compelled to order a retrial, so that the parties are back at square one after spending tens of thousands of pounds at the original trial and on the appeal.

The injustice that this can cause can be illustrated by the case Dr J P R Williams, the former Welsh International rugby fullback, brought against the *Daily Telegraph*. In 1979 the *Daily Telegraph* published two articles suggesting that Williams, by then an orthopaedic surgeon, had infringed his amateur status by accepting money for his autobiography. The £25,000 he obtained from the book was used to set up a sports clinic in his home town of Bridgend. Somewhat surprisingly the issue between Williams and the

Daily Telegraph was whether he had intended all along to give this money to charity or whether he only decided to do so after the *Daily Telegraph* articles were published. The jury accepted J P R Williams's account and awarded him £20,000, slightly less than the £25,000 he had given away.

However, eighteen months later this award was set aside, as the Court of Appeal held that the trial judge had misdirected the jury on the interpretations of the rules as to amateur status in rugby. The unfortunate consequence of this had been that the trial judge had poured 'something like scorn' on the *Daily Telegraph*'s interpretation of the rules of amateur status, which was that the player was professionalized if he signed a contract under which money was payable to him, whatever his ultimate intentions might have been.

Justice had not been done to the newspaper's defence, but equally it was arguable that, had the jury been properly directed, they would still have come down in Williams's favour. As it was, Williams was unwilling to incur the expense of a further trial. He lost his damages and was left with a bill of £30,000 legal costs and the newspaper with one of £50,000. It was a result that can scarcely have pleased anyone. The newspaper had wanted to introduce some new evidence against Williams regarding some alleged payments of boot money, but this was not upheld by the Court of Appeal.

While it is unwise to place too much emphasis on one particular case, it would appear that injustice could be lessened by giving the Court of Appeal a wider power to alter the amount of damages and to impose its decision on the parties. That might have been difficult on the particular facts of the Williams case, but it may not have been impossible, as the Court of Appeal had listened to the case for six and a half days as opposed to the four days which the trial took. It would no doubt have been somewhat arbitrary to order a reduced sum of damages, taking account of each party's chances of success, but it would in most cases seem preferable.

If a retrial has to be ordered for reasons that are not the

fault of either party, such as in a recent case (Llewellyn v Rendall *see* Appendix) where a juror was discovered in the course of the trial to be of doubtful mental health, thus invalidating the verdict in favour of the plaintiff, it would seem only just to allow the parties to have their costs paid out of central government funds, as can happen in criminal cases.

Legal aid is not available in libel cases, and contingency litigation is illegal in this country. (In the United States lawyers operate on a 'no foal, no fee' system, by which they only receive a fee if the action is successful – when normally they would receive about 25 per cent of the damages.) The result is that libel actions are very much the preserve of the wealthy. Any reduction in the potential expense of a retrial would go some small way to reducing the disadvantage faced by the less well off party to the litigation.

Leaving aside the question of the expense of libel litigation, the law is at present unfairly weighted in favour of a plaintiff. He will know that resisting and disproving his claim will place a considerable burden on the defendant and that the cost of the litigation and the risk of an enormous award of damages will make an early settlement of his case an attractive course for the defendant. There are two particular aspects of the law that operate unfairly against defendants. The first is that a plaintiff can demand the withdrawal of a book without making any corresponding proposal to pay the costs of this expensive process, should his claim for libel ultimately fail. It is normal practice to require a defendant who in other types of litigation obtains an injunction before the trial of the action to give an undertaking that he will pay the damages occasioned by the grant of the injunction, should his action prove to be unsuccessful. It would seem only just that a plaintiff who weighs in with a demand that a book be withdrawn, should likewise be called upon to pay the costs of this being done and compensate the author for any loss of sales, if the court ultimately decides that the book did not contain a libel. The second disadvantage a defendant may face is that, even if he successfully defeats the plaintiff's action, he may be substantially out of pocket. The plaintiff can compel the defendant to 'tax his costs', that is to say to have them scrutinized by a court official who is unlikely to allow the defendant to recover more than seventyfive per cent of his costs from the plaintiff and quite possibly much less. The defendant would still have to pay the balance to his lawyers.

Another vexed question is whether it is right to permit the dead to be libelled. Certainly it seemed very harsh in the case of *Webb v Holder* (*see* chapter 1) that the case should come to an abrupt halt and proceed no further, when the plaintiff collapsed and died after he had given his evidence. In such a case, each side would have to bear their own legal costs irrespective of the merits. There seems to be a case for letting such actions continue, if they were started before one of the parties died. No doubt they would almost invariably be settled, but probably on more just terms than under the present arrangement.

Bringing libel actions on behalf of those who are already dead is a difficult matter. The besmirching of a person's reputation after they have died is obviously distressing for his relatives. However, allowing libel actions to be brought by the dead man's family seems highly undesirable. Without the deceased's testimony but with the emotion of the distress caused to the relatives, it is doubtful whether the right result would necessarily be obtained. The present law is very protective of reputation and there seems no very good reason for continuing that protection beyond the grave other than delicacy or taste. While some questioned the taste of the attack by Bernard Levin on the former Lord Chief Justice Lord Goddard immediately after his death and in terms which *The Times* would no doubt have been unwilling to print during his lifetime, it must surely be preferable to allow uninhibited comment on a man's life and to enable obituaries to be written free of the fear of libel. It has been suggested that there should be a period of, say, five years during which close relatives could bring libel actions on behalf of the deceased, but that seems a most unsatisfactory line to draw.

It may be unedifying to see pencils being sharpened to

write after a person's death what could not be written in his lifetime, and it may be quesionable whether the *Mail On Sunday* should, as was done under the unambiguous headline 'Did this man get away with mass murder?', virtually republish the libel for which its sister newspaper, the *Daily Mail* had paid £50,000 damages, the moment Dr Bodkin Adams had died and it was safe to do so, (*see* chapter 1). However, this may in some measure be due to the restraints imposed by the law of libel and the very occasional dancing on someone's grave seems preferable to further restraints on the press. Practically the only thing that deceased relatives can do in such circumstances is to complain to the Press Council, although in the Bodkin Adams case the Press Council ruled that there was an overriding public interest in the case which justified the publication.

Certainly the time has come to review the workings of the law of libel and to implement many of the recommendations made by the Faulks committee. There seems little purpose in preserving the technical distinctions between libel and slander. As has been seen in chapter 9 the defence of unintentional defamation has proved far too cumbersome. There are a number of other rules of evidence in the law of libel which could be changed. Without embarking on what is a highly technical subject, it is for instance very difficult for a defendant to establish that the plaintiff has a bad reputation. The defendant is not allowed to call evidence of other acts of misconduct. He has instead to produce witnesses who merely say that they know the plaintiff is a man of bad general reputation.

At present there are a number of highly technical and complex cases which go for trial by jury which could more easily and less expensively be heard by a judge alone. If one party feels that there is some tactical advantage in seeking trial by jury, it will only be very rarely that the court can order trial by judge alone. An extension of the court's powers in suitable cases which do not involve personal liberty or honour would result in speedier, less costly and more predictable justice.

There are a number of areas where the balance of the law of libel should be shifted in favour of the press. One is in the area of qualified privilege (*see* chapter 1), where the categories of case to which the defence applies need revision. In the thirty years since the Defamation Act 1952 was passed, we have joined the Common Market. It would seem desirable to amend the categories so as to ensure that the press is suitably protected when reporting controversial matters relating to the European Economic Community.

Secondly, there should also be a shift in favour of the media by permitting a defence of fair information on a matter of public interest. At present local newspapers, for example, run a considerable risk in ventilating some matters of local controversy if the information they are given and publish in good faith turns out to be inaccurate. Under the law at present they might be at some risk in publishing a story about local residents' complaints about a company disposing of toxic chemicals in the district, as the company probably can afford skilled libel lawyers and the local residents, with the best will in the world, may have got some of their facts wrong. However, unquestionably it would be a matter of considerable public interest and it seems wrong that the newspaper has to gamble on whether all the facts are right.

In 1960 it looked as if the English courts might allow a defence of fair information on a matter of public interest. This arose in a case brought by a Mrs Cynthia Webb against *The Times*. She had been married to, but had divorced Donald Hume, who had been convicted of being an accessory after the fact to the murder of Stanley Setty whose dismembered body had been thrown out of an aeroplane onto an Essex marsh. This earned Hume a twelve-year prison sentence rather than the death penalty he would have received if he had been convicted of Setty's murder. He subsequently boasted in a newspaper that he had in fact murdered him.

After serving his sentence, Hume was again arrested and was put on trial on charges of murder, attempted murder and armed robbery in Switzerland. He was also wanted by the English police on charges of attempted murder and armed robbery. In those circumstances *The Times* felt it right to report his trial as being of considerable interest to its readers.

In the course of his trial in Switzerland Hume admitted he had killed Setty in 1950 out of jealousy, going on to say that Setty was the father of his child. This was false and was no doubt offered as an excuse for Hume having despatched Setty. However, *The Times* had no means of forming a judgment on these matters, which had taken place over ten years ago. Furthermore it seemed only fair that, at the risk of causing distress to innocent parties, the newspaper should be entitled to publish a report of these foreign court proceedings. The report was particularly unfortunate in that not only did it raise an issue of paternity, but it carried the implication that Mrs Webb's evidence at the Central Criminal Court in 1959 that she had never met Setty in her life was less than truthful. *The Times* immediately published a denial by Mrs Webb that there was any truth whatsoever in the allegation by Hume.

The question was whether Mrs Webb should receive damages for these undoubtedly false statements or whether the newspaper's right to publish fair reports of foreign proceedings should be upheld. Such a report would be protected by privilege if it had concerned an English court, but this privilege did not extend to reports of proceedings in foreign courts. The judge, Mr Justice Pearson, came down in favour of the newspaper, saying that qualified privilege could attach to fair information on a matter of public interest. Unhappily for the press, this principle was not followed in the recent case of *Blackshaw v Lord*, the facts of which follow in the Appendix.

The courts are reluctant to amend the law of libel and understandably feel that this is a matter for Parliament.

Appendix

Selected Recent Libel Awards

There follows a selection of significant libel awards in the last decade. Only brief details can be given for reasons of space and it should be noted that in each case the words complained of were found to be defamatory. A number of the larger awards were in fact settled for an undisclosed sum prior to an appeal. (Source of information in brackets in column two.) I am grateful to Mr Peter Carter-Ruck author of *Libel and Slander* for the lay-out.

'I'll drink to Private Eye's 500th issue –
I'm a libel lawyer...'

Name of Case	Date	Nature of Publication
Pulley v Odhams Newspapers	29 April 1972 (*Times*)	Sunday newspaper
Prchal v Hochhuth	4 May 1972 (*Times*)	play, book and foreign newspaper
Hardwick v Beaverbrook Newspapers	21 December 1972 (*Times*)	national daily newspaper
Floris v BBC	23 October 1973 (*Times*)	television current affairs broadcast
Ingham Engineering Ltd v Linkhouse Publications Ltd	5 February 1974 (*Times*)	specialist car magazine
Brooks v IPC Newspapers Ltd	6 November 1974 (*Times*)	Sunday newspaper
Clift v IPC Newspapers Ltd	5 February 1975 (*Times*)	magazine

Details of Libel	Award
An article entitled 'The Good Policeman Pulley' suggested that the police constable's transfer would ease racial tension in the Notting Hill area	£5,000
Hochhuth alleged in his play and book entitled *Soldiers* and in a German Sunday newspaper that Prchal had deliberately crashed an aeroplane in 1943 to kill the Polish prime minister. Case proceeded in Hochhuth's absence	£50,000 (divided £5,000, £25,000 and £20,000 respectively)
Allegations that a headmaster had banned a six year old girl from the Christmas party for wearing a trouser suit with suggestion that he was an unreasonable and unfeeling man	£1,000
Allegations regarding health hazards at a bakery called Floris Gruhn previously owned by the House of Floris which held a warrant from the Queen as bakers and confectioners. Floris Gruhn twice referred to in programme as Floris	£10,000 to Christopher Floris and £5,000 to the House of Floris
The company specializing in the tuning and conversion of Renault cars was described as 'a fairly unspeakable bunch of grease monkeys'. It was suggested that readers should take their custom elsewhere	£5,000
Article suggesting that a solicitor was 'a menace to young girls'	½p
An article about Christmas thieving at Smithfield was illustrated by the plaintiff engaged in the innocent activity of a meat-carrying race during Smithfield Centenary celebrations	£1,500

Name of Case	Date	Nature of Publication
Shulman *v* Gaventa	5 March 1975 (*Times*)	report to Tattersalls
Bernstein *v* The Observer Ltd	24 April 1975 (*Times*)	Sunday newspaper business section
Millward *v* Hamilton	12 February 1976 (*Times*)	book
Scargill *v* Sheffield Newspapers Ltd	25 March 1976 (*Times*)	provincial newspaper
Savalas *v* Associated Newspapers Ltd	16 June 1976 (*Times*)	national newspaper
Wigg *v* Ingrams	17 June 1976 (*Times*)	article in *Private Eye*

Details of Libel	Award
False allegations by bookmaker and complaint to Tattersalls regarding the payment of a betting debt by the theatre critic punter	£1,200
Suggestion that the chairman of Granada television and leisure group was involved in what the article termed 'The £25 million Barranquilla scandal'. Barranquilla was a subsidiary of Granada	£35,000 upheld by the Court of Appeal as 'not too high'
Member of Parliament in his book *My Queen and I* suggested that a tutor to the Prince of Wales was associated with a political party which he alleged supported terrorist activities	£1,000
Allegation that the Yorkshire miners' leader had, during the 1974 miners' strike, shown favouritism to a group of miners in the Barnsley area by allocating them the plum picketing jobs in East Anglia	£3,000
Allegations that the actors' wild nightlife on location in Berlin caused him to forget his lines and keep his co-star waiting	£34,000, but settled at a lower undisclosed figure prior to an appeal
Allegation that a former chairman of the Horserace Betting Levy Board had intervened in a stable lads' dispute to enable the Derby to be run at the behest of bookmakers	£5,000 (a further award of £2,500 was made on 1 February '78 against Nigel Dempster for remarks on the BBC that the original settlement was without his knowledge or consent)

Name of Case	Date	Nature of Publication
Herbert v BBC	30 November 1976 (*Times*)	current affairs television programme
Jenkins v Foot	25 February 1977 (*Times*)	limited circulation newspaper
Bloom v Stephens	11 March 1977 (*Times*)	article in Sunday newspaper
Cosmos Air Holidays v BBC	23 March 1977 (*Times*)	television holiday programme
Mullett v Odhams Newspapers	20 December 1977 (*Times*)	Sunday newspaper

Details of Libel	Award
Allegations that an Abergavenny landowner, magistrate and member of the Executive Committee of the National Trust was an inhumane landlord who harassed his tenants	£30,000
General secretary of a trade union was satirized in a left-wing publication, the *Socialist Worker*, for the union's proposals to provide cheap holidays for their members in Spain in an article entitled 'Spain? Fly me, I'm Clive.' The article implied that the plaintiff condoned political oppression under the Franco régime and was prepared to take ghoulish pleasure in visiting jails and watching garrotting	£1,000 to Mr Jenkins and £100 to the union (plus £1,000 each for breach of copyright regarding the use of facsimiles of Mr Jenkins's signature and the union emblem)
Article criticizing an elderly doctor for signing a certificate for a therapeutic abortion	½p
Criticism of facilities offered in hotels used by a holiday tours firm – accompanied by the theme music of the 'Colditz' television series	'Several thousands of pounds'. (Settled out of court)
Allegations in the *Sunday People* against a detective sergeant (who was promoted in the course of the trial to detective inspector) under the headline 'Caught a Crooked Cop'. The officer was not named but was easily identifiable. Virtually 'a trial alleging corruption.'	£20,000

Name of Case	Date	Nature of Publication
Obote *v* Listowel	23 February 1978 (*Times*) and 21 July 1979 (*Daily Telegraph*)	book
Chapple *v* S W Litho Ltd	2 March 1978 (*Times*)	pamphlet
Jewish Telegraph Ltd *v* Jewish Gazette Ltd	23 September 1978 (*Times*)	limited circulation newspaper
Russell *v* Bank of America National Trust & Savings Ass.	21 October 1978 (*Times*)	endorsement on cheques

Details of Libel	Award
Allegations made in a book of corruption and abuse of power against the then deposed President of Uganda and his former Planning Minister and his former general service officer. The Planning Minister did not attend the trial	£40,000, £8,500 and £17,500. An appeal was settled on the basis of not enforcing the awards in excess of the modest sums paid into court, although this agreement was not to imply that the substantial sums were unjustified
Allegations in a left-wing publication that the general secretary of a trade union had pursued policies contrary to union members' interests and had gagged criticism within the union. The pamphlet was published when he was standing for re-election. By the time of the trial the publishers were in voluntary liquidation and took no part in the proceedings and damages were assessed by the judge.	£22,500
False allegation in a rival newspaper that the paper had declined to publish a photograph of a winning soccer team in a competition it had sponsored because it contained seven non-Jewish boys, with a suggestion that it may have breached the Race Relations Act	£1,000 and £5 each for three of its directors
On four cheques presented by the plaintiff the bank wrote 'account closed', whereas the account had been transferred from London to its Jersey bank	£50,000

Name of Case	Date	Nature of Publication
Coxall v Miller	10 November 1978 (*Times*)	letter
Davey v BBC	20 June 1979 (*Daily Telegraph*)	BBC television programme
Hyams v Associated Newspapers Ltd	20 June 1979 (*Daily Telegraph*)	gossip column of national newspaper
Day v United Newspapers Ltd	6 October 1979 (*Daily Telegraph*)	provincial daily newspaper
Graham v Crampton	6 October 1979 (*Daily Telegraph*)	letter
Lawford & Co v Leveller Magazine Ltd	24 November 1979 (*Times*)	limited circulation magazine
Horobin v Daily Telegraph Ltd	17 December 1979 (*UK Press Gazette*)	national newspaper

Details of Libel	*Award*
Letter to the editor of *Dog World* which was published naming her and to the *Sunday People* which published an article not naming her, falsely accusing her of dyeing her champion apricot poodle at Crufts. The claim was not contested	£4,000
False allegation in course of documentary on a police informer that plaintiff had conspired with criminals to stage a bogus burglary and defraud the insurance company of £10,000	£15,000
False suggestion that the yacht *Shemara* had been impounded because of unpaid repair bill	£5,000
Newspaper reported allegation of lying by chief superintendent in relation to enquiry into allegations of misconduct by a chief constable	£10,500
Police officer accused by motorist of harassing and hounding him over driving offences	£100
Allegation in left-wing magazine that a firm of solicitors, specializing in trade union matters, had improperly supported a faction within a client trade union and had disloyally backed an employers' pressure group	£5,000
Allegation that a chief superintendent had been transferred from CID to uniformed duties because of his handling of the kidnapping and murder of four hostages, whereas he had previously applied for such a transfer	£4,000

Name of Case	Date	Nature of Publication
Stern v Beauprez	6 February 1980 (*Times*)	letter
Dempster v BBC	21 March 1980 (*Times*)	radio chat show
Angel v More	7 May 1980 (*Times*)	book and Sunday newspaper
Samuels v *West Indian World*	8 May 1980 (*Daily Telegraph*)	weekly newspaper
Ronay v Bernstein	25 June 1980 (*Times*)	slander

Details of Libel	*Award*
Letter by an accountant alleging that plaintiff, who was described as 'the world's biggest bankrupt', was trying to buy back assets of liquidated companies at artificially low prices in a secretive and underhand way	£2,000
Offensive jibes by a journalist employed by the *National Enquirer* about well-known gossip columnist. 'There is a lot of dirt about Nigel we could tell'	Substantial damages described by Mr Dempster as 'Four figures – less than a Ferrari but more than a Mini'. Settled out of court.
Allegations in an actor's autobiography serialized in a Sunday newspaper about the producer of his film, *Reach for the Sky*, and the question whether he influenced Kenneth More's prospects of being offered part in the film, *Guns of Navarone*	£200 for book and £100 for newspaper article
Jocular article about pasties – 'Charlie's Tasties – Look before you bite – it could be Rover from next door – there has been a noticeable lack of strays.' Identifiable café owner sued. Defence that this was a harmless joke	£2,125
Comments by Chairman of Granada Motorway Services Ltd, regarding critical comments made by Egon Ronay in 1978 guide concerning meals served at Granada operated motorway service areas. Ronay's competence as a caterer questioned	£5,000 (damages given to Hotel and Catering Benevolent Association)

Name of Case	Date	Nature of Publication
Pond v Newsgroup Newspapers Ltd	12 July 1980 (*Times*) and 9 December 1982 (*Guardian*)	Sunday newspaper
MacGibbon v Squires	17 February 1981 (*Times*) and 19 May 1982 (*Times*)	slander
Blackshaw v Lord	26 February 1981 (*Daily Telegraph*) and 21 February 1983 (*Times*)	national newspaper
MacGibbon v Dempster	6 May 1981 (*Times*)	national daily newspaper
Squires v Newsgroup Newspapers Ltd	27 June 1981 (*Times*)	national Sunday newspaper

Details of Libel	*Award*
Pregnancy testing business collapsed after a *News of the World* article on abortion, falsely alleging that the plaintiff advised a reporter who was not pregnant to have an abortion. He obtained a further £22,000 damages of which £15,000 were exemplary damages for allegation in a book (entitled *Babies for Burning*) that he was an abortionist's tout	£40,000
False allegation in the singer's autobiography that a highly reputable publisher had spent 2 years in jail. Injunction granted against her. This followed case on 30 January 1981 where Dorothy Squires had unsuccessfully alleged that a letter written to Harold Robbins by MacGibbon implicated her in a payola scandal	£10,000 upheld on appeal
False suggestion that former undersecretary in charge of offshore supplies office of Department of Energy was responsible for grants which resulted in loss of £52 million to the Exchequer and that he had been compelled to resign. In fact, not responsible and had voluntarily resigned to become business consultant and author. Newspaper report based on erroneous information given at a press conference	£45,000 – upheld on appeal. Court would not interfere with such awards unless sum was one which no twelve reasonable jurors could have awarded if properly directed
Allegation in gossip column that the managing director of a publishing company had wrongfully withheld money from Dorothy Squires	£15,000 upheld on appeal
False allegation in *News of the World* that the singer had been involved in a payola record plugging scandal and had bribed the producer of a BBC radio record request programme	£30,000

Name of Case	Date	Nature of Publication
Elahi v *Daily Millat*	27 June 1981 (*Times*)	limited circulation newspaper
Chaim Schreiber v Thames Television Ltd	1 July 1981 (*Times*)	television current affairs programme
Longmores v BBC	22 December 1981 (*Times*)	radio plays
Bremner v Odhams Newspapers Ltd	4 February 1982 (*Times*)	Sunday newspaper
Ward v *Time Out*	12 February 1982 (*Daily Telegraph*)	weekly magazine
Watson v *Yachting World*	18 February 1982 (*Times*)	specialist interest magazine

Details of Libel	Award
Former Pakistan Minister of Labour accused in the London-published Urdu newspaper *Daily Millat* of forging work permits for immigrants in Switzerland. Libel admitted	£25,000
Head of Schreiber Furniture and Hotpoint alleged to have contravened Resale Price Maintenance Act by threatening to withhold Hotpoint appliances from discount warehouse company unless it agreed to sell them at manufacturer's minimum price	Schreiber £5,000 Hotpoint £500
Two plays involving fictitious firm of solicitors, Longmore Page & Longmore ('not the kind of firm people would wish to entrust their business to'). Accidental association in minds of listeners with reputable and well-established firm of Longmores, although no particular partner identified. No such link intended, but BBC criticized for failing to take action after complaint following first broadcast	£8,000 Appeal settled out of court
Allegations against a footballer that he had offered bribes to other players to 'fix' results of matches	£100,000
Allegation against director of film processing firm that company paid appalling wages and treated workers badly	£1,250 to him £1,000 to company
Picture of dentist mending his outboard motor on a French quayside with a caption headed 'Marina Thief'. Magazine claimed it was all a harmless joke	½p

Name of Case	Date	Nature of Publication
Rhoden v Noor	19 February 1982 (*Daily Telegraph*)	letters
Douglas-Home v Ashmore	20 February 1982 (*Times*)	letter
Williams v Daily Telegraph Ltd	26 February 1982 (*Daily Telegraph*)	national daily newspaper

Details of Libel	*Award*
Allegations by community worker against headmaster in letters to Secretary of State for Education and Prime Minister of India accusing him of being a racist and second allegation in letter to Lord Chancellor that he was unfit to be a magistrate	£3,500 and £1,500
Award on counterclaim for libel in copyright action unsuccessfully brought against playwright. Allegation of plagiarism in letter to producer of Douglas-Home's play, *The Kingfisher*	£100
Two articles suggesting well-known Welsh rugby international fullback and an honorary surgeon to Welsh team had infringed his amateur status by accepting money for his autobiography and was guilty of 'shamateurism'. In fact the £25,000 he received from the book was used to set up a sports clinic in Bridgend	£20,000 This award was set aside and a retrial ordered by the Court of Appeal owing to a misdirection of law by trial judge. The case was not then proceeded with by Dr Williams. It cost him £30,000 in legal fees and the newspaper £50,000

Name of Case	Date	Nature of Publication
Rendall v Llewellyn	12 March 1982 (*Daily Telegraph*)	letters to newspaper
Jeffrey v Associated Newspapers Ltd	16 March 1982 (*Daily Mail*)	national daily newspaper

Details of Libel	*Award*
Allegation by Dai Llewellyn, brother of one of Abergavenny's better-known gardeners, night club entrepreneur and greeter, that a rival social entrepreneur, Liz Brewer, was 'a plain and simple hustler' and unprofessional and incompetent at her job	£13,000 This award was set aside owing to a procedural mishap during the trial when one of the jurors went to the Court of Protection which, owing to her mental state of health, was administering her affairs, to ask for her expenses as a juror. This raised questions as to her suitability to serve on the jury and she was discharged. The defendant appealed on this procedural point and the verdict was, by consent, set aside. The retrial was settled out of court on undisclosed terms with all allegations against the plaintiff being withdrawn
Article in gossip column suggesting that he could not afford a house he was buying and that the locals did not want him	£25 A larger offer in settlement had been rejected and the plaintiff reputedly had to pay costs of the order of £10,000

Name of Case	Date	Nature of Publication
Wilcox v Ingrams	7 May 1982 (*Times*)	*Private Eye*
Dickinson v Webster Publications Ltd	20 July 1982 (*Times*)	racing weekly newspaper
Hain v Webster	20 November 1982 (*Times*)	magazine
Eaton v Horsley	11 February 1983 (*Times*)	letters

Details of Libel	*Award*
Allegation that he misused position as head of BBC General Features to put himself forward as writer of book based on BBC 2 series. In fact, reluctantly persuaded to put his name forward. Damages reduced because some allegations of breach of copyright found proved. Costs estimated at £80,000. (He and his wife Esther Rantzen recovered undisclosed damages on 30 June 1983 for suggestions that they received favourable terms for the purchase of a Rover motor car in return for favourable treatment of British Leyland in the 'That's Life' programme)	£14,000
Allegation in *Racing Specialist* against former National Hunt jockey and then trainer that he had sat virtually motionless on horse in race at Catterick in 1977	£7,500 Appeal settled out of court
Allegation against a Labour supporter by an official of the National Front in the National Front magazine that he supported violence and brutality	£5
Letters sent by a college art teacher to his college head with copies to six other members of staff and to plaintiff's solicitors accusing the plaintiff, a gym mistress and his former mistress at the same school, of blackmail and sexual harassment	£12,000, but the defendant declared himself bankrupt after paying £2,000

Name of Case	Date	Nature of Publication
Callaghan *v* Express Newspapers Ltd	15 March 1983 (*Times*)	national daily newspaper
Mason *v* William Hill Ltd	17 March 1983 (*Times*)	slander
Dryden-Brownlee and Pearson *v* Thames Valley Newspapers	19 March 1983 (*Daily Telegraph*)	provincial evening paper

Name of Case	Date	Nature of Publication

Allegation in 1980 in two gossip column articles that the plaintiff, a well-known racehorse trainer, had back in 1975 remained seated during the Royal toast and said 'Stuff the Queen' and 'Up the IRA'. The article had caused the plaintiff to receive a number of anonymous threatening letters. Defendants' witnesses rejected by the judge as 'almost incoherent', 'deaf', recollections at fault', 'medical and drink problem' and 'unimpressive'. The plaintiff denied doing anything other than drinking the Royal toast		£15,000 £12,000 for first article, £3,000 for second)
Fleet Street landlord accused of altering bet by changing an X to a 2 so as to increase his winnings from £468 to £3,150. Acts complained of were: 1 slander by action, viz being frog-marched out of betting office by William Hill security men; 2 an incident in the betting office where security men said in hearing of others 'This bet has been altered'; 3 outside the shop plaintiff accused of placing a crooked bet; 4 crooked bet allegation repeated in bookmaker's head office. Allegations caused well-known personalities to snub him and boycott his pub and he had to buy his own drinks at El Vino's		£44,000 divided for the incidents complained of 1 £30,000 2 £10,000 3 £3,000 4 £1,000 Appeal subsequently settled out of court
Former council architect and the clerk of works accused of malpractice regarding the building of civic offices at Basingstoke		£28,000 (architect) and £12,500 (clerk of works)

Name of Case	Date	Nature of Publication
Cartland *v* BBC	4 May 1983 (*Times*)	television documentary
Carpenter *v* Granada Television Ltd	15 June 1983 (*Guardian*)	television documentary
Boden *v* Long	15 October 1983 (*Sun*)	letter
Pamplin *v* Express Newspapers Ltd	18 October 1983 (*Times*)	national Sunday newspaper

Details of Libel	*Award*
In their 'Escape' series, which had also dealt with Lucan and Kim Philby, the BBC produced a dramatized documentary about the murder of the plaintiff's father in France in 1973. Although the BBC accepted Cartland was entirely innocent, the jury found that the programme raised a question mark over his innocence. Never shown script as promised	£50,000
'World in Action' programme investigated the results of Operation Countryman. The plaintiff was a plainclothes police officer attached to the Clubs Office at West End Central police station. As the commentator said 'Since 1969 repeated investigations have shown some CID men take bribes'. In a 2½-second film clip the plaintiff was shown emerging from the police station. Not otherwise identified in programme and no suggestion that he was guilty of such conduct. However, programme led to an internal police investigation and damaging remarks from colleagues	£20,000
Allegation by her workmate Joyce Long, who accused the plaintiff, Joan Boden, of touching her in a disgusting manner by giving her a New Year peck on the cheek	£500
Legal executive who had sought to avoid parking tickets by registering his car in his small son's name had been called 'a slippery unscrupulous spiv'. £5 offer of settlement made by newspaper rejected	½p At the first trial a jury awarded £12,000. This was set aside by the Court of Appeal, Mr Pamplin had to pay most of second trial costs, all the first trial costs and the appeal costs

Name of Case	Date	Nature of Publication
Weinstock *v* IPC Magazines	20 October 1983 (*Daily Mail*)	magazine
Riches *v* News-group Newspapers Ltd	10 February 1984 (*Daily Telegraph*)	Sunday newspaper

Details of Libel	*Award*
Managing director of GEC accused in an article in *New Scientist* of wrongfully seeking to influence the government against improving the status of engineers	£40,000
Claim in July 1978 by all the male members of the Banbury CID against the *News of the World* for their front page story headlined 'Siege Man tells us why he did it' and marked 'exclusive'. The article was published during a five and a half day siege by a gunman called David Brain who was holding hostages in the village of North Aston. He had made a number of lurid allegations against the police that they had raped and beaten his wife and threatened his five-year-old son to keep his wife quiet. The newspaper's defence was that readers would realize that these allegations were the product of a deranged mind and in fact Brain was subsequently sent to Broadmoor following his conviction. They also said that by publishing the allegation they had helped end the siege without any loss of life. The article had not named the police officers and the newspaper denied that the letter referred to the plaintiffs. The police officers saw it rather differently and accused the paper of publishing juicy and scandalous allegations, which they knew were untrue	£300 compensatory damages and £25,000 exemplary damages for each officer from Chief Inspector to Constable making £25,300 each and a total of £253,000. On appeal the award of exemplary damages was set aside and a new trial ordered on the amount of exemplary damages

Name of Case	Date	Nature of Publication
Sasse and Turnball v Daily Telegraph Ltd	13 March 1984 (*Standard*)	national daily newspaper
Entwistle v Channel 4	11 April 1984 (*Times*)	television programme
Gooch v Newsgroup Newspapers Ltd	11 July 1984 (*Daily Telegraph*)	national newspaper
Steinberg v Selfridges	15 November 1984 (*Standard*)	slander
Pitts v Millivres Ltd	7 February 1985 (*Times*)	gay magazine

Details of Libel	Award
Allegation in City Page article entitled 'Underwriters Suspended in Lloyds Purge', following losses of £14,000,000 by the Sasse syndicate, that 'three underwriters connected with the Sasse syndicate' were facing 'criminal proceedings'. The two plaintiffs were not named, but were clearly identifiable. In fact the losses of the syndicate had been investigated and no charges were ever brought	£37,500 to Mr Sasse and £32,500 to Mr Turnball
Popstar's wife called 'a dog' on television programme, a remark which her counsel observed implied she was a 'contemptible and repulsive woman of loose morals'. Her husband had apologized profusely and asked for the remark to be cut. She did not sue him for libel but she did file for divorce	Undisclosed but in four figures
English test cricketer banned from playing for his country for three years after going on a rebel tour of South Africa was accused in the *Sun* of being too busy helping the Springboks to worry about England's humiliation in Australia	£25,000
Racehorse owner and breeder falsely accused of shoplifting (but not charged) and contents of her handbag searched in the street by a department store. Incident lasted five minutes	£1,500
Article in the magazine *Mister* accompanied by the plaintiff's photograph described the love affairs of 'Jeremy Spits' omitting to point out that they were with women	£11,000

Name of Case	Date	Nature of Publication
White v Scott	22 February 1985 (*Times*)	press release
Gee v BBC	24 April 1985 (*Times*)	current affairs television programme
Nkoana v Penguin Books	7 May 1985 (*Times*)	book
Peters v The Observer Ltd	24 July 1985 (*Daily Telegraph*)	Sunday newspaper

Details of libel	*Award*
Former headmistress falsely accused of caning children in her Clacton-on-Sea infants' school by education secretary of anti-caning campaign. Press release said to make her resemble Wackford Squeers in *Nicholas Nickleby*	£6,000
Harley Street doctor who specialised in slimming treatment was falsely made out by *That's Life* to be a 'profiteering unscrupulous quack' who was unfit to remain in practice after allegedly prescribing drugs that nearly killed a patient	Case settled after 87 day trial with BBC paying agreed damages of £75,000. Costs were estimated to be £1,000,000. Subsequently the two doctors who had made the allegations against Dr Gee paid a further £15,004 and £10,003 damages respectively. His total damages of £100,007 is the largest publicly announced award to date
South African political exile wrongly accused in a book by a South African spy called *Inside Boss* of spying for BOSS (the South African Bureau of State Security) and of supplying them with information that led to the execution of a man who was executed for placing a bomb in a railway station	£12,000 (as a greater sum had been paid into court, he did not recover all his legal costs)
Detective Superintendent in the Flying Squad falsely accused of corruption in relation to investigations of a £3,000,000 silver bullion robbery	£10,000

Name of Case	Date	Nature of Publication
Roberts v Pressdram Ltd	7 August 1985 (*Times*)	*Private Eye*
Tomalin v Waugh	11 September 1985 (*Standard*)	*Private Eye*
Hart v Scripglow Ltd	14 November 1985 (*Times*)	video film
Cornwell v Odhams Newspapers Ltd	19 November 1985 (*Times*)	Sunday newspaper

Details of Libel	*Award*
Solicitor falsely accused of involvement in a fraud relating to Bob Hope British Golf Classic tournament which it was alleged consisted of trying to bury the failure of the tournament without any official investigation. The journalist Jack Lundin making the allegations did not attend the trial to substantiate these allegations	£20,000 After a 25 day trial *Private Eye* was ordered to pay Mr Roberts costs on a higher scale than normal because of its conduct of the case
Article written by Auberon Waugh falsely accusing the *Sunday Times* literary editor Claire Tomalin of lesbian sympathies after Waugh received a spoof invitation to review an anthology of 'recent gay and lesbian fiction' which added for good measure that Waugh was the right man for the job and could be relied upon for a sympathetic review	Case settled on payment of £2,500 damages plus costs
Unauthorised use of a clip from actress' appearance in *Games That Lovers Play* in what was described as a pornographic video clip called *Electric Blue 002* depicting the plaintiff as looking through a two-way mirror as her daughter in the film cavorts in bed with her lover	£15,000
The television critic of the *Sunday People*, in reviewing the Plaintiff's performance in the series *No Excuses*, referred to her as 'an ugly middle-aged rock star whose bum is too big'	£10,000 (comfortably beating the £5 paid into court)

Name of Case	Date	Nature of Publication
Howe v Times Newspapers Ltd	28 November 1985 (*Daily Telegraph*)	Sunday newspaper and magazine
Halil v Guardian Newspapers Ltd	26 February 1986	national newspaper
Bennett v Pressdram Ltd	4 March 1986 (*Daily Telegraph*)	*Private Eye*

Details of Libel	*Award*
Allegation in *Sunday Times* and *Time Out* that a political aide to the Prime Minister tried to obstruct an enquiry into a housing association when he was on its management committee	£2,500 *v Sunday Times* and £500 *v Time Out*. As he recovered less than *Time Out* had paid into court he had to pay a substantial part of the costs of the five week trial
Article in the *Guardian* accused a 60-year-old Turkish Cypriot Assistant Solicitor in the Department of Employment of being racially prejudiced and of discriminating against coloured members of his staff. He resigned from his job, losing £19,266 in salary. He conducted his case in person with some skill against the *Guardian's* lawyers, calling Professor Eynseck to support his idiosyncratic views on racial matters	£61,266
Conservative Member of Parliament and Privy Councillor compendiously accused of supporting genocide in Bangladesh, introducing gambling to the Cayman Islands in association with the Mafia, making dishonest claims for expenses and trying to conceal losses made by the Crown Agents	Undisclosed substantial damages reported to be £25,000

Name of Case	Date	Nature of Publication
Stark *v* Sightline Publications Ltd	25 March 1986 (*London Standard*)	soft-porn magazine

Details of Libel	*Award*
Penthouse magazine published an alleged interview about the plaintiff's love life under the heading '*Koo Stark exclusive: Sex Star Tells*'. This purported to be an interview by, as she was described in court, the internationally-known actress, following the break-up of her romance with Prince Andrew. This falsely gave the impression that she had been prepared to sell her story to a magazine like *Penthouse*. In fact what had happened was that she had spoken somewhat frankly about her life to a freelance writer in 1977 following her appearance in a soft porn film. She said the conversation was not accurately reported. As in the Docker case the fact the interview had been given some years ago was not to be found in the published story	Substantial but undisclosed figures

Bibliography

Jerome K. Jerome, *My Life and Times*. Hodder and Stoughton. 1926.

Alfred Moss, *Jerome K. Jerome, His Life and Work*. Selwyn & Blount. 1928.

W. Teignmouth Shore, *The Baccarat Case*, William Hodge, 1932.

Sir Basil Thomson, *The Story of Scotland Yard*. Grayson & Grayson. 1935.

Patrick Hastings, *Cases in Court,* Heinemann, 1949.

E. Napier, *Winter is in July,* Jonathan Cape, 1949.

Clark Gavin, *Foul, False & Infamous*, Abelard Press, 1950.

Joseph Dean, *Hatred, Ridicule & Contempt,* Constable, 1953.

Julian Symons, *Horatio Bottomley*, Cresset Press, 1953.

Hugh Cudlipp, *Publish and be Damned,* Arthur Barker, 1953.

Captain S. W. Roskill, *The War at Sea,* HMSO, 1956.

Randolph Churchill, *What I Said About the Press*, Weidenfeld & Nicolson, 1957.

Harold Abrahams, *The Advertisement that Upset the Golfer,* Country & Sporting Publication, 1959.

H. Montgomery Hyde, *Patrick Hastings: His Life & Cases,* Heinemann, 1960.

John Welcome, *Cheating at Cards,* Faber, 1963.

Dennis Bardens, *Famous Cases of Norman Birkett,* Robert Hale, 1963.

Iain Adamson, *The Old Fox,* Frederick Muller, 1963.

H. Montgomery Hyde, *Norman Birkett,* Hamish Hamilton, 1964.

Michael Hamlyn, 'How the Dering dossier was built up', *Sunday Times,* 10 May 1964.

Iain Adamson, *A Man of Quality,* Frederick Muller, 1964.

Jack Winocour, *Points of the Compass.* Encounter. 1964.

Mavis Hill & Norman Williams, *Auschwitz in England*, MacGibbon & Kee, 1965.

A. Hinds, *Contempt of Court,* Bodley Head, 1966.

David Irving, *The Destruction of Convoy PQ17,* Popular Library (New York), 1968.

Robert Connor, *Cassandra,* Cassell, 1969.

James Fox, 'The Luck of the Lucans', *Sunday Times,* 2 March 1969.

H. Montgomery Hyde, *Their Good Names,* Hamish Hamilton, 1970.

Michael Rubinstein, *Wicked, Wicked Libels,* Routledge & Kegan Paul, 1972.

Allan Hyman, *The Rise and Fall of Horatio Bottomley,* Cassell, 1972.

Graham Greene, *The Pleasure Dome,* Secker & Warburg, 1972.

P. F. Carter-Ruck, *Libel & Slander,* Faber, 1972.

Michael Foot, *Aneurin Bevan,* vol 2, Davis-Poynter, 1973.

David Leigh & Peter Chippendale, *The Thorpe Committal,* Arrow, 1975.

Christopher Sykes, *Evelyn Waugh,* Collins, 1975.

Fenton Bresler, *Lord Goddard,* Harrap, 1977.

Neville Faulks, *No Mitigating Circumstances*, William Kimber, 1977.

J. R. Spencer, 'Criminal Libel – A Skeleton in the Cupboard', *Criminal Law Review,* 1977.

Piers Paul Read, *The Train Robbers,* W. H. Allen/The Alison Press & Secker & Warburg, 1978.

Barrie Penrose and Roger Courtier, *The Pencourt File,* Secker & Warburg, 1978.

Anthony Powell, *Messengers of Day,* Heinemann, 1978.

Neville Faulks, *Law Unto Myself,* William Kimber, 1978.

Lewis Chester & Jonathan Fenby, *Fall of the House of Beaverbrook,* André Deutsch, 1979.

Richard Ingrams, *Goldenballs,* Coronet, 1979.

Lewis Chester, Magnus Linklater & David May, *Jeremy Thorpe, A Secret Life,* Fontana, 1979.

Lord Denning, *The Discipline of the Law,* Butterworth, 1979.

Peter Bessell, *Cover Up,* Simons Books (San Diego, California), 1980.

Janet Morgan (ed.), *Back Bench Diaries of Richard Crossman,* Hamish Hamilton/Jonathan Cape, 1981.

J. C. C. Gatley, *Libel & Slander,* 8th ed., Sweet & Maxwell, 1981.

Geoffrey Wansell, *Sir James Goldsmith – The Man and the Myth*, Fontana, 1982.

Law Commission, Working Paper No. 74 – *Criminal Libel*, *HMSO, 1982.*

Patrick Marnham, The Private Eye Story, André Deutsch, 1982.

Eric Newby, *A Traveller's Life*, Picador, 1982.

Muriel Box, *Rebel Advocate:* Biography of Gerald Gardiner, Victor Gollancz, 1983.

Oliver Woods & James Bishop, *The Story of The Times*, Michael Joseph, 1983.

Elizabeth of Toro, *African Princess*, Hamish Hamilton, 1983.

C. Duncan & B. Neill, *The Law of Defamation*, 2nd ed., Butterworth, 1983.

Richard Hough, *Edwina, Countess Mountbatten of Burma*, Weidenfeld & Nicolson, 1983.

Percy Hoskins, *Two Men Were Acquitted*, Secker & Warburg, 1984.

Index